Dear Alanna,

Best wishes for a sustainable and rewarding career!

Sincerely,

Joe Powell

SUSTAINABLE DEVELOPMENT IN THE PROCESS INDUSTRIES

SUSTAINABLE DEVELOPMENT IN THE PROCESS INDUSTRIES

Cases and Impact

Edited by

JAN HARMSEN
JOSEPH B. POWELL

AIChE

WILEY

A JOHN WILEY & SONS, INC., PUBLICATION

A Joint Publication of the Center for Chemical Process Safety of the American Institute of Chemical Engineers and John Wiley & Sons, Inc.

Published by John Wiley & Sons, Inc., Hoboken, New Jersey.
Published simultaneously in Canada.

For general information on our other products and services or for technical support, please contact our Customer Care Department within the United States at (800) 762-2974, outside the United States at (317) 572-3993 or fax (317) 572-4002.

Wiley also publishes its books in a variety of electronic formats. Some content that appears in print may not be available in electronic formats. For more information about Wiley products, visit our web site at www.wiley.com.

Library of Congress Cataloging-in-Publication Data:

Sustainable development in the process industries : cases and impact / edited by Jan Harmsen, Joseph B. Powell.
      p. cm.
   Includes index.
   ISBN 978-0-470-18779-1 (cloth)
   1. Industrial ecology. 2. Sustainable development. I. Harmsen, Jan, 1950– II. Powell, Joseph B., 1956–
   TS161. S87 2010
   670–dc22

                                                                 2009033993

Printed in the United States of America

10 9 8 7 6 5 4 3 2 1

CONTENTS

CONTRIBUTORS

Carina Maria Alles, DuPont Engineering and Research Technology, Wilmington, Delaware

Paul M. Ayoub, Shell Technology Centre, Amsterdam, The Netherlands

L. W. Baas, Erasmus Centre for Sustainability and Management, Erasmus University, Rotterdam, The Netherlands; Linköping University, Linköping, Sweden

Nitosh Kumar Brahma, Indian Institute of Technology, Kharagpur, W. Bengal, India; IGE-Badu-Kolkata, India

Johannes Fresner, STENUM GmbH, Graz, Austria

Jan Harmsen, State University Groningen, Groningen, The Netherlands

Robin Jenkins, DuPont Engineering and Research Technology, Wilmington, Delaware

G. Korevaar, Delft University of Technology, Delft, The Netherlands; Institute of Environmental Sciences, Leiden University, Leiden, The Netherlands

Jean-Paul Lange, Shell Technology Centre, Amsterdam, The Netherlands

Iris Lewandowski, Shell Technology Centre, Amsterdam, The Netherlands

Andrew Mangan, U.S. Business Council for Sustainable Development, Austin, Texas

Michael Narodoslawsky, Institute for Process Technology, Graz University of Technology, Graz, Austria

Elsa Olivetti, Massachusetts Institute of Technology, Cambridge, Massachusetts

W. Prins, Biomass Technology Group, Enschede, The Netherlands; Ghent University, Ghent, Belgium

Joseph B. Powell, Shell Global Solutions, Houston, Texas

Jan Sage, STENUM GmbH, Graz, Austria

Johan T. Tinge, DSM Research, Technology and Analysis Geleen, SRU Industrial Chemicals, Geleen, The Netherlands

Tjien T. Tjioe, DSM Research, Technology and Analysis Geleen, SRU Industrial Chemicals, Geleen, The Netherlands

R. H. Venderbosch, Biomass Technology Group, Enschede, The Netherlands

Qingzhong Wu, Environmental Technology Center, The Dow Chemical Company, Plaquemine, Louisiana

FOREWORD

The book offers an important industry perspective on how companies develop and design innovative solutions to complex environmental and societal challenges. It goes well beyond theory, offering case studies with quantifiable results that illustrate how companies can save money while improving the environment and helping local communities. It shows how small, medium-sized, and large companies are using resources more efficiently, sometimes by teaming up with other industries, to achieve results that balance the triple bottom line of people, planet, and prosperity.

This richly detailed study should be of great interest to industry leaders, policymakers, scholars, and students of sustainable development.

ANDREW MANGAN

Executive Director
U.S. Business Council for Sustainable Development

PREFACE

This book presents examples and approaches to the application of sustainability in the process industries. Before describing some ways in which the book can be used in courses and in industry, let's look at the evolution of the concept of sustainable development and how industry has played its role in this evolution.

The term *sustainable development* was redefined and became globally known through the publication of *Our Common Future*, commonly called the "Brundtland report" (WCED 1987), which states:

> Sustainable development is not a fixed state of harmony, but a process of change in which the exploitation of resources, the direction of investments, the orientation of technological development and institutional change are made consistent with future as well as present needs. Sustainable development is development that meets the needs of the present generation without compromising the ability of future generations to meet their own needs.

It is clear from this description that sustainable development contains social, cultural, environmental, and economic aspects and takes worldwide and long-term perspectives into account.

After publication of the definition in 1987, the concept of sustainable development was debated broadly and deeply by those in a variety of scientific and academic fields (de Beer and Swanepoel 2000). It survived this discussion and became broadly accepted by many governments. The financial and business world also adopted the concept, but defined it further by introducing three essential dimensions of sustainable development: the social, ecological, and economic dimensions (Serageldin 1993; Hart 1997; WBCSD 1997). Elkington (1997), in turn, transformed the concept into the *triple bottom line* of people, planet, and profits. Soon after, a number of companies began to use it (Shell 2000).

According to the triple-bottom-line concept, in corporate activities equal weight should be given to:

- *People:* the social consequences of its actions
- *Planet:* the ecological consequences of its actions
- *Profits:* the economic profitability of companies (being the source of "prosperity")

The main point is that the "bottom line" of an organization is not only an economic–financial one—an organization is responsible for its social and ecological environment as well. From this "triple P" perspective, an organization that considers a strategy of sustainability must find a balance between economic goals and goals with regard to the social and ecological environment.

The adoption of triple-bottom-line concepts in industry helped to forward its popularity by governments. In the United Nations World Conference on Sustainable Development in Johannesburg, South Africa in 2002, the "triple P" description was adopted and modified, with *profit* changed to *prosperity.* To quote:

> We, the representatives of the peoples of the world, assembled at the World Summit on Sustainable Development in Johannesburg, South Africa, from 2 to 4 September 2002, reaffirm our commitment to sustainable development. We commit ourselves to act together, united by a common determination to save our planet, promote human development and achieve universal prosperity and peace (UN 2002).
> —Johannesburg Declaration on Sustainable Development

Thus, industry helped make the concept of sustainable development more applicable and, perhaps even more important, easier to remember, by introducing the terms *triple P* and *triple bottom line.* Moving beyond definitions to actual implementation can be a challenge for any organization given the expanded array of considerations required by the triple-bottom-line concept and the frequent lack of quantitative metrics available for use in decision making. Although some attention is paid to an overview of the current status of metrics and methodologies in beginning chapters, the examples and case studies that follow help us to focus on the more specific set of drivers that affect decision making in applications across the process industries and related disciplines. Topics include the design of industrial parks and synergistic industrial networks, mining, chemicals, water treatment, and new domains, such as biofuels, which are driven by a desire for more sustainable industries.

The book can be used in courses on sustainable development, regional planning and development, industrial ecology, industrial metabolism, process design, and innovation. It can, for example, be used in exercises to apply a specific analysis or assessment method to a selected case study. It can also be used to analyze and compare the approaches used to implement and apply sustainability principles. Finally, it can be used in process design by giving it as an exercise to improve a specific case process.

The book should also be useful in industry: by implementing approaches described in the case-study processes, or by using the sustainable development metrics and methods described. The cases come from small, medium-sized, and large enterprises. The reader may notice interesting differences in the methods used, depending on the size of the company or industrial branch. Cross-fertilization may happen in this way.

ACKNOWLEDGMENTS

We thank the authors of and contributors to the chapters. Given the breadth of the subject of sustainability, the variety of perspectives and insights presented by our fellow authors has made the preparation of this book an enriching exercise. We trust that you will find it similarly insightful.

G. JAN HARMSEN
JOSEPH B. POWELL

REFERENCES

de Beer, F., and H. Swanepoel. 2000. *Introduction to Development Studies*. Oxford, UK: Oxford University Press.

Elkington, J. 1997. *Cannibals with Forks*. Oxford, UK: Capstone.

Hart, S. 1997. Beyond greening: strategies for a sustainable world. *Harvard Bus. Rev.*, Jan.–Feb., pp. 66–76.

Serageldin, A. 1993. Making development sustainable. *Finance Dev.*, 30(4):6–10.

Shell. 2000. *People, Planet & Profit*, The Shell Report 2000.

UN (United Nations) Department of Economic and Social Affairs, Division of Sustainable Development). 2002. Johannesburg Declaration on Sustainable Development, Sept. 2–4, 2002. Accessed Jan.2009 at http://www.un.org/esa/sustdev/documents/WSSD_POI_PD/English/POI_PD.htm.

WBCSD (World Business Counsil for Sustainable Development). 1997. *Exploring Sustainable Development: Global Scenarios, 2000–2050*, London, UK.

WCED (World Commission on Environment and Development). 1987. *Our Common Future*. Oxford, UK: Oxford University Press.

1

INTRODUCTION

JAN HARMSEN

State University Groningen, Groningen, The Netherlands

1.1 REASON FOR THIS BOOK

The editors of this book have long industrial experience in process develop-ment and novel commercial-scale process implementations. In the past decade we became convinced that sustainable development (SD) is a good driver for innovation, as it makes good business sense to provide for the needs of people in an ecological, economical, and socially acceptable way. Our company, Shell, was adopted sustainable development as one of its business principles, as have many other companies. Formation of the World Business Council for Sustainable Development, with its large number of contributing companies worldwide, is a good indicator of this new direction in global businesses.

However, we felt the lack of reported industrial cases necessary to convince and inspire our colleagues, academics, and students that, indeed, sustainable development has entered the process industry. We assumed that industrial cases existed not only in our company but were also present in other compa-nies. Evidence for this was obtained from the overwhelming response to a proposed session of the American Institute of Chemical Engineers in the spring of 2006 in Orlando, Florida, on "Sustainability in Practice," which ulti-mately swelled into a four-session topical conference. So when we asked our peers in the process industry to provide written cases from their companies to serve as chapters in this book, they responded quickly. All of them had to

Sustainable Development in the Process Industries: Cases and Impact, Edited by Jan Harmsen and Joseph B. Powell
Copyright © 2010 John Wiley & Sons, Inc.

write the cases at least partially in their spare time, but they were sufficiently motivated to do so. Obtaining permission to publish the case descriptions presented another hurdle, but that hurdle was also overcome. So what you find in this book are true industrial cases of novel processes or systems that contribute to sustainable development based on the "triple bottom line" or "triple P" dimensions of "people, planet, and profits."[1]

1.2 SCOPE OF THE BOOK

To make the book as useful as possible, we obtained cases from a variety of:

- *Industries:* oil and gas, bulk chemical, specialty chemical, material and mineral processing
- *Global regions:* Asia, Europe, and the United States
- *Systems:* industrial ecopark, regional development, domestic-industrial ecology, individual corporate operating sites

To the example cases we added methods and metrics that can be used by industry to assess processes as to sustainability. All examples are real industrial cases. Some of the processes are in the pilot-plant stage, but most have already been implemented at a commercial-scale capacity.

1.3 USE IN EDUCATION

The book can be used in many different academic educational programs and courses and in many different ways. Perhaps the first use is to motivate students to work on sustainable development, because it is a real business driver, as shown in the industrial cases. In undergraduate courses, the book can be used to provide students with real examples of industrial sustainable systems and processes. Chapters 12 and 14 illustrate the concept of industrial ecology with the closing of material cycles. A very simple and clear case on domestic wastewater used as feed for boiler feedwater production is described in Chapter 14. A further example, on by-product synergy, is provided in Chapter 6. Also, the translation of the high-level "triple P" dimensions into qualitative and quantitative methods and metrics to assess real processes and their life cycles are illustrated in the cases. In graduate-level courses, the book can be used as test cases and scenarios for the evaluation of theories and frameworks for sustainable development.

---

[1]The origins of "triple P" (or "3P"), encompassing "people, planet, and profits," and "triple bottom line," denoted as "TBL" or "3BL," are described in the preface and are attributed to John Elkington in publications such as *Cannibals with Forks: The Triple Bottom Line of 21st Century Business* (Oxford, UK: Capstone, 1997).

The benefit of incorporating all three dimensions of sustainable development (ecology, economy, and society) in solutions is highlighted by the examples provided in Chapters 3 to 6. For industrial ecology courses, Chapters 4 to 6 and 14 will be useful. The cases presented can be used to illustrate the practical use of the corresponding principles.

Courses on renewable energy can benefit from Chapters 7 to 9. Courses on process design can benefit from any of the industrial cases. In particular, the closing of material cycles is illustrated in Chapter 12, a case study from an anodizing company.

Courses on life-cycle assessment can use Chapter 8, based on an integrated biorefinery, and Chapter 14, a case on industrial symbiosis in wastewater management, where an end-of-cycle wastewater stream is upgraded to a feedstock for chemical processes. Cases throughout the book can be used to analyze the various emission types and emission reductions obtained by the synergy between a local society's waste and the use of that waste by a company, compared to the choice of a conventional solution.

1.4   USE IN INDUSTRY

The book can be used by anyone in industry to convince others in a company that working on innovative processes and systems that contribute to sustainable development makes good business sense and to demonstrate that many other companies are already doing it. An excellent treatment of value added is presented in Chapter 6 using such an innovative process. The book can also be used to apply sustainable development metrics to rank existing and novel process alternatives for sustainability, and to give direction and guidance to process innovation, and small and medium-sized enterprise companies can use the very practical strategy provided to implement sustainable development in their companies. In addition, the book can be used to obtain specific ideas and insights on how to modify processes to direct them toward more sustainable deployment of technology within an industry.

2

SUSTAINABILITY METRICS, INDICATORS, AND INDICES FOR THE PROCESS INDUSTRIES

JOSEPH B. POWELL

Shell Global Solutions, Houston, Texas

2.1 OVERVIEW AND SCOPE

This book is devoted to *sustainability in practice*, or how one translates the often vague and high-level concepts of sustainability into action. It has been said that a person can manage only that which can be measured and defined.[1] How then do we define and measure sustainability? In the following review we look at broad definitions and indicators of sustainability, followed by a focus on a more specific subset of metrics and tools relevant to the process industries.

The emergence of sustainability science and engineering as a meta-discipline is described in a recent academic-center review (Mihelcic et al. 2003); a more in-depth review of sustainability metrics for the chemical and process industries may be found in the book *Transforming Sustainability Strategy into Action* (Beloff et al. 2005). Batterham (2006) presents a hierarchical perspective of sustainability for the practicing chemical engineer: from global objectives, through enterprise and corporate strategies, to individual work tasks. Practices and approaches recommended for use by the process industries are

---

[1]"Measure what is measurable, and make measurable what is not"—quote attributed to Galileo (Sikdar 2009).

Sustainable Development in the Process Industries: Cases and Impact, Edited by Jan Harmsen and Joseph B. Powell
Copyright © 2010 John Wiley & Sons, Inc.

also available from chemical engineering institute working groups (AIChE 2000; ICheme 2002; Schuster 2007). A number of recent reviews of sustainability metrics, indicators, and frameworks with assessment of state-of-the-art implementation strategies have appeared from leaders in environmental agencies, nonprofit institutes, and universities. In this chapter we provide an overview of the current state of the art and best practices, with updates as to recent trends and assessments. An extensive reference list is provided for use in the implementation of sustainability frameworks and the use of metrics.

2.1.1 Definition of Sustainability

Although it is frequently stated that there is no agreed upon definition of *sustainability*, the original definition of the United Nations' Brundtland Commission (WCED 1987) is most often quoted and is widely accepted: "'Sustainable' development is development that meets the needs of the present without compromising the ability of future generations to meet their own needs." This is quite a broad definition if one is looking for a directive for tangible action.

Further clarification is afforded by consideration of three impact areas (Figure 2.1): (1), environmental, (2) economic, and (3) societal, or "people, planet, and profits," as part of the *triple bottom line* concept for corporate and governmental responsibility (Elkington 1994, 1997). *Sustainability* is a consideration of societal and environmental performance, on top of a broadened concept of financial performance that considers economic cost–benefit impacts beyond corporate profits. The need for sustainability results from the fact that economic systems are imperfect and do not reflect total costs or values, including environmental and social impacts. Sustainability metrics thus attempt to "measure the immeasurable" (Pintér et al 2005; Böhringer and Jochem 2007)

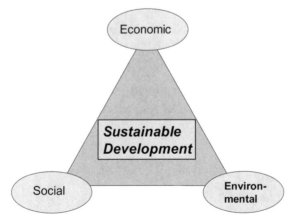

Figure 2.1 Triple bottom line of sustainability, or "triple P": people, planet, and profits.

by including those costs and values that defy traditional economic analysis (Goodstein 1999; AIChE 2000; Sagoff 2000).

The triple-bottom-line concept seeks to address the interests of all stakeholders affected by project implementation or deployment. While traditional corporate shareholder interests are reflected through well-established financial performance indicators, stakeholders also include customers, neighboring communities, employees, and (for the case of global warming) society at large. Sustainable development strives to address the composite and varying needs of stakeholders beyond simply the traditional financial interests of shareholders. To the extent that this reduces future risks and liabilities and extends future viability, sustainability can be a means to enhance shareholder value as well, in a win–win manner. A number of sustainability indices seek to measure or quantify the intangible impact of actions or policy for use in financial or investment decision making (Cobb et al. 2007, 2009; Pernick and Wilder 2007).

Other formulations have the triangle constrained within a three-dimensional cone of environmental carrying capacity (Mauerhofer 2008), which reflects the breath of opinion on the prioritization of trade-offs among often-conflicting criteria as well as differing perspectives on which stakeholders may be allowed to decide or indeed *be* stakeholders.

2.2 HIERARCHY OF SD METRICS, INDICES, AND INDICATORS

Given the complexity of attempting to define sustainable development, it is no surprise that there is no uniform consensus on metrics, indices, or frameworks (Sikdar 2007). The problem has given rise to an "industry" of indicators, metrics, and tools (Wilson et al. 2007), with the current status characterized as an "indicator zoo," comprising 500 to 650 or more indicators with limited cross-standardization (Pintér et al. 2005; IISD 2009). Awareness of the broad scope of sustainability is valuable in setting goals and strategies to ensure that the most important impact areas are being addressed for a given entity or organization. Indices often overlap partially with differing levels of aggregate subindices.

2.2.1 National and International Public Policy-Level Indicators

At the international, national, or strategic policy level, Böhringer and Jochem (2007) identified and analyzed 11 of the most popular or widely used indices among the more than 500 reported:

1. *Living planet index:* tracks 1100 species (World Wildlife Federation)
2. *Ecological footprint:* water and land use per capita
3. *City development index:* infrastructure, waste handling, health, education
4. *Human development index:* life expectancy, education, gross national product

5. *Environmental sustainability index:* preserving environmental resource
6. *Environmental performance index:* environmental stressors
7. *Environmental vulnerability index:* fragile ecosystems
8. *Index of sustainable economic welfare:* consumption, income distribution
9. *Well being index:* aggregate index of all sustainable development
10. *Genuine savings index:* economic "rents" required to sustain a lifestyle
11. *Environmental adjusted domestic product*

The findings of this study were that the metrics in general were in many cases weak in scientific underpinnings, with a large degree of arbitrariness in assessment, which limits credible use for decision making, especially for decisions requiring trade-offs between competing interests. Discussion of the way forward in sustainability indices and indicators, despite inherent complexity, is provided in the International Institute for Sustainable Development's United Nations' report (Pintér et al. 2005). Recommendations include further development of aggregate and goal-oriented indices, improved standardization of reporting, and identification of gaps in current indicator assessment methodologies. Dependence of results on context-sensitive scenarios, lack of consensus on scientific bases, and differences in relative value judgments across societies and cultures all complicate the development of universal indicators. A further review of global policy-level metrics is also available (Wilson et al. 2007).

For process industry impacts at the national and international levels, the Environmental Sustainability Index (Esty et al. 2005), indicators developed by the European Environmental Agency (EEA; www.eea.europa.eu), assessments and performance measures reported by the U.S. Environmental Protection Agency (USEPA; www.epa.gov/Sustainability) under materials and toxics, and the environmental performance index method of the Association of the Dutch Chemical Industry (VNCI 2000) are examples of relevant indicator sets and methodologies for use in footprint assessment. An approach to consideration of material and energy constraints in public policy has also been prescribed (Thomas and Graedel 2003).

2.2.2 Broader Corporate-Level Indicators, Indices, and Best Practices

Corporations across industries can be compared relative to sustainability commitments and performance, despite variations in specific product lines and businesses. A number of indices and organizations exist to share best practices and metrics in sustainability. The World Business Council for Sustainable Development is a corporate-led global association of some 200 companies in more than 35 countries that deals exclusively with businesses and sustainable development (www.wbcsd.org). The organization is supported by a number of regional councils, with a focus on energy and climate, development, the business role in sustainable development, and ecosystems.

Gemi is a nonprofit organization for benchmarking and best practices in sustainability and in environmental health and safety, with 37 member companies representing 22 types of businesses (www.gemi.org). The Sustainability Consortium of the Society for Organizational Learning, formed in 1999 to foster sustainability in the three dimensions of people, planet, and profits, offers a number of tool kits and benchmarks for cross-industry sustainability (www.solsustainability.org). The International Institute for Sustainable Development (IISD) is a nonprofit organization dedicated to biodiversity, global warming, and world poverty issues (www.iisd.org). Financial indicators focused on or including sustainability include the Dow Jones sustainability index, the FTSE4Good environmental index, and the Calvert social index (Cobb et al. 2007).

2.2.3 Corporate-Level and Management System Indicators and Indices

Although diverse, corporate-level indices and indicators can provide more specific, actionable goals for management, which to some degree transcend specific industries. Relative to the generic triad of societal, environmental, and economic performance indicators, the Institute for Sustainability of the American Institute of Chemical Engineers (AIChE) proposes the following sustainability index, directed toward corporate management and governance (Cobb et al. 2007):

- Strategic commitment to sustainability
- Safety performance (employee and process)
- Environmental performance (resource use; emissions, including greenhouse gases)
- Social responsibility (community investment, stakeholder engagement)
- Product stewardship (product safety, Responsible Care/Reach)
- Innovation (in sustainability)
- Value chain management (supplier and customer standards)

As part of this initiative, a review of the tools available for assistance in organizational sustainability programs was recently completed (Schuster 2007). Responsible Care is a voluntary initiative within the chemical industry under which companies work together continuously through their national associations to improve their health, safety, and environmental performance and to communicate with stakeholders about their products and processes. This is an industry-wide initiative to help to establish credibility in corporate responsibility for the chemical industry in general, with an emphasis on compliance (www.responsiblecare.org). Reach (EC2007), a more recent program in the European Union (EU), places additional responsibility on industry to ensure testing and risk management of all chemicals marketed and used in the EU. These programs focus on human and environmental health aspects of sustainability.

2.3 PRACTICAL TOOLS FOR THE PROCESS INDUSTRIES

Other than compliance requirements for chemical products as defined by Responsible Care and Reach, the indicators and indices above provide only a framework for organizational goals and targets. More specific information is needed to make decisions between competing alternatives and options.

2.3.1 Toolkits from ICHEME and AIChE

One tool publically available from the Institution of Chemical Engineers is a spreadsheet of metrics recommended for use in the process industries (IChemE 2002):

1. Environmental indicators
    a. Energy
    b. Material intensity
    c. Water
    d. Land
    e. Emissions
        i. Atmospheric
            (1) Acidification
            (2) Global warming
            (3) Human health
            (4) Ozone depletion
            (5) Photochemical ozone (smog)
        ii. Aquatic
            (1) Acidification
            (2) Oxygen demand
            (3) Ecotoxicity
            (4) Eutrophication
        iii. Land
            (1) Toxic waste disposal
            (2) Nontoxic waste disposal
2. Economic indicators
    a. Profit, value, taxes
    b. Investments
3. Social indicators

a. Workplace (jobs, training, safety)
b. Society

The metrics are structured based on the triple-bottom-line framework for sustainable development. Weighting factors are provided for environmental impacts of a large list of components in each emissions category, such that environmental burden is calculated on the basis of a potency factor times a quantity of emissions (in metric tons).

In 1999–2000 the American Institute of Chemical Engineers developed a framework entitled Total Cost Analysis as part of the Center for Waste Reduction Technologies (AIChE 2000). The approach uses life-cycle inventory and assessment for an environmental footprint, together with process economics and workshop-derived assessments of risk and future costs (Bendixen 2002; Lauren 2007). The objective is to place environmental and social costs on the same basis as economic costs, such that businesses can use standard economic and cost tools in decision making. Costs are categorized as follows:

I. Direct costs
   a. Capital
   b. Fixed (labor)
   c. Feedstock (raw materials)
   d. Waste disposal
   e. Operating and maintenance
II. Indirect costs
   a. Nonallocated and overhead costs
III. Future liabilities
   a. Fines, penalties, legal fees
   b. Business interruptions
   c. Cost of environmental cleanup
IV. Intangible internal costs
   a. Reputation
   b. Customer acceptance and loyalty
   c. Employee morale and safety
V. Intangible external costs
   a. Costs borne by society
   b. Environmental costs within compliance

The methodology is available for download (AIChE 2000). Automated total cost assessment tools, including case studies, were developed further into software known as TCAce, which was refined through industrial applications. The software is available for purchase along with other life-cycle assessment tools and resources to assist in deploying this methodology.[2] Estimations of type I to III costs are relatively straightforward. Types IV and V cost estimations are substantially more difficult. A workshop approach using experienced environmental and external-relations expertise can be used to provide cost-impact estimates. Additional benchmarking and tools are under development by AIChE's Institute for Sustainability (Cobb et al. 2007), including the Center for Sustainable Technology Practices, which serves as the corporate-led project development arm.[3]

The specific impact of sustainable areal land use has been considered (Krotscheck and Narodoslawsky 1996). Special considerations for the consumer products industries have also been reviewed (Saurs and Mitna 2009). Principles of industrial ecology were introduced by Garner and Keoleian (1995), including a life-cycle inventory checklist and a case study of industrial symbiosis in Kalundborg, Denmark. The latter entails a synthesis of electrical power, oil refining, biotechnology, and fiberboard manufacture. A simple framework for sustainability metrics has been developed in a collaboration between the U.S. EPA and academia (Martins et al. 2007).

2.3.2   Resources for Conducting Life-Cycle Assessment

Life-cycle inventory (LCI) and assessment (LCA) approaches are used widely to assess sustainability and environmental footprints. The following categories are considered relevant for life-cycle inventory and assessment by the U.S. EPA (SAIC 2006):

- Ozone depletion
- Global warming
- Smog formation
- Acidification
- Eutrophication
- Human health cancer
- Human health noncancer
- Human health criteria pollutants
- Ecotoxicity
- Fossil-fuel depletion
- Land use
- Water use

---

[2]TCAce is available from Earthshift (www.earthshift.com). Two third-party firms offering services featuring total cost assessment and related tools are Bridges to Sustainability (www.bridgestos.org/) and Sylvatica (www.sylvatica.com).

[3]Institute for Sustainability of the AIChE: http://www.aiche.org/IFS/index.aspx; also contains links to the Center for Sustainable Technology Practices.

Land and water use are simply reported on an absolute basis. Other stress factors are assessed relative to a reference standard. The tool is useful for assessing the relative impact of emissions as environmental stressors. More specific tools are also available to estimate the relative impact of toxic emissions. The U.S. offers TRACI (tool for reduction and assessment of chemical and other environmental impacts) (Bare et al. 2003). The Association of the Dutch Chemical Industry (VNCI) has prepared a methodology based on environmental performance indicators (VNCI 2000).

Normalization and Weighting Factors   Relative impacts of emissions can in principle be assessed via normalization, which was not included in the 2003 TRACI release but is reported in a 2006 assessment (Bare et al. 2006). Netherlands and Western European weighting factors, along with those for the rest of the world, have also been reported (Huijbregts et al. 2003). Normalization is often dependent on regional emission profiles. The normalization factors are used as a precursor to LCA weighting exercises and entail normalizing the impact of a given environmental stress factor within a given category (e.g., ozone depletion) relative to total emissions and stress factors for that category. For example, the differences in global warming potential for different chemical species (methane vs. CO_2) can be considered for each molecular unit discharged. Weighting of the relative importance of different categories of stress factors for LCA trade-off comparisons (e.g., importance if global warming vs. ozone depletion) is subject to stakeholder opinion and varies with different stakeholder groups. Normalization factors allow for consistent comparison among different sources within a category. Weighting factors attempt to assign relative values to the importance of each category. A preference index has been proposed (Robèrt 2000) as one means of addressing the latter trade-offs. Alternatively, attempting to place each stress factor impact on an estimated cost basis [e.g., Total Cost Analysis (AIChE 2000)] provides a means of comparison, at least in principle.

As indicated above, many of the more specific metrics involved in the practical implementation of sustainability are associated with environmental footprint assessment and natural resource depletion. A partial list of methodologies available for impact and footprint assessments relevant to the chemical and process industries is given in Table 2.1.

2.3.3   Green Chemistry and CleanTech Frameworks

Green chemistry and CleanTech are two subdisciplines under the sustainable development umbrella as it pertains to the process industries. Green chemistry (Poliakoff and Anastas 2001) seeks to develop more benign chemical processes, according to the following 12 principles (Anastas and Warner 1998):

1. Prevent waste.
2. Design safer products.

TABLE 2.1   Life-Cycle Inventory and Assessment Tools and Methodologies[a]

Tool	Web Site
TRACI: Tool for the Reduction and Assessment of Chemical and Other Environmental Impacts (U.S. EPA)	http://www.epa.gov/nrmrl/std/sab/traci/
Boustead Model: Computer Model and Database for life-cycle Inventory (UK)	http://www.boustead-consulting.co.uk/ products.htm
CMLCA: Chain Management by Life-Cycle Assessment (Leiden University)	http://www.leidenuniv.nl/interfac/cml/ ssp/software/cmlca/index.html
Ecoinvent: Extensive life-cycle inventory database (Swiss Center for LCI)	http://www.ecoinvent.com/
U.S. Life Cycle Inventory Database: National Renewable Energy Lab	http://www.nrel.gov/lci/
SimaPro: LCA Software	http://www.pre.nl/simapro/default.htm
Spine: LCI database (Chalmers University)	http://www.globalspine.com/
SPOLD: Society for the Promotion of Life Cycle Assessment	http://lca-net.com/spold/
Umberto: Life-cycle assessment (Hamburg)	http://www.umberto.de/en/index.htm
Team: Life-cycle inventory and assessment tool (Pricewaterhouse Coopers)	http://www.ecobalance.com/uk_team.php
EIO-LCA: (Carnegie-Mellon University)	http://www.eiolca.net/
Gabi4: LCA (University of Stuttgart)	http://www.gabi-software.com/
GREET: Greenhouse Gases, Regulated Emissions, and Energy Use in Transportation (U.S. DOE)	http://www.transportation.anl.gov/ software/GREET/
TCACE: Total cost analysis	http://www.earthshift.com/tcace.htm

[a]Additional compendia of resources and tools: http://www.gdrc.org/uem/lca/lca-japan.html (Japan) http://www.epa.gov/ORD/NRMRL/lcaccess/resources.html#Software (U.S.)

3. Design less hazardous chemical syntheses.
4. Use renewable feedstocks.
5. Use catalysts, not stoichiometric reagents.
6. Avoid chemical derivatives or protecting groups.
7. Maximize atom economy.
8. Use safer solvents and reaction conditions.
9. Increase energy efficiency.
10. Design chemicals and products to degrade after use.

11. Implement real-time analysis and control to prevent pollution.
12. Minimize the potential for accidents.

Metrics commonly used in green chemistry include (Anastas et al. 2001):

1. Effective mass yield
2. Carbon efficiency
3. Atom economy
4. Reaction mass efficiency
5. Environmental factor

These metrics are indeed subsets of material intensity and environmental toxicity factors for life-cycle assessment. The concepts of atom efficiency and maximum environmental impact factor have been combined to look at generic reaction classes to assess greenness (Andraos 2005; Manley et al. 2008). A methodology for life-cycle chemistry impact assessment has also been described (Lankey and Anastas 2002).

Green engineering is a related concept (Anastas 2003; Anastas and Zimmerman 2003), whose principles are summarized as follows:

1. Minimize hazards in material and energy inputs.
2. Prevent waste rather than cleaning it up.
3. Minimize energy and materials consumption in the separation and purification steps.
4. Design products and processes to maximize mass, energy, and space–time efficiency.
5. For optimal efficiency, select and remove outputs rather than forcing mass and energy inputs.
6. Embedded entropy and complexity must be considered when making choices on recycle, reuse, or disposition.
7. Targeted durability should be a design goal, not infinite life.
8. Avoid unnecessary capacity or capability.
9. Promote recycling by minimizing the compositional diversity of products.
10. Optimize heat and material integration.
11. Where plausible, products, processes, and systems should be designed for use in a commercial "afterlife."
12. Use renewable material and energy inputs where possible.

Ecoefficiency and green engineering seek to ensure that products or processes meet the same defined customer benefit, that the entire life cycle is considered, and that both environmental and economic assessments are carried out. Approaches include (Allen and Shonnard 2001, 2002; Shonnard et al. 2003):

- Calculation of total cost from a customer viewpoint
- Preparation of a specific life-cycle analysis for all products or processes investigated according to the rules of the ISO's regulation 14040
- Determination of impacts on the health, safety, and risks to people
- Weighting life-cycle analysis factors against societal factors
- Determination of the relative importance of ecology versus the economy

CleanTech is another initiative under sustainable development (www.ct-si.org/about), which has a somewhat broader focus but emphasizes the following drivers espoused by Pernick and Wilder (2007):

1. Promotion and commercialization of new sustainable and clean technologies
   a. Renewable energy
   b. Biofuels
   c. Systems integration
   d. Environment and water
   e. Public policy
2. Promotion of reduced footprint practices in traditional industries
   a. Traditional power generation
   b. Exploration, extraction, and refining
   c. Transportation
   d. Building and construction
   e. Industrial processes
   f. Industry initiatives and best practices

This began as an investment index for clean technologies (www.cleantech.com) but has grown into a synonym for sustainable technologies and development, and green technology.

2.3.4 Calculational Tools and Frameworks

A number of calculational approaches to optimization and decision making have also been published (Thurston and Srinivasan 2003; Piluso et al. 2008). Optimization theory (e.g., to minimize an objective function describing an environmental footprint) can be employed, provided that adequate metrics are available. Use of computable general equilibrium models for public policy sustainability impact assessment, including guidance on the selection of indicators and metrics, has been described (Böhringer and Löschel 2006).

Schwarz et al. (2002) describe the use of metrics for material, water, and energy usage intensity, plus toxic, pollutant, and greenhouse gas emissions, computed on the basis of mass per unit mass of product and per unit economic value added, as a means of discerning the economics, footprint, and risks of two closely competing process options. The concept of stacking impacts across supply chains is introduced as an important consideration. For comparison of closely competing options, metrics along the economic–environmental axis can often be defined with sufficient precision to guide investment decisions.

Bode et al. (2006), through practical examples, describe an approach to dealing with uncertainty in input assumptions for a similar comparison of options, trading off direct economics and eco-indicators. Sensitivity studies to test the impact of input parameter assessment and stochastic dominance principles were applied to assess the level of risk associated with high uncertainty in input parameters. For the latter, inputs are modeled as distributions and allowed to propagate through the model to provide a distribution of outputs allowed. The importance of fully characterizing the disposition of all streams and all impacts on materials and energy consumption is clearly evident.

Allen and Shonnard similarly describe the use of green engineering principles and metrics in process design, where answers are often ambiguous due to unique footprints and the impact of alternate routes (Allen and Shonnard 2001). A calculational methodology for plant retrofits has also been described (Carvalho et al. 2008), including an example assessment for production of vinyl chloride monomer. Quantitative treatments are presented for environmental indicators and metrics as well as an inherent safety index. A road map and principles for sustainable construction and engineering have also been presented (Vanegas 2003).

Energy-efficiency improvement can often be considered "low-hanging fruit" in the reduction of a CO_2 footprint, as shown in the CO_2 cost abatement curve reported by McKinsey and associates (Sylvester 2009). Given the direct and quantifiable economic incentives provided by energy savings, ambiguity in metrics and decision making is reduced.

The use of scenarios and metrics for assessment of future sustainable energy options has been examined (Darton 2003), with a note that "renewable" does not necessarily mean "sustainable."

Trade-offs along the economic–environmental axis can thus be put on an approximate numerical basis via a number of approaches, as a guide for decision making. This is especially valuable in the early stages of process development. Evaluation of the relative preferences (e.g., for reducing energy use and global warming, vs. the impact on ecotoxicity and footprint) can remain partially subjective. However, published indicators and metrics can provide guidance in decision making to allow selection between competing options.

2.4 SUMMARY AND CONCLUSIONS

In this chapter we have summarized the current state of the art in sustainability metrics (e.g., "measuring the immeasurable") and have reviewed indices, indicators, and frameworks used for benchmarking and program implementation in the process industries. Findings can be summarized as follows:

1. There exist a myriad of sustainability indices, indicators, and metrics, as well as tools and methodologies for implementation. Although awareness of the breadth of sustainability is valuable, on a practical basis it is necessary to focus on a subset pertinent to the particular business, program, or project under consideration. Comparison of options and benchmarking against competitors requires the use of a consistent set of metrics and indicators. There is no "one size fits all" program for relevant sustainability indicators and metrics for a given company, business unit, or entity. Frameworks developed by ICheme and AIChE, reviews and guidelines relevant to the process industries, and principles developed under the context of green chemistry or engineering or CleanTech provide guidelines and checklists of value in this domain.

2. Although economic and some elements of environmental performance can typically be quantified, the relative importance of environmental stressor categories and societal impacts remains largely nonquantitative, often subjective, and open to debate. These are best handled by focused workshops and debate among specific stakeholder representatives prior to project delivery, whereas published normalization data can be used as a guide in process screening. Given the inability to calculate rigorous metrics, sustainability and active consideration of triple-bottom-line concepts require an organizational mindset and structure. Leadership commitment and organizational frameworks to promote consideration of sustainability in decision making are important components.

3. Life-cycle inventory and assessment tools, along with normalization databases, provide a basis for direct assessment of environmental stressors, as well as a checklist and framework to ensure that relevant stress factor categories are considered. Use of these numerical tools can be an important input to decision making, requiring trade-off of competing factors and footprints. Where input data are weak, use of scenarios, sensitivity studies, and risk assessment approaches can be valuable in assessing distributions of possible outcomes for overall risk–benefit comparison.

The relationships among concepts, tools, metrics, and frameworks of sustainable development have been reviewed by several authors, (e.g., Robèrt 2000; Norris 2001; Darton 2003; Jain 2005; Batterham 2006) with Robèrt (2000) indicating that multiple approaches are needed because they "represent different levels of strategic planning." As one example, the natural step process seeks to link strategic objectives via "backcasting" from "basic principles of success" to determine which steps should be taken today to drive toward identified strategic objectives and outcomes, using metrics as a means of assessment. Thus, a flexible methodology is sought whereby decision making supports strategic goals, independent of inherent system complexity.

Elements of practical sustainable development implementation within organizations require:

- A flexible management system, network, or initiative championed by senior leaders whereby sustainability or triple-bottom-line impacts are actively considered in decision making and trade-offs
- Frameworks and checklists to identify key considerations, augmented by numerical assessment where possible
- Mechanism for external and internal stakeholder engagement, awareness, or representation for proper weighing of alternatives

There is no single recipe or aggregate metric that will fit or describe all situations or trade-offs. Rather, sustainability is an organizational mindset that strives to make use of collective awareness and anticipation of stakeholder expectations and needs, both today and in the future. "Getting it right" means better decisions via anticipation of total costs, future liabilities, and opportunities. Life-cycle inventory assessment for human and environmental stress factors provides the primary tools for implementation. Sustainability metrics or indicators can either enter indirectly as the deciding vote between competing options or programs, or directly by comparing total costs for those cases where the latter impact can be estimated.

To the extent that these principles and approaches become embedded in the corporate psyche and affect day-to-day decision making (Wade and Machado 2005), comprehensive tracking of individual performance metrics may not be required. Rather, effects will be seen by means of the impact on brand, reputation, license to operate, market acceptance of products, and market valuation. Performance in these arenas can be validated by external benchmarking and positioning relative to one or more of the published sustainability indices.

REFERENCES

AIChE (American Institute of Chemical Engineers). 2000. *Total Cost Assessment Methodology Manual*. New York: AIChE Center for Waste Reduction Technology, Institute for Sustainability. Accessed Apr. 2009 at http://www.aiche.org/uploadedFiles/IFS/Products/TCAM.pdf.

Allen, D. T., and D. R. Shonnard. 2001. Green engineering: environmentally conscious design of chemical processes and products. *AIChE J.*, 47(9):1906–1910.

———. 2002. *Green Engineering: Environmentally Conscious Design of Chemical Processes*. Upper Saddle River, NJ: Prentice Hall.

Anastas, P. T. 2003. Green engineering and sustainability. *Environ. Sci. Technol.* 37(23):423A.

Anastas, P., and J. Warner. 1998. *Green Chemistry: Theory and Practice*. New York: Oxford University Press.

Anastas, P. T., and J. B. Zimmerman. 2003. Design through the 12 principles of green engineering. *Environ. Sci. Technol.* 37(5):95A–101A.

Anastas, P. T., M. M. Kirchhoff, and T. C. Williamson. 2001. Catalysis as a foundational pillar of green chemistry. *Appl. Catal. A*, 221(1–2):3–13.

Andraos, J. 2005. Unification of reaction metrics for green chemistry: II. Evaluation of named organic reactions and application to reaction discovery. *Org. Process Res. Dev.*, 9(4):404–431.

Bare, J. C., G. Norris, D. W. Pennington, and T. McKone. 2003. TRACI: the tool for the reduction and assessment of chemical and other environmental impacts. *J. Ind. Ecol.*, 6(3):49–78.

Bare, J., T. Gloria, and G. Norris. 2006. Development of the method and U.S. normalization database for life cycle impact assessment and sustainability metrics. *Environ. Sci. Technol.*, 40(16):5108–5115.

Batterham, R. J. 2006. Sustainability: the next chapter. *Chemi. Eng. Sci.*, 61(13): 4188–4193.

Beloff, B., M. Lines, and D. Tanzil. 2005. *Transforming Sustainability Strategy into Action*. Hoboken, NJ: Wiley.

Bendixen, L. 2002. Integrate EHS for better process design. *Chem. Eng. Prog.*, 98(2):26–32.

Bode, G., K. Hungerbuhler, G. J. McRae, and R. Schomaecker. 2006. Get your investment decisions right. *Chem. Eng. Prog.*, 102(2):49–56.

Böhringer, C., and P. E. P. Jochem. 2007. Measuring the immeasurable: a survey of sustainability indices. *Ecol. Econ.*, 63(1):1.

Böhringer, C., and A. Löschel. 2006. Computable general equilibrium models for sustainability impact assessment: status quo and prospects. *Ecol. Econ.*, 60(1):49.

Carvalho, A., R. Gani, and H. Matos. 2008. Design of sustainable chemical processes: systematic retrofit analysis generation and evaluation of alternatives. *Process Saf. Environ. Prot.*, 86(5):328.

Cobb, C., D. Schuster, B. Beloff, and D. Tanzil. 2007. Benchmarking sustainability. *Chem. Eng. Prog.*, 103(6):38–42.

———. 2009. The AIChE sustainability index: the factors in detail. *Chem. Eng. Prog.*, 105(1):60–63.

Darton, R. C. 2003. Scenarios and metrics as guides to a sustainable future: the case of energy supply. *Trans IChemE* 81(P B.):295–302.

EC (European Commission, Environment Directive General). 2007. Reach in Brief: Why Do We Need Reach? Accessed at http://ec.europa.eu/environment/chemicals/reach/pdf/2007_02_reach_in_brief.pdf.

Elkington, J. 1994. Towards the sustainable corporation: win–win–win business strategies for sustainable development. *Calif. Manag. Rev.*, 36(2):90–100.

———. 1997. *Cannibals with Forks: The Triple Bottom Line of 21st Century Business*. Oxford, UK: Capstone.

Esty, D. C., M. A. Levy, T. Srebotnjak, and A. de Sherbinin. 2005. *Environmental Sustainability Index (ESI):Benchmarking National Environmental Stewardship*. New Haven, CT: Yale Center for Environmental Law and Policy (www.yale.edu/esi).

Garner, A., and G. A. Keoleian. 1995. *Industrial Ecology: An Introduction*. Ann Arbor, MI: National Pollution Prevention Center for Higher Education, University of Michigan. Accessed Apr. 2006 at http://www.umich.edu/~nppcpub/resources/compendia/INDEpdfs/INDEintro.pdf.

Goodstein, E. S. 1999. *Economics and the Environment*. Upper Saddle River, NJ: Prentice Hall.

Huijbregts, M. A. J., L. Breedveld, G. Huppes, A. de Koning, L. van Oers, and S. Suh. 2003. Normalisation figures for environmental life-cycle assessment: The Netherlands (1997/1998), Western Europe (1995) and the world (1990 and 1995). *J. Cleaner Prod.*, 11(7):737.

IChemE (Institution of Chemical Engineers). 2002. *Sustainable Development Progress Metrics: Recommended for Use in the Process Industries*, ed. A. Azapagic. Rugby, UK: ICHEME. Accessed Apr. 2009 at http://www.icheme.org/sustainability/metrics.pdf.

IISD (International Institute for Sustainable Development). 2009. *Compendium of Sustainability Indicators*. Winnipeg, Manitoba, Canada: IISD. Accessed at http://www.iisd.org/measure/compendium/searchinitiatives.aspx.

Jain, R. 2005. Sustainability: metrics, specific indicators and preference index. *Clean Technol. Environ. Policy*, 7:71–72.

Krotscheck, C., and M. Narodoslawsky. 1996. The sustainable process index: a new dimension in ecological evaluation. *Ecol. Eng.*, 6:241–258.

Lankey, R. L., and P. T. Anastas. 2002. Life-cycle approaches for assessing green chemistry technologies. *Ind. Eng. Chem. Res.*, 41(18):4498–4502.

Lauren, L. 2007. Sustainability: keeping the competitive edge. *Chem. Eng. Prog.*, 103(6):44–46.

Manley, J. B., P. T. Anastas, and B. W. Cue, Jr. 2008. Frontiers in green chemistry: meeting the grand challenges for sustainability in R&D and manufacturing. *J. Cleaner Prod.*, 16(6):743.

Martins, A. A., T. M. Mata, C. A. V. Costa, and S. K. Sikdar. 2007. A framework for sustainability metrics. *Ind. Eng. Chem. Res.*, 46(16):5468–5468.

Mauerhofer, V. 2008. 3-D sustainability: an approach for priority setting in situation of conflicting interests towards a sustainable development. *Ecol. Econ.*, 64:496–506.

Mihelcic, J. R., J. C. Crittenden, M. J. Small, D. R. Shonnard, D. R. Hokanson, Q. Zhang, H. Chen, S. A. Sorby, V. U. James, J. W. Sutherland, and J. L. Schnoor. 2003. Sustainability science and engineering: the emergence of a new metadiscipline. *Environ. Sci. Technol.*, 37(23):5314–5324.

Norris, G. 2001. Integrating economic analysis into LCA. *Environ. Qual. Manage.*, 10(3):59–64.

Pernick, R., and C. Wilder. 2007. *The Clean Tech Revolution: The Next Big Growth and Investment Opportunity*. New York: Harper Collins.

Piluso, C., Y. Huang, and H. H. Lou. 2008. Ecological input–output analysis-based sustainability: analysis of industrial systems. *Ind. Eng. Chem. Res.*, 47(6): 1955–1966.

Pintér, L., P. Hardi, and P. Bartelmus. 2005. *Indicators of Sustainable Development: Proposals for a Way Forward*. Discussion paper prepared under a consulting agreement on behalf of the UN Division for Sustainable Development. UNDSD/ EGM/ ISD/2005/CRP.2. Winipeg, Manitobe, Canada: International Institute for Sustainable Development.

Poliakoff, M., and P. Anastas. 2001. Green chemistry: a principled stance. *Nature (London)*, 413(6853):257.

Robèrt, K.-H. 2000. Tools and concepts for sustainable development, how do they relate to a general framework for sustainable development, and to each other? *J. Cleaner Prod.*, 8(3):243–254.

Sagoff, M. 2000. Environmental economics and the conflation of value and benefit. *Environ. Sci. Technol.*, 34(8):1426–1432.

SAIC (Scientific Applications International Corporation). 2006. Life Cycle Assessment: Principles and Practice, US EPA/600/R-06/060. Washington, DC: US EPA.

Saurs, L., and S. Mitra. 2009. Sustainability innovation in the consumer products industry. *Chem. Eng. Prog.*, 105(1):36–40.

Schuster, D. 2007. The road to sustainability. *Chem. Eng. Prog.*, 103(6):34–36.

Schwarz, J., B. Beloff, and E. Beaver. 2002. Use sustainability metrics to guide decision-making. *Chem. Eng. Prog.*, 98(7):58–63.

Shonnard, D. R., A. Kicherer, and P. Saling. 2003. Industrial applications using BASF eco-efficiency analysis: perspectives on green engineering principles. *Environ. Sci. Technol.*, 37(23):5340–5348.

Sikdar, S. K. 2007. Sustainability perspective and chemistry-based technologies. *Ind. Eng. Chem. Res.*, 46(14):4727–4733.

———. 2009. Achieving technical sustainability. *Chem. Eng. Prog.*, 105(1):34–39.

Sylvester, R. W. 2009. A personal perspective on sustainability through energy efficiency. *Chem. Eng. Prog.*, 105(1):54–59.

Thomas, V., and T. E. Graedel. 2003. Research issues in sustainable consumption: toward an analytical framework for materials and the environment. *Environ. Sci. Technol.*, 37:5383–5388.

Thurston, D. L., and S. Srinivasan. 2003. Constrained optimization for green engineering decision-making. *Environ. Sci. Technol.*, 37(23):5389–5397.

Vanegas, J. A. 2003. Road map and principles for built environment sustainability. *Environ. Sci. Technol.*, 37(23):5363–5372.

VNCI (Association of the Dutch Chemical Industry). 2000. *Guideline: Environmental Performance Indicators for the Chemical Industry: The EPI-Method.* Leidschendam, The Netherlands.

Wade, M., and J. Machado. 2005. Business value from sustainable development at Shell. In *Transforming Sustainability Strategy into Action*, ed. B. Beloff, M. Lines, and D. Tanzil. Hoboken, NJ: Wiley.

WCED (World Commission on Environment and Development). 1987. United Nations General Assembly document A/42/427. Accessed at http://www.worldinbalance.net/pdf/1987-brundtland.pdf. Also published in *Our Common Future*. Oxford, UK: Oxford University Press, 1987.

Wilson, J., P. Tyedmers, and R. Pelot. 2007. Contrasting and comparing sustainable development indicator metrics. *Ecol. Indicators*, 7(2):299–314.

3

RESOURCE EFFICIENCY OF CHEMICAL MANUFACTURING CHAINS: PRESENT AND FUTURE

JEAN-PAUL LANGE

Shell Technology Centre, Amsterdam, The Netherlands

3.1 INTRODUCTION

Since the Earth Summit in Rio de Janeiro in 1992, the concept of sustainable development has been adopted widely in the energy and chemical industries (Eissen et al. 2002; Watkins 2002). Increasingly, business options are evaluated on their triple bottom line of economic, environmental, and societal responsibilities. This is often called the strategy of the 3P's: people, planet, and profits (or prosperity). Accordingly, sustainability must contribute to the prosperity of communities and industry, it must preserve the planet by utilizing natural resources efficiently and by protecting the environment from waste disposal, and it must respect people by respecting their values and communities. In the specific case of manufacturing processes, sustainability can be reduced effectively to four basic dimensions—resource, waste, hazard, and cost—which have been applied to a few industrial processes for illustration purpose (Lange 2009). Key aspects of manufacturing costs, resourse utilization, and waste (polymer disposal or recycling) have been discussed in some length in earlier papers (Lange 2001, 2002). The present contribution will review and complement these discussions, and will address the potential of renewable feedstock.

Sustainable Development in the Process Industries: Cases and Impact, Edited by Jan Harmsen and Joseph B. Powell
Copyright © 2010 John Wiley & Sons, Inc.

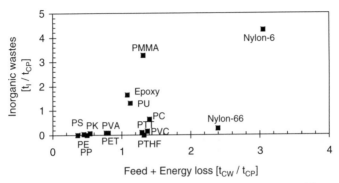

Figure 3.1 Resource utilization of polymers, expressed as wastes of inorganics and total carbon integrated over the entire manufacturing chain. (Adapted from Lange 2002.)

3.2 RESOURCE EFFICIENCY

3.2.1 Conventional Manufacturing Chains

Fifty large chemical processes have been analyzed in terms of their efficiency in utilizing feedstock, chemicals, and energy (Lange 2002). This approach extends Sheldon's pioneering analysis of the environmental (E) factor (Sheldon 1994) by using real process data and considering energy consumption. These 50 processes were linked to one another to compose 15 complete manufacturing chains that convert crude oil to large-volume polymers such as polyolefins, polystyrene, poly(vinyl chloride) (PVC), polyurethane, polyesters, polycarbonates, epoxy resins, polymethacrylate, and nylon (Lange 2002).[1] The overall losses of hydrocarbons (C) and inorganics (I) of these integral chains are reported in Figure 3.1.

According to the figure, integrated manufacture of polyolefins [e.g., polyethylene (PE) and polypropylene (PP)] and polystyrene (PS) proceeds fairly efficiently with integral hydrocarbon waste of less than 0.5 metric ton of carbon (t_{CW}) per metric ton of carbon in products (t_{CP}), and inorganic waste production of less than 0.1 metric ton (t_I) per metric ton of carbon in products (t_{CP}). This is expected to hold for most of the commodity hydrocarbon polymers used in commerce. Other integral production chains appear much less efficient, however. The production of PVC appears to be energy intensive, with hydrocarbon losses of about $1.4\,t_{CW}$ per metric ton of product. As shown in Figure 3.1, large amounts of inorganic can also be consumed during the

---

[1]The initial study did not account for the co-production of NaOH during Cl_2 manufacture. The present revision spreads the waste over both products, which results in lower hydrocarbon consumption for Cl_2 manufacture (50% reduction), PVC (25% reduction), and epoxy resins, polycarbonate, and polyurethane (<10% reduction).

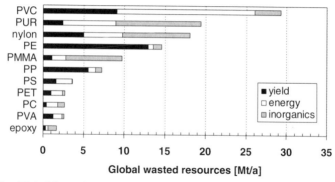

Figure 3.2 Global loss of carbon and inorganic during the manufacture of 11 major polymers (1995–2000).

manufacture of high-performance polymers such as polyamide (nylon 6 and nylon 6,6), poly(methyl methacrylate) (PMMA), epoxy resins, polyurethane (PU), and polycarbonate (PC).

Specific waste production, expressed per ton of carbon in the polymer, can be used to estimate the global waste production simply by multiplying it by the volume of polymer produced. The result, shown here in Figure 3.2, reveals that global waste production is dominated by the manufacture of PVC, polyurethane nylon, and polyethylene: PVC and PE because of hydrocarbon losses; PU and nylon because of high additional inorganic losses.

Except for polyolefins, hydrocarbon losses are usually dominated by energy consumption. Indeed, PE and PP waste more feedstock than fuel, by downgrading part of the feed to fuel during steam cracking. As for inorganic losses, the largest contributions come from polyurethane, nylon, and poly(methyl methacrylates). The overall losses due to these major polymers are distributed almost equally over yield loss [41 megatons/yr (Mt/a)], energy consumption (38 Mt/a), and inorganic wastes (33 Mt/a).

The consumption of integrated chains can be broken down into individual process steps in an attempt to identify the most inefficient or those that need most improvement. Table 3.1 summarizes the major contributions of the seven most conspicuous chains, and Figure 3.3 reports the overall efficiency of the major chemical intermediates, integrated from the primary hydrocarbons to the target intermediates. These analyses reveal seven conspicuous intermediates: five that consume much inorganic resources—caprolactam (CPL), methyl methacrylate (MMA), epichlorohydrin (ECH), toluene diisocyanate (TDI) and its precursor dinitrotoluene (DNT), and two that consume much hydrocarbon—hexyldiamine (HDA) and phosgene (Cl_2CO). High inorganic waste is often related to the use of stoichiometric reagents such as H_2SO_4, $Ca(OH)_2$, NH_3, and Cl_2. High hydrocarbon waste can be related to poor selectivity, energy-intensive separation processes, or a high consumption of hydrogen,

TABLE 3.1   Major Contribution to the Resource Inefficiency of the Seven Most Conspicuous Polymers

Major Hydrocarbon Waste			Major Inorganic Waste		
Product	Feed	Contribution (%)	Feed	Product	Contribution (%)
Nylon 6,6					
Butadiene	HDA	38	Butadiene	HDA	42
Benzene	Adipic acid	21	Benzene	Adipic acid	53
Nylon-6					
Cyclohexane	CPL	51	Cyclohexane	CPL	98
CH_4	NH_3	21			
PMMA					
MMA	PMMA	23	DMK	MMA	98
Epoxy					
Phenol	BPA	27	Propene	ECH	74
Benzene	Phenol	20	BPA + ECH	Epoxy	25
PUR					
DNT	TDI	36	Toluene	DNT	88
PVC					
NaCl	Cl_2	35	NaCl	Cl_2	40
Ethene	VCM	32	Ethene	VCM	58
PC					
BPA	PC	91	BPA	PC	32
			Phenol	BPA	27

ammonia, and/or Cl_2, which are made from methane. These seven intermediates are obvious targets for further research.

Neelis et al. (2006) have published a study that confirms and complements these results. They confirmed the chemical intermediates that are manufactured with large energy losses. They also estimated that chemical manufacturing in Europe and worldwide is contributing to 2000 and 10,000 pJ/yr, respectively, of energy loss. Neelis et al. did not consider the consumption of inorganics, however. For comparison, the 79 Mt/a of hydrocarbon losses estimated here for 11 major polymers corresponds to 3300 pJ/yr of energy loss (i.e., to a third of Neelis's estimate for the total chemical industry).

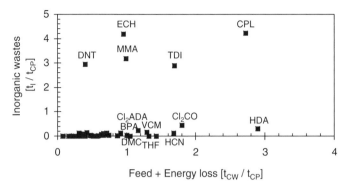

Figure 3.3 Resource utilization of chemical intermediates, expressed as wastes of inorganics and total hydrocarbon integrated over the entire manufacturing chain. (Adapted from Lange 2002.)

3.2.2 New Manufacturing Chains Based on Petrochemical Feedstocks

Based on this analysis, it is not surprising to see the seven conspicuous intermediates being subject to extensive research. For example, alternative routes are being investigated for caprolactam, adipic acid, methyl methacrylate, and vinyl chloride (Chauvel and Lefebvre 1989; ECN 1999; Bellussi and Perego 2000; Dahlhoff et al. 2001; Morgan 2002). Similarly, the substitution of phosgene by diphenyl carbonate, for example (Ono 1997; Plotkin and Glatzer 2002), is also aimed at improving the manufacture of diisocyanate and polycarbonates. However, less effort appears to be being put toward improving the manufacture of epichlorohydrin or dinitrotoluene. Efficiency analyses, as reported here and by Neelis et al. (2006) would be instrumental in comparing various routes and identifying the most efficient. For example, Neelis et al. showed that the energy efficiency of hexyldiamine manufacture is highest for the route based on adipic acid, followed by that based on butadiene, and finally, that based on acrylonitrile. Inorganic wastes were omitted but should be considered in future analyses.

High-performance polymers are usually based on functionalized monomers that provide polarity, hydrogen bonding, and/or cross-linking. Building such properties from hydrocarbons usually requires significant resource inputs at some point in the value chain. Consequently, one can identify a clear research driver aimed at achieving these performance attributes through other, less resource-intensive means. A few examples are worth mentioning. In a first approach, the properties of polyolefins and polystyrene can be improved significantly by changing the tacticity and microstructure and/or by incorporating simple apolar and polar co-monomers (Morse 1998; Dubois 2001; Mecking 2001; Tullo 2002). Alternatively, polystyrene can be hydrogenated to polycyclohexylethylene to obtain a glassy polymer with performances that can compete with polycarbonate or poly(methyl methacrylate) in certain applications (Reisch 2000, 2001; Tullo 2002). As a third example, some properties of polyamides are now duplicated by a new polyester, poly(trimethylene terephthalate) (PTT), which is based on monomers that consume many fewer resources than those of polyamides: namely, 1,3-propane diol and terephthalic acid (Figure 3.1). The resource consumption of PTT is expected to decrease further in the future, when operational experience allows for further optimization of the manufacturing process. Finally, engineering-type performance has been achieved by co-polymerizing the simplest monomers (i.e., alkenes and CO) into regular polyketones (Drent et al. 1996; Tullo 2002). This high-performance polymer is characterized by very low integral wastes of approximately 0.5 metric ton of hydrocarbon waste and 0.03 metric ton of inorganics per metric ton of carbon in product (Figure 3.1).

3.2.3 New Manufacturing Chains Based on Renewable Feedstocks

Polar monomers might be obtained more efficiently from natural resources such as carbohydrates. Natural carbohydrate polymers such as starch, hemicellulose, and cellulose can be chemically modified to produce valuable materials such as fibers, adhesives, and additives (Kola et al. 1995; Grüll et al. 2006). Several companies are also commercializing aliphatic polyesters based on natural hydroxyalkanoates that are produced by and accumulated in certain plants (Baker 2002; BenBrahim 2002; Tullo 2002; Brown 2006). Alternatively, polymeric carbohydrates can be hydrolyzed to elementary sugars and subsequently converted to a variety of chemical intermediates, as illustrated in Figure 3.4. Fermentation processes can convert sugars to ethanol, lactic acid (Gruber et al. 2006), 1,3-propane diol (Nakamura and Whited 2003), or succinic acid (Ritter 2004; Werpy et al. 2006). Chemical processes can also be applied to upgrade sugars to ethane and propane diols (Crabtree et al. 2006) or to platform molecules such as levulinic acid, furfural, and hydroxymethyl furfural (Kamm et al. 2006). These can subsequently be converted to numerous chemical intermediates: for example, to monomers for nylon or monomers for metacrylate- and terephthalate-type polymers (Wool 1999; Kamm et al. 2006; Lichtenthaler 2006; Lange 2007a). Kamm et al. (2006) have reported comprehensive trees of derivatives for furfural, hydroxymethyl furfural, and levulinic acid. Figure 3.4 is limited to oxygenated intermediates. However, a wealth of nitrogen-containing building blocks can also be obtained by reacting these intermediates (e.g., with NH_3 or amines).

Natural triglycerides are also a promising feedstock for the chemical industry. The fatty acids are already converted to detergents, emulsifiers, emollient, and a variety of specialty chemicals (Wool 1999; Hill 2006). More recently, however, they are also being modified for incorporation in polyurethane and polyester resins (Tullo 2007). Glycerol, which is a frequent co-product of triglyceride upgrading, is also a promising chemical. It can be applied as an additive in various formulations or be converted to numerous intermediates (e.g., to 1,2- and 1,3-propane diol, epichlorohydrin, or acrylic acid) (Dasari et al. 2005; Crabtree et al. 2006; Hill 2006; McCoy 2006; Wilke 2006; Sels et al. 2007).

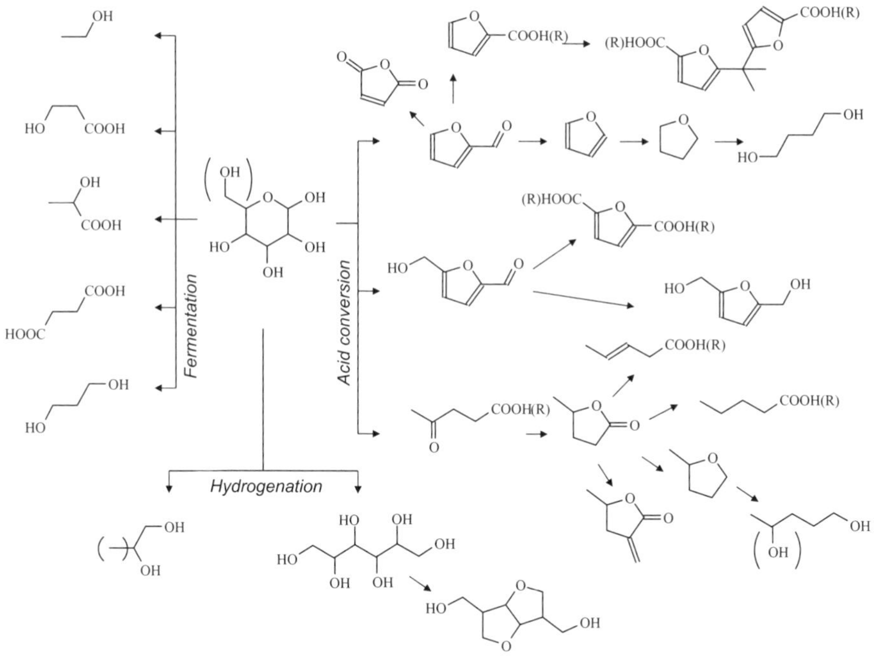

Figure 3.4 Oxygenated chemical intermediates produced by fermentation or chemical conversion of sugars (nitrogen-containing derivatives were omitted for the sake of simplicity).

Some of these efforts are targeting alternative, more efficient routes to existing intermediates. Others are investigating new intermediates and polymers to replace those applied today. The fact that novel chains are derived from renewable feedstock does not guarantee high resource efficiency or low environmental impact. Figures 3.3 and 3.1 indicate the monomers and polymers that offer the largest room for improvement in resource utilization. They therefore represent the weakest competitors in terms of environmental and cost performance (cost performance will be discussed later). These intermediates and polymers should be the first targets for renewable chemicals. Nice examples are the conversion of sugars to nylon intermediates or the conversion of glycerol to epichlorohydrin. Resource-efficient polymers such as the polyolefins and polystyrene are more difficult targets for renewable feedstock. Preliminary analysis of the integral production chain, from biomass to polymer, suggests indeed that such renewable routes may consume more energy than do their oil-based alternatives (Gerngross and Slater 2000).

3.2.4 Polymer Recycling

Another way to reduce the footprint of polymer manufacture consists of recycling spent resins back to the manufacturing chain to save virgin material (Figure 3.5). Recycling can be done via:

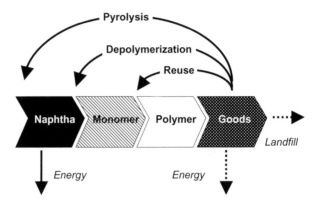

Figure 3.5   Options for disposing of spent polymers. (From Lange 2002.)

- Reuse of the polymer after simple cleaning or after cleaning and reprocessing to equal- or lower-grade material
- Depolymerization back to the monomer(s)
- Conversion to a general feedstock such as naphtha or synthesis gas (e.g., via pyrolysis) of gasification

If none of these options is technically or economically feasible, one can always exploit the heating value of the spent polymer by burning it instead of burning fossil fuels.

Intuitively, one expects the shorter recycle loop in Figure 3.5 to offer larger savings in waste production during manufacture. This is not always the case, however, for the recycling process also consumes resources such as energy. The optimal recycling option depends on many factors, some technical, some economic, and some societal (Kaminsky 1992; Borchardt 1998). Such a life-cycle analysis is clearly outside the scope of the present conceptual analysis. However, a simple conceptual framework has been proposed to help discriminate between theoretically preferred options (Lange 2002). This framework was based on two indices. The first index is the integral waste production of polymer manufacture as developed above. The second index is the enthalpy of depolymerization: The lower the enthalpy requirement, the easier the depolymerization, and probably, the lower the consumption of energy and chemicals. The combination of these two indices shows contrasting characteristics for condensation and addition polymers (Figure 3.6). The former are generally characterized by high waste production and easy depolymerization, whereas the latter are characterized by low waste production but demanding depolymerization.

In fact, Figure 3.6 can be divided into four quadrants according to the disposal options that are theoretically preferred (Lange 2002). The upper two quadrants (1 and 2) regroup polymers that release much waste during virgin manufacture. They should therefore be recycled as much as possible,

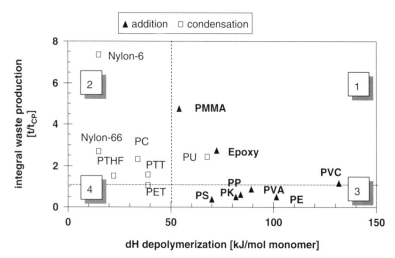

Figure 3.6 Environmental friendliness of polymers, expressed as the ease of depoly-merization and the resources wasted during virgin manufacture. The four quadrants represent theoretically preferred options for the disposal of spent polymer: (1) reuse, (2) reuse or depolymerization, (3) reuse or gasification/pyrolysis, and (4) all of the above + landfill. (Adapted from Lange 2002.)

preferably by reuse (quadrants 1 and 2) but also via depolymerization when feasible (quadrant 2). The polymers of the lower two quadrants do not release much waste upon virgin manufacture. Recycling options include reuse (quad-rants 3 and 4), depolymerization (quadrant 4), or pyrolysis (quadrant 3). However, it might not save significant resources compared to virgin manufac-ture. Combustion could therefore be considered as well, as it might save resources by avoiding the burning of fossil fuels. These four quadrants have arbitrary boundaries and do not account for all aspects of polymer disposal. Nevertheless, they seem to offer a reasonable framework for the purpose of mapping the appropriate disposal options adopted by responsible industries, as illustrated elsewhere (Lange 2002).

The present discussion did not address the potential of biodegradation because it is not a recycling or valorization option. Like landfill, biodegrada-tion is a disposal option. In fact, it requires very specific conditions to allow microorganisms to digest the biodegradable wastes efficiently. Recycling should be preferred when technically and economically feasible.

3.2.5 Life-Cycle Analyses

The present analysis compares polymers with one another during manufacture and recycle. However, it neglects their applications and the alternatives for these applications. It would be much better to compare the alternative materials based on the service provided rather than on mass or volume used. The chemical industry and chemical associations have performed such comparisons to highlight the true benefits of synthetic materials (O'Discroll 2005, 2007). For example, plastic packaging and polystyrene containers are claimed to save 30% energy over their entire life cycle compared to paper and paperboard alternatives. Plastic bags have been reported to produce fewer air and water pollutants than are produced by paper bags (Jones 2007). The substitution of light plastics for metals in cars is claimed to improve the fuel economy by 7% and, thereby, to save 2 tons of fuel over a car's life. Polymer insulation is claimed to save five times more energy than is consumed during manufacture. These few examples illustrate the need to compare materials based on the service provided. Such life-cycle analyses provide true evaluation of the resource efficiency of products and services.

3.3 ECONOMIC IMPACT

3.3.1. Cost of Inefficiency

Resource-efficient chains are not only friendlier to the environment but are also often more economical than inefficient ones. Indeed, the cost of polymers appears to increase with the increasing amount of hydrocarbon wasted throughout the entire manufacturing chain (Figure 3.7). Notice that for the sake of consistency, the costs and wastes have been expressed per ton of carbon in the final polymer. Why this relationship between resource and cost efficiency?

Efficient chains often require less feedstock and chemicals. They thereby have lower feedstock cost. Energy-efficient chains often require lower investment as well. The investment cost of manufacturing plants has been shown to depend primarily on the energy efficiency and energy-transfer duty of the

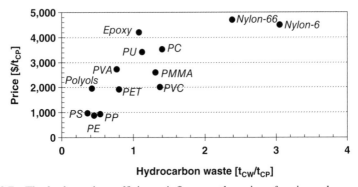

Figure 3.7 The hydrocarbon efficiency influences the price of major polymers (1975–1995 average oil price of about $23 per barrel).

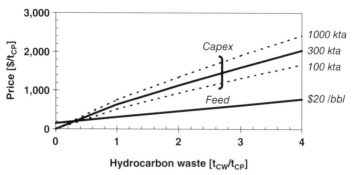

Figure 3.8 Impact of resource efficiency on feed cost and capital costs (based on a model chain of four steps of identical scale and a capex energy loss correlation. (From Lange 2001.)

manufacturing processes (Lange 2001): The more efficient the chemistry, the lower the energy transferred during manufacture and, consequently, the lower the investment cost.

Figure 3.8 illustrates these points by displaying typical increases in feed and investment costs that have been determined using a reference oil price of $20 per barrel (or $150/t) and the investment–duty correlation reported by Lange (2001). According to the figure, a manufacturing chain that operates with an overall waste of 2 t_{CW}/t_{CP} would require a feedstock cost of some $500/$t_{CP}$ (product carbon). With a capital cost of about $1100/$t_{CP}$ (on a scale of 300 kilotons/yr), the total fixed and capital costs would amount to about $1500/$t_{CP}$, which would raise the total manufacturing cost to about $2100/$t_{CP}$ (i.e., already half the market price displayed in Figure 3.7).

These calculations assumed that the manufacturing chain consists of four process steps of identical scale (i.e., 100, 300, and 1000 kilotons/yr). Obviously, representative calculations should consider the real number and scale of the process steps. The number usually increases and the scale usually decreases with increasing complexity of the monomer, which makes the product more expensive. The calculations should also consider the cost of catalyst and chemicals, which can be significant in the case of processes that produce much inorganic waste. Finally, the calculations used an oil price of $20 per barrel, to be consistent with Figure 3.7. When considering higher oil prices, one needs to raise not only the feed cost but also the investment costs (e.g., because of the increased steel price), as we have witnessed over recent years.

3.3.2 Economic Potential of Bio-Based Chemicals

Returning to renewable feedstocks, we need to recognize and exploit the high functionality of the feedstock. In the petrochemical industry, much effort has been devoted to incorporating oxygen into hydrocarbons selectively, often using expensive oxidation processes. This has resulted in a general

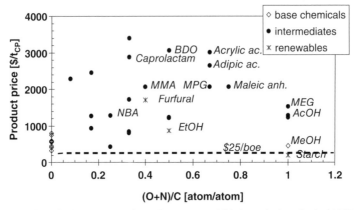

Figure 3.9 Historical average price of petro- and biobased chemicals (1975 to 1995 average oil price of about $23/bbl). (From Lange 2007b.)

increase in product cost with increasing oxygen content, as shown in Figure 3.9 (Lange 2007b).

In contrast, renewable feedstocks are often too rich in oxygen. They will probably require novel processes to remove excessive oxygen selectively. We can reasonably expect that intermediates that require moderate deoxygenation will also require moderate investment. Furthermore, they will better valorize the oxygen that has been paid for when purchasing the feedstock. Hence, renewable feedstock might best be used when aiming at producing highly functionalized intermediates and polymers. The future will tell us whether selective deoxygenation of carbohydrates is more efficient and cost-effective than selective oxygenation of hydrocarbons.

Figure 3.9 suggests that the conversion of renewable feedstock to hydro-carbon polymers is not economically attractive. At about $20 per barrel of oil, the conversion of starch to ethanol and, subsequently, ethene does not look at all attractive. The picture is likely to change at high crude oil prices, however, as indicated by the recent announcement by Dow and Crystalsev of their intention to build a PE plant based on Brazilian sugarcane ethanol (Bryner and Westervelt 2007).

As a final point, we need to address the dilemma of existing versus new building blocks. The renewable feedstocks do not lead easily to intermediates that are presently used in the petrochemical industry. They lead more readily to novel building blocks and novel materials such as aliphatic or furanic poly-esters. Deployment of such novel materials is a slow and difficult process, however. It requires the creation and development of new markets, often starting with niche applications that value specific properties but accommodate small volumes. It is therefore essential to direct the renewable feedstock to existing intermediates if one wishes to make a rapid and large impact on the industry.

3.4 CONCLUSIONS

Integrated manufacturing chains applied in the petrochemical industry have been analyzed in terms of their consumption of feed, energy, and chemicals. Commodity hydrocarbon polymers such as polyolefins and polystyrene appear to make efficient use of natural resources, with overall releases of less than 0.5 metric ton of hydrocarbon waste and 0.05 metric ton of inorganics per metric ton of carbon product. Other polymers are either wasting more hydrocarbons (e.g., PVC and nylon 6,6) and/or more inorganics (e.g., nylon 6, methyl methacrylate, polyurethane, and epoxy resins). Worldwide, the major polymers considered here are responsible for wasting annually some 110 megatons of resources, which are distributed fairly equally over waste of feedstock, energy, and inorganic materials. These resource inefficiencies are related to the production of seven major and conspicuous intermediates: caprolactam, hexyldiamine, methyl methacrylate, toluene diisocyanate, epichlorohydrin, vinyl chloride, and phosgene.

The resource inefficiencies also have economic penalties, for the least efficient routes lead to the more expensive polymers. Improving the resource efficiency is therefore of paramount economic importance. Beyond efficient manufacturing, clean and efficient disposal of spend products also needs to be addressed. Two indices are proposed for the preliminary evaluation of the recycle options of major polymers: the heat of depolymerization and the overall waste production of virgin polymers.

Areas that warrant more research include improvements in critical manufacturing steps, development of alternative chains, and exploration of alternative products. In particular, renewable feedstocks seem to offer excellent opportunities for delivering high-value, oxygen-rich polymers.

REFERENCES

Baker, J. 2002. *Eur. Chem. News*, Feb. 18, p. 24.

Bellussi, G., and C. Perego. 2000. *CatTech*, 4:4.

BenBrahim, A. 2002. *Chembytes Ezine*, Apr., www.chemsoc.org.

Borchardt, J. K. 1998. In *Kirk–Othmer Encyclopedia of Chemical Technology*, 4th ed. New York: Wiley, p. 460.

Brown, R. C. 2006. In *Biorefineries: Industrial Processes and Products*, Vol. I, ed B. Kamm, P. R. Gruber, and M. Kamm. Weinheim, Germany: Wiley–VCH, p. 227.

Bryner, M., and R. Westervelt. 2007. *Chem. Week*, July 25, p. 13.

Chauvel, A., and G. Lefebvre. 1989. Petrochemical processes: 1. Synthesis gas derivatives and major hydrocarbons; 2. Major oxygenated, chlorinated and nitrated derivatives. Paris: Editions Technip, Institut Français du Petrole.

Crabtree, S. P., R. C. Lawrence, M. W. Tuck, and D. V. Tyers. 2006. *Hydrocarbon Proc.*, Feb., p. 87.

Dahlhoff, G., J. P. M. Niederer, and W. F. Hoelderich. 2001. *Catal. Rev.*, 43:381.

Dasari, M. A., P.-P. Kiatsimkul, W. R. Sutterlin, and G. J. Suppes. 2005. *Appl. Catal. A*, 281:225.

Drent, E., J. A. M. van Broekhoven, and P. H. M. Budzelaar. 1996. In *Applied Homogeneous Catalysis with Organometallic Compounds*, ed. B. Cornils and W. A. Hermann. New York: VCH, p. 333.

Dubois, Ph. 2001. *Chim. Nouv.*, 75:3297.

ECN. 1999. *Eur. Chem. News*, Oct. 18, p. 26.

Eissen, M., J. O. Metzger, and E. Schmidt. 2002. Schneidewind. *Angew. Chem. Int. Ed.*, 41:414.

Gerngross, T. U., and S. C. Slater. 2000. *Sci. Am.*, Aug., p. 25.

Gruber, P., D. E. Henton, and J. Starr. 2006. In *Biorefineries: Industrial Processes and Products*, ed. B. Kamm, P. R. Gruber, and M. Kamm. Weinheim, Germany: Wiley–VCH, p. 381.

Grüll, D., F. Jetzinger, M. Kozich, M. M. Wastyn, and R. Wittenberger. 2006. In *Biorefineries: Industrial Processes and Products*, ed. B. Kamm, P. R. Gruber, and M. Kamm. Weinheim, Germany: Wiley–VCH, p. 61.

Hill, K. 2006. In *Biorefineries: Industrial Processes and Products*, Vol. II, ed. B. Kamm, P. R. Gruber, and M. Kamm. Weinheim, Germany: Wiley–VCH, p. 291.

Jones, P. 2007. *ICIS Chem. Bus.*, July 16, p. 36.

Kaminsky, W. 1992. In *Ullmann's Encyclopedia of Industrial Chemistry, A21.* Weinheim, Germany: VCH, p. 153.

Kamm, B., M. Kamm, M. Schmidt, T. Hirth, and M. Schulze. 2006. In *Biorefineries: Industrial Processes and Products*, Vol. II, ed. B. Kamm, P. R. Gruber, and M. Kamm. Weinheim, Germany: Wiley–VCH, p. 97.

Kola, R., O. von Elsner, W. Riepe, and K. Reuter. 1995. In *Ullmann's Encyclopedia.* Weinheim, Germany: VCH, p. 153.

Lange, J.-P. 2001. *CatTech*, 5:82.

———. 2002. *Green Chem.*, 4:546.

———. 2007a. *Chem. Commun.*, 3488.

———. 2007b. In *Catalysis for Renewables*, ed. by G. Centi and R. van Santen. Hoboken, NJ: Wiley.

———. 2009. Sustainable chemical manufacturing: a matter of resources, wastes, hazards and costs. *ChemSusChem* 2:587–592.

Lichtenthaler, F. W. 2006. In *Biorefineries: Industrial Processes and Products*, Vol. II, ed. B. Kamm, P. R. Gruber, and M. Kamm. Weinheim, Germany: Wiley–VCH, p. 3.

McCoy, M. 2006. *Chem. Eng. News*, Feb. 6, p. 7.

Mecking, S. 2001. *Angew. Chem. Int. Ed.* 40:531.

Morgan, M. 2002. *Eur. Chem. News*, Feb. 11, p. 20.

Morse, P. M. 1998. *Chem Eng. News*, July 6, p. 11.

Nakamura, C. E., and G. M. Whited. 2003. *Curr. Opin. Biotechnol.*, 14:454.

Neelis, M., M. Patel, K. Blok, W. Haije, and P. Bach. 2006. *Energy 2007*, 32:1104.

O'Discroll, C. 2005. *Eur. Chem. News*, Oct. 3, p. 24.

———. 2007. *Chem. Ind.*, July 9, p. 24.

Ono, Y. 1997. *Appl. Catal. A*, 155:133.

Plotkin, J., and E. Glatzer. 2002. *Eur. Chem. News*, July 8, p. 32.

Reisch, M. 2000. *Mod Plast. Int.*, July 7, p. 17.

———. 2001. *Chem. Eng. News*, Sept. 17, p. 22,

Ritter, S. K. 2004. *Chem. Eng. News*, May 31, p. 31.

Sels, B., E. d'Hondt, and P. Jacobs. 2007. In *Catalysis for Renewables*, ed. G. Centi and R. van Santen. Hoboken, NJ: Wiley.

Sheldon, R. A. 1994. *ChemTech*, Mar., p. 38.

Tullo, A. H. 2002. *Chem. Eng. News*, May 20, p. 13.

———. 2007. *Chem. Eng. News*, Aug. 20, p. 36.

Watkins, K. S. 2002. *Chem. Eng. News*, Apr. 22, p. 15.

Werpy, T., J. Frye, J. Holladay, and R. Bush. 2006. In *Biorefineries: Industrial Processes and Products*, ed. B. Kamm, P. R. Gruber, and M. Kamm. Weinheim, Germany: Wiley–VCH, p. 367.

Wilke, T. 2006. In *Biorefineries: Industrial Processes and Products*, Vol. I, ed. B. Kamm, P. R. Gruber, and M. Kamm. Weinheim, Germany: Wiley–VCH, p. 385.

Wool, R. P. 1999. *ChemTech*, 6:44.

4

REGIONAL INTEGRATION OF PROCESSES, AGRICULTURE, AND SOCIETY

MICHAEL NARODOSLAWSKY

Institute for Process Technology, Graz University of Technology, Graz, Austria

4.1 THE FORMATIVE CHARACTER OF RAW MATERIALS

The challenge to make the process industry more sustainable starts at the very beginning of any process—the raw material base. Raw materials determine many aspects of processes. Their provision will cause a number of environmental impacts and will have a major effect on the social situation of those providing them. Their qualities and properties will structure logistics as well as process technology. Their abundance or scarcity and their availability in the long term will have a profound impact on global issues such as security and peace. Finally, they will determine the quality of products and their environmental impact.

Humankind will always have to rely on resources provided by nature, and there will always be a diversity of resources at the disposal of industry to fulfill human desires to sustain and improve living conditions. No class of resources will be "off limits" for human use. Sustainable development will, however, cause rethinking regarding the rational use of various resources. Fossil and mineral resources, even radiating material, will all find their place in a sustainable society. The challenge will be to assign them their particular place as well as to design the right structures and processes for their use and possible treatment when the products they make up have outlived their useful life span.

Sustainable Development in the Process Industries: Cases and Impact, Edited by Jan Harmsen and Joseph B. Powell
Copyright © 2010 John Wiley & Sons, Inc.

In this chapter we deal particularly with the use of renewable resources within the framework of sustainable development. Even more specifically, we deal with processes based on biogenic resources. Within the framework of sustainable development, this class of resources will have to provide a wide range of products and services. It will play a considerable role in the provision of energy, especially when energy has to be stored. It will provide the base for most products with a short life span used in society and for products that will be released to nature, such as fertilizers or pest control agents. Products based on biogenic resources will also play a considerable role in construction and infrastructure. As a matter of fact, biogenic raw materials will take over many applications and services provided currently by fossil raw materials, and quite a few that are now covered by mineral resources. Biogenic raw materials, together with the direct utilization of solar energy in the form of photovoltaic, thermal solar collectors, and wind and hydro power will become the most important "rising stars" of the technical system on which a sustainable society will be based.

4.1.1   Biogenic Raw Material Properties

The structure of the technological system that utilizes a particular class of raw materials will be defined by inherent properties of these resources. It is therefore important to analyze the characteristic properties of biogenic raw materials in order to understand the forces that will form the technologies utilizing them. Comparing these properties with those of the prevailing raw materials of process technology will also help to highlight the necessary changes in the technological structure on its way toward sustainability. In the following paragraphs we summarize briefly some of these characteristic properties of biogenic resources, at least as far as they are important for the task of describing the structures and challenges for process technology in a sustainable society.

Limited Infinity   The term *limited infinity* seems at first glance a paradox, but it describes very precisely the most important sustainability property of biogenic raw materials: They are renewable, but not unlimited in availability. Biogenic raw materials are nothing other than a result of the influx of solar radiation. Any natural growth process needs energy that is eventually provided by the sun. It also needs material resources such as water, carbon, and oxygen. All these materials partake in enormous global cycles, again driven by solar radiation. Without the sun, there is no life on our planet, and consequently, no biogenic resources to utilize.

The sun is obviously the "infinite" aspect of biogenic raw materials. For all practical considerations, there is no end to solar radiation. What is limited is the capacity of our planet to catch solar radiation. Our planet receives solar radiation on its surface, and this surface is limited. This means that at any given time, there is only a limited *flow* of solar energy reaching our planet, which will drive enormous but still limited global material cycles that will, in turn, provide abundant but still limited *growth* of biogenic material. From the (limited) material grown in, say, a year, we may harvest and utilize a part for our human needs. Next year we are again entitled to our share of the bounty, but not to more.

The deeper meaning of the term *limited infinity* is that despite the fact that they are renewable, the utilization of biogenic raw materials is always competitive. We as a species have to compete with other species and other natural processes for our share of the sun. In more practical and technological terms, this means that biogenic raw material utilization will always have to be efficient, making the most out of an inherently limited flow. It also means that we have to make sure that this flow will not be diminished by our activities. We certainly will not influence the capacity of the sun to send us life-supporting energy. We may, however, degrade our planet's ability to take advantage of it by reducing the quality of the land (and possibly also the sea), and thereby diminish the overall bounty of biomass production.

To highlight the competitive character of the use of biogenic resources, some numbers may be informative: Overall global biomass production, measured as carbon, stands at about 60×10^9 metric tons of carbon per years. Current use of biomass from agriculture is approximately 6×10^9 metric tons/yr, and current fossil raw material consumption in 2008 stands at about 7×10^9 metric tons of carbon per year. If we factor in a global population increase to 9 billion people by 2050, demand for agricultural biomass will surpass 9×10^9 metric tons/yr. If we just want to replace fossil resource utilization at the same per capita rate as today, this would amount to an additional resource demand of over 10×10^9 metric tons/yr. This estimate is very conservative, as no increase in per capita energy demand is factored in. According to other sources (Siirola 2007), even according to this very modest estimate, appropriation of yearly natural biomass production by humankind would come to almost a third of the total. The sustainability of an increase in humans' take from a tenth to a third of nature's bounty remains to be seen.

These numbers should not be seen as an argument against a shift toward biogenic resources as the main source of industrial processes. It should, however, reinforce the argument for utmost efficiency in its use as well as for wise management of the "machines" that provide us with these resources: namely, intact ecosystems.

Decentralized Resources   The sun shines everywhere and it does so moderately and evenly. Therefore, this natural income can be harvested at almost any place on our planet. This aspect of decentralized resource provision is markedly different from other types of raw materials, especially fossil resources. Crude oil, natural gas, and coal all come from mines or oil and gas fields, which constitute clearly delimited spatial areas, most of them removed from the areas where the products and services gained from these raw materials are consumed. A larger share of biogenic resources as input to our industry also means a dramatic change in the resource logistics. The logistics will have to shift from point sources to a spatially spreadout resource base. This means

TABLE 4.1   Humidity, Calorific Value, and Density for Some Renewable Resources Compared to Fuel Oil

Material	Humidity (% w/w)	Calorific Value (kWh/kg)	Bulk Density (kg/m³)
Straw (gray) baled	15	4.17	100–135
Wheat	15	4.17	670–750
Rapeseed	9	6.83	700
Wood chips	40	2.89	235
Split logs (beech)	20	4.08	400–450
Wood pellets	6	4.90	660
Light fuel oil	0	11.86	840

that we have to build up a logistical system that no longer ships resources via giant installations such as oil terminals, tankers, and pipelines to our consumption points, but that collects raw materials from fields, forests, and possibly the sea, and brings them to us.

Low Densities   As they come from the fields and forests, biogenic raw materials have low densities and high humidity compared to fossil oil, which now constitutes the main base for industrial production (Table 4.1). In addition, biogenic resources have not gone through the aging process of fossil materials, which leaves them with markedly lower calorific values. From the point of raw material logistics, this property (energy density) is important. As resources become more bulky and less rich in usable content, transport volume, not tonnage, becomes limiting.

The consequence of this will add to the dramatic change in the technosocial system that becomes necessary when the share of biogenic raw materials as input to our industry is increased. Figure 4.1 compares the energy necessary to ship 1 MJ provided by a certain resource a distance of 1 km, for different transport systems. The energy content here may be taken as an indicator of the value content of a certain resource for industrial utilization. From this figure it follows that transporting straw over 30 km or wood over 150 km will consume 1% of the energy content of the material transported. So does transporting crude oil over 2500 km per ship or pipeline!

Time Limitations   Biogenic resources are derived from living organisms and are therefore coupled to the cycles of life: the cycle of planting, growing, and harvesting, as well as the cycle of growth and degradation. Again, this is a marked difference to almost all other types of resources. Neither mineral nor fossil resources are subject to any change in quality over time. The only time dependence experienced by those resources is the exhaustion of reserves that may be exploited economically. This property adds to the complexity of the technical and logistical system that utilizes biogenic raw materials. Cyclical supply combined with limited shelf life results in the fact that most biogenic

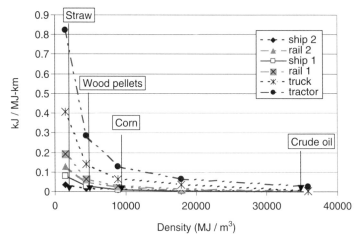

Figure 4.1 Energy necessary to transport 1 MJ over 1 km for various volumetric energy densities.

raw materials are not available at all times: There is an abundance at harvest time and relative scarcity in between.

4.1.2 Regional Biogenic Resources

The properties discussed above point toward the fact that biogenic raw materials are context specific. According to its natural endowment, every region will offer a distinctly different resource portfolio. According to its logistical parameters, raw material transport over long distances will become less attractive, keeping resources "in the region." Finally, the requirement to keep fields and forests fertile calls for conscious management of whatever remains after processing the raw material, and returning to the soil in a proper way all nutrients that have not been utilized. Such a material management program, coupled with conscious care for ecosystems and agricultural productivity, can only be realized on the local and regional level, involving a large spectrum of actors.

The importance of the regional context for biogenic raw material generation and provision results in a regional contextualization of technology. Regional differences in the raw material supply, as well as the necessity of shortening transport between raw material generation and technical treatment, call for regionally adapted technologies. At first glance this seems to contradict the general drive toward globalization of the economy. On a closer look, however, it becomes obvious that a stronger contextualization of technology just means that one of the major tenets of a global economy—that the competitive advantage of regions will define their economical activity—will be served in a more systemic manner. Goods and services required by society will be provided by optimized networks of technologies, based on optimized utilization of renewable resources, taking into account the spatial dimension of resource provision and the structural dimension of social and economical networks of actors.

It is important to state here that regional adaptation and contextualization of technologies do not imply regional autarky. There will still be global markets for goods and services. There will still be central processing units for a wide array of products, from computers to cars to pharmaceuticals and possibly also some bulk products such as polymers. What will be changed is the spatial distribution of sources for most energy services as well as intermediate chemicals. These services and products will be supplied much more decentrally than in our current fossil-based economy.

4.2   THE SYSTEMIC ENGINEERING CHALLENGE

The arguments discussed above boil down to three hypotheses that will define the development discourse in process engineering in the twenty-first century:

1. Dwindling fossil resources and increasing concern about global climate change and other environmental concerns will make this century a transition period from a fossil past to renewable future resources.
2. This change will necessitate reconstruction of much of the process industry that currently provides energy services and materials for society, as the types of raw material defines the technologies that are utilizing them.
3. This reconstruction will affect not only the technologies used, but also the structure of industry and the logistical system employed in material flow management.

From these three hypotheses we may deduce the engineering challenge for process engineers in the twenty-first century. This challenge will have to include the contextualization of technologies regarding their regional settings. If we concentrate on regional contextualization (which is the topic of this chapter), aspects that follow will become increasingly important for process engineers.

4.2.1   The Enlarged Process Concept

The challenge for engineers in the twenty-first century is to optimize the transformation of renewable resources into products and services for society. This means that engineers have to take into account raw material generation, the conversion of raw materials to products and services, and the reintegration of waste and by-products into the ecosphere in a meaningful way. Thus, the process to be designed by the engineer does not start and stop at the factory gate, but comprises the entire cycle from raw material generation, to production processes, to distribution, to recycle and/or reuse. From the aspect of regional contextualization, this means that the engineer has to serve actively as the interface with resource provision (i.e., agriculture, forestry, and aquaculture) and to participate in the design of regional material flow management.

4.2.2   The Resource Efficiency Challenge

Given the strong competition for renewable resources that results from their limited-infinity property and the increasing demand to substitute for fossil resources, resource efficiency will become a key success factor for future technologies. In particular, this requires engineers to design utilization technologies (or, better, technology networks) that will utilize the resources entirely. Every gram of the resource harvested has to be transformed into a salable product, has to provide a service for society, or has to be returned to the biosphere and support fertility for the generation of further resources.

Contextualization requires the engineer to deal with different resources in different regions. These resources will offer different constituents for utilization but will also pose different technological challenges to make them available. On top of this, agricultural production factors such as fields, grasslands, and forests will require different qualities and quantities of materials to be returned to them if they should maintain or increase their productivity.

4.2.3   The Variety Challenge

Natural systems provide neither single resources nor resources in cookie-cutter homogeneity. They provide a variety of resources in ever-differing qualities. Dealing with this variety in a way that optimizes resource provision in the long term (e.g., avoiding monocultures) and solving the quality control issues posed by wider quality variations in renewable resources compared to fossil resources will become critical success factors for engineers. Again, it is obvious that regional contextualization is a key to this challenge. Every region will provide its own rich diversity of resources and requires a certain variety of land and resource use for maintaining its productivity. Each region will have its particular bandwidth of variation in the quality of its primary renewable resources.

4.2.4   The Network Challenge

Utilizing renewable resources optimally requires not only highly efficient single technologies, but networks of technologies. The challenge to design technology networks has two interesting aspects when seen from the vantage point of regional contextualization. On the one hand, the approach to optimizing networks differs from that to optimizing single technologies. It will lead to an optimal output of the network, whereas subsystems might well be suboptimal. In a concrete regional setting, this requires an informed discourse between the actors, as the spoils of optimization have to be distributed within the network, taking into account the overall goal of the network. The engineer must contribute to this discourse to provide a factual base for the economic and social sharing of burdens as well as profits. On the other hand, networks consist of sources, processing units, consumers, and the logistics that connect these nodes of the network. The last item here, the logistical aspect of renewable resource utilization, will become an especially decisive factor, as renewable resources require a more sophisticated logistical system, taking into account low transport densities and time-dependent resource provision. Engineers will therefore be well advised to include logistics into their process concept.

From the point of view of regional contextualization, it is clear that logistics is always dependent on regional resources and their qualities, but also on regional infrastructure and regional actors. An industrial system depending increasingly on renewable resources will have to integrate logistical factors on the ground into the design and choice of technologies.

4.3   REGIONAL INTEGRATION OF TECHNOLOGIES

These challenges need new methodological approaches to process design. The methodological toolbox for process engineers, that is, the methods of mass and energy balances (e.g., Schnitzer 1991), material flow management (e.g., Brunner and Rechberger 2004), and methods such as pinch analysis, which generate heat transfer networks (e.g., Kemp 2006), may be adapted to the enlarged process concept described above. These tools will take the process engineer a long way toward solving the problems of regional adaptation of technologies.

Some salient questions regarding regional contextualization will, however, be addressed in the remaining parts of this contribution. One concerns the overall approach to generating regional technology networks based on renewable resources. Another question concerns the choice of the right size of processes based on renewable resources. Both are addressed briefly in this contribution. The methods employed here have proven to be adequate; however, there may still be methodological development in these fields. The methods and case studies presented below are not so much intended to present final solutions as to point to approaches to solving the challenges of the twenty-first century. It is worthwhile to state at this point that there still is some time left to find a sure footing for process engineering in this century. However, discourse regarding its future must begin now.

4.3.1   Regional Technology Networks: The Case Study of Eastern Styria

The key question here is to transform a set of boundary conditions (e.g., the natural endowment of a region), requirements (e.g., the energy and nutritional demands of a certain region), technologies, and chances (e.g., export of materials and energy services) into a technology and material flow network that optimizes the value generated by the natural resources of a particular region. It is obvious that this task requires contextualization of technologies. It will therefore be exemplified in a concrete case study.

The viewpoint here opens regional production networks to treatment with process synthesis methods as a means of rational optimization in order to construct sustainable production systems. In the case study that follows a highly effective combinatorial method introduced by Friedler et al. (1992a), based on a process graph representation and on the axioms of combinatorially feasible process structures and combinatorial algorithms (Friedler et al. 1992b) [e.g., a maximal structure generator (Friedler et al. 1993), a solution structure generator, and decision mapping (Friedler et al. 1995)], was applied to the problem.

It goes without saying that implementation of technology networks in a region is a complex social and economic process. What is shown here has to be understood as the provision of scenarios for this discourse. This task can be based on solid methodological frameworks. The real challenge for engineers, however, is to participate in this discourse and to contribute to the implementation of sustainable utilization of the region's resources.

The case study addresses a region in southeastern Austria bordering on Slovenia and Hungary. East Styria is a predominantly agricultural region with 268,000 inhabitants, 61,000 hectares (ha; defined as $10,000\,m^2$; equals 2.41 acres) of fields, 41,000 ha of grassland, and 155,000 ha of forest (mostly coniferous). It comprises five "Bezirke" (an Austrian administrative level between a municipality and a federal state) and has a long and successful history of utilizing renewable energies. The case study examined technology networks that may be based on regional agriculture. Agriculture was seen as a material flow system encompassing growing of crops, grassland, stock breeding, forestry, orchards, and wine production as well as the provision of energy and auxiliary materials (pesticides, fertilizers). Regional households were seen as primary consumers of food, heat, and electricity. Any surpluses generated by the farming sector (such as excess food, electricity, energy carriers, and bio-based industrial products) were exported to marketplaces outside the region. Subsidies were not taken into account.

4.3.2   Starting Point

Today's agriculture in the region is characterized by small structures with a high input in working hours, machine hours, and money. Calculated at full cost and without subsidies, the agricultural sector has a negative added value, as shown in Figure 4.2. At full costs, most crop production, grassland cultivation, and husbandry produce an economic loss. Only forestry, orchards, and wine production have a positive added value. Alternative utilizations such as bio-based heat networks have a positive added value, whereas biogas on a base of corn silage (i.e., traditional biogas) has a negative net value. Other forms of

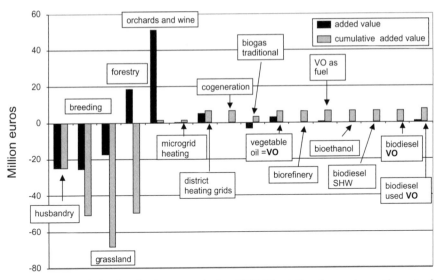

Figure 4.2 Added value in the scenario for 2005. The left column shows the actual added value of the activity; the right column is the cumulative added value of all activities, counting from the left. SHW, slaughterhouse waste.

utilization depicted in the figure (e.g., biorefineries, heat and electricity contracting, production of biofuels such as vegetable oil, biodiesel, and bioethanol) have not yet been used, but show potential for future development.

One reason for the negative added value in crop production (and hence in husbandry based on these crops) is the high demand for fossil fuel per hectare, as shown in Figure 4.3. Biological and low-tillage farming can reduce the fossil input per hectare considerably. A large factor in fossil energy demand (and hence costs as well as ecological impact) is drying of some crops, especially corn, which is the main crop in the region.

4.3.3 Scenario Development

Developing scenarios for regional technology networks requires a definition of possible economic frameworks, especially considering the level of exchange with other regions and the responsibility of the farming sector in a region to supply food to urban centers outside the region. Scenario C1 deals with the situation where the amount of agricultural goods imported into the region remains on the current level, and food is provided according to the demand of the region and of the nearby urban center of Graz. Overall, this reduces the amount of crops and animals going to the food sector compared to the current situation. This reduction, in turn, reduces the necessity for intensive farming and husbandry, opening acreage for alternative land utilizations, such as oil crops and energy plants, which have higher added value. On top of that,

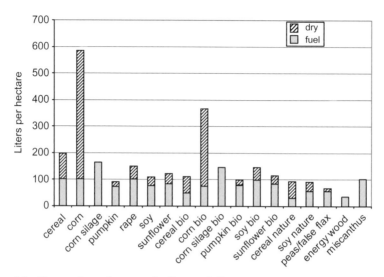

Figure 4.3   Demand per hectare (in liters of diesel and heating oil) for drying and mechanical energy.

there is room for biological and natural farming, which has a lower yield but also needs less energy and material input.

Grass silage that is not used for feeding of cows is utilized in biorefineries to produce lactic acid, proteins, and fibers. The latter are then fed into a biogas plant to produce heat and electricity or clean natural methane gas that is injected into the raw gas network. The latter form of biorefinery dominates the technology network as heat production is bound on demand. With most distance heating systems in the region already using biomass, demand for extra heat generation is limited.

Biofuels are produced in three different ways. The production of biodiesel from used vegetable oil remains on the same level (there exists an 8000-metric ton/yr site in the region already), whereas vegetable oil is used directly, without transesterification, in agricultural vehicles. In a new method of producing biodiesel, tallow from slaughtering is converted to fuel. The reduced fuel demand of agriculture can be met to a large extent by the amount of biodiesel and vegetable oil produced in the region.

With these optimizations, the agriculture of the region can produce 100% of the heat that is needed in private households and in agriculture. Furthermore, wood pellets from forestry can be exported. Figure 4.4 shows a dramatic change in the economic situation of the region in this scenario, with an overall increase in revenue from the agricultural sector and decentralized energy and industrial production sites linked to renewable resources.

A second long-term scenario (C2) deals with the aspect of an autarkic region, at least as far as food, energy for private households, and demand for agricultural products is concerned. (Transport not linked to agriculture itself

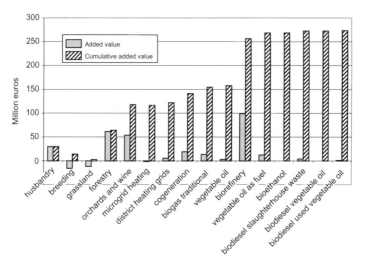

Figure 4.4   Added value for scenario C1.

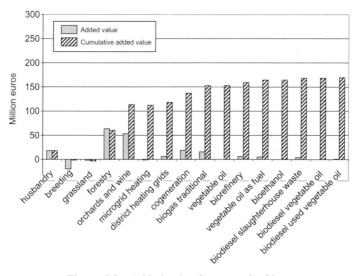

Figure 4.5   Added value for scenario C2.

is excluded.) All food, as well as energy, has to be produced within the region. The scenario reveals that it is possible to supply energy for households (electricity as well as heating) and for sustaining farming while also supplying food to the region (Figure 4.5). From an economic point of view, it is, however, not an appealing scenario. The necessity to supply products with low added value for the sake of achieving autarky blocks the use of acreage for more profitable uses.

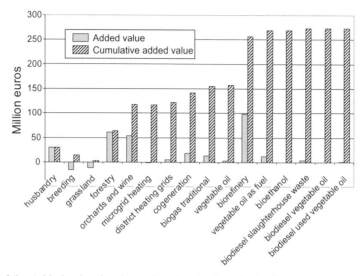

Figure 4.6   Added value for the regional agriculture in the long-term scenario (C3).

The final scenario (C3) represents an unhindered free-trade scenario, with the region free to import and export goods and services. This leads to a situation where low-value-added goods (e.g., corn or cereals) are imported, utilizing the acreage for energy provision and for the production of bulk products such as lactic acid, fibers, and amino acids (Figure 4.6).

4.3.4   Integrating Technologies into Regional Settings: Getting the Scale Right

It is an almost undisputed "truth" for the process industry that the larger the plant, the more profitable the operation. Economies of scale usually rein for the design decisions in this sector. Using renewable resources, the picture becomes considerably more complicated, especially if the ecological side of design decisions is also taken into account. Providing the energy for processes on the base of renewable resources either requires additional raw material input (approximately 25 to 38% of corn or wheat for ethanol production) or the utilization of wastes and by-products. Given the low transport density of many cheap agricultural by-products (e.g., straw), possibilities to utilize them in processes far from the fields would imply high transport loads. The amount of straw necessary to provide the heat for a 60,000-metric ton/yr ethanol plant is about 1,100,000 m^3/yr, requiring 55,000 tractor transports per year (150 per day). This requires larger, more central process sites to utilize other energy sources, mainly fossil energy carriers such as natural gas. In this section, bioethanol production is used as a reference process to investigate the impact of size on the environmental as well as the economic performance of renewable-resource-based production systems (Gwehenberger et al. 2007).

TABLE 4.2   Assumed Crop Rotation Systems and Yields for Corn and Wheat

Crop	Corn	Wheat
Corn	3 years; 8.9 metric tons/ha corn; 14.2 metric tons/ha straw	
Clover	2 years; 12.0 metric tons/ha	1 year; 12.0 metric tons/ha
Wheat	—	1 year; 5.6 metric tons/ha corn; 4.6 metric tons/ha straw
Barley	—	1 year; 5.0 metric tons/ha corn; 4.0 metric tons/ha straw
Rape	—	1 year; 2.2 metric tons/ha corn; 3.7 t/ha straw

Defining the Case Study   Four different scales of production have been investigated for fuel-grade bioethanol: 60,000, 10,000, 5,000, and 1000 metric tons/yr. The 60,000-metric ton/yr scale marks the lower margin of conventional industrial production, deriving its energy from natural gas and electricity from the (Austrian) grid (Eurostat 2004). Economic data as well as material and energy balances were taken from the literature (Friedl 2005). Three other scales are obtained from small-scale installations deriving their energies from by-products of farming, crop rotation, or from the process itself. If these sources did not suffice to cover the demand, the same assumptions were made for energy "imported" from the outside, as in the 60,000-metric ton/yr case. Transport was in all cases supplied by conventional fossil fuels. For all scales, corn as well as wheat as raw materials have been investigated, following a crop rotation system designed to make farming sustainable. This crop rotation system is summarized in Table 4.2.

For small-scale cases, three different technology options were included in the calculations:

1. *Ethanol production in combination with a biogas combined heat and power (CHP) plant.* Heat and electricity from the biogas CHP are utilized for ethanol production, while surplus electricity is supplied to the grid. The size of the biogas CHP that utilizes mash, clover, and straw is chosen such that its heat provision exactly covers the demand of the ethanol plant. Results are shown in Figure 4.4.

2. *Ethanol production in combination with biogas production.* In this case the biogas is utilized directly to supply process heat for the ethanol production. The biogas unit utilizes only the mash generated by the ethanol process. Excess biogas (in facilities with capacities of 5000 and 10,000 metric tons/yr) will be utilized to generate electricity by means of a small biogas CHP unit. Results are shown in Figure 4.5.

3. *Ethanol production combined with straw combustion.* For these cases, process heat is generated by burning a part (27 to 52% for wheat or

15 to 28% for corn, depending on the size of the plant) of the straw produced to provide the input to ethanol fermentation. In these cases mash will be utilized as a fertilizer since drying and selling as distillers' dried grains with solubles has a large energy demand and an ever-narrowing market as ethanol production increases globally. Results are shown in Figure 4.6.

Four ethanol-production-optimized technologies, depending on the size of the plant, have been considered. Detailed information on the technological features of the configuration in each case is available in a report of Friedl's (2007).

Economic and Ecological Evaluation The 18 small-scale options (three technological options, three capacity options, and two raw material options) and the 60,000-metric ton/yr corn and wheat plant were subjected to an economic and ecological evaluation. The economic evaluation was a straightforward calculation of the cost of 1 L of fuel-grade ethanol (using an azeotropic distillation process), given the running costs as well as the investment cost (where a payback time of seven years was assumed). Any products from the crop rotation not utilized by the ethanol plant were assumed to be sold at market prices.

The ecological pressure was calculated for the entire life cycle, including the agricultural production as well as all transport induced by the technologies, using the sustainable process index (SPI) (Krotscheck and Narodoslawsky 1996). This index describes the aggregated ecological pressure of a certain process by the area needed to embed this process sustainably into the ecosphere, rendering an "ecological footprint." The SPI calculates the areas necessary to provide raw materials and process energy as well as the area required to dissipate emissions and wastes from any process step sustainably. The general idea of this measure is that sustainability requires that all global material cycles (e.g., the global carbon cycle) are strictly closed and that any dissipation must be kept within the limits of natural variations in the air, water, and soil compartments. The SPI is able to distinguish between the ecological pressure of renewable and fossil raw materials based on closing the global carbon cycle, which is important to cases involving both resource types. The SPI has already been applied successfully to biofuels (Niederl and Narodoslawsky 2004). Allocation of the ecological pressure to the products was based on the income from the various agricultural products calculated at market prices.

Ecological impacts include transport from the fields to the site of ethanol production as well as any necessary transport of residues from the site back to the fields. Transport was assumed to be carried out by tractors for distances up to 15 km. Above that, trucks (40 metric tons) took over. Figure 4.7 shows some results of the ecological evaluation of various fuel systems. This figure reveals some interesting insights:

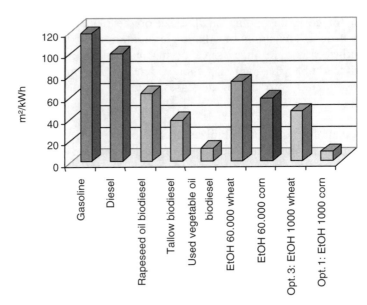

Figure 4.7 Ecological footprint (calculated using the SPI method) for different fuel options (60,000-metric tons/yr options with DDGS production).

1. There is a clear ecological advantage of biofuels compared to fossil competitors. All biofuels show a lower SPI value than those for gasoline and diesel. (This is also true for all other options not shown in the figure.)

2. The differences in the ecological impact of biofuels are considerable. They depend partly on the raw material (see the differences in the biodiesel cases and the difference between ethanol from the 60,000-metric ton/yr plant with corn and wheat as raw material). Corn has clear advantages over wheat. This advantage is linked to the higher yield per hectare of corn compared to wheat, reducing the agricultural impact calculated per kilogram of ethanol.

3. Small-scale options have a clear advantage in terms of the ecological impact. The best alternative (option 1, 1000 metric ton/yr capacity, using corn) has only 7.6% of the impact of fossil gasoline and only 15% of the impact of ethanol from the 60,000-metric ton/yr plant using the same raw material.

The latter result motivated a closer look into the influence of size on ecological as well as economic performance. Figure 4.8 presents, for the options considered, the cost of 1 L of ethanol based on corn as a raw material, with the assumptions that all by-products are sold at market prices, and that surplus electricity is sold as tariffs for green electricity. The effect of the economies of scale can be seen clearly. The smallest-scale plants produce at approximately double the cost of the 60,000-metric ton/yr plant.

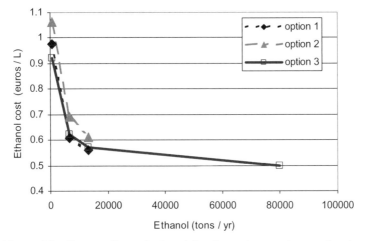

Figure 4.8   Cost per liter of ethanol for the various options and scales.

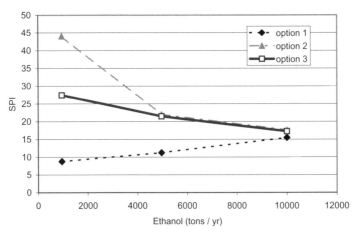

Figure 4.9   Sustainable process index (m^2/yr per liter) as a function of ethanol capacity.

A look into the ecological performance of the various options at different sizes (Figure 4.9) reveals another interesting insight. With options 2 and 3, the ecological impact decreases with the size of the plant. This is a result of increasing efficiencies linked to larger production units. With option 1, however, the ecological footprint calculated with SPI increases with the capacity of the plant. This result is linked primarily to the fact that in this option the residues of the biogas unit are redistributed to the fields in liquid form, requiring intensive transport effort. This recycles important nutrients to a much larger extent, however, than in the other two options.

The increased transport footprint is more than outweighed by the fact that less fertilizer is required in option 1. Transport to the fields is, however, responsible for the increase in the ecological footprint per kilowatt-hour of ethanol produced, with increasing production capacity. An interesting aspect is shown in Figure 4.9. At a capacity of 10,000 metric tons/yr, the economic and ecological performances of all three small-scale options become relatively similar, and the influence of the size becomes less pronounced. This indicates that this capacity may be optimal in terms of the trade-off between economy and ecology.

4.3.5   Region and Technology: How to Succeed

The regional context becomes increasingly important as renewable resources shift toward center stage as industrial raw materials in the twenty-first century. This requires a new set of engineering tenets that govern the development and design of future technologies. Among them are:

1. Successful integration of technologies into regions can only be achieved if the region itself is seen as a process network, based on its natural resources as well as its infrastructure. As we have learned in other fields of process technology, optimizing subprocesses will always lead to suboptimal solutions. Therefore, technology networks have to strive for optimal profits for the entire region.

2. Utilizing biogenic raw materials requires more thorough material flow management as well as management of natural resources. This, together with the properties of biogenic raw materials such as high water content and low transport density, requires the integration of logistical considerations into the design of processes.

3. A complete life-cycle approach is a necessity for regional integration of technologies and the development of regional technology networks. Ecologic and economic impacts of agriculture, the logistical chain, and the reintegration of by-products into the biosphere have to be taken into account for any contextualization of technologies.

4. The optimal size of plants will be more complicated to define. Decentralizing the production until by-products of the agricultural production of the raw materials can be used for process energy provision always lowers the ecological impact. The more transport capacity that is needed for resources to, and by-products from, a plant, the greatest the advantage of decentralization. For processes that either utilize process by-products or that require moderate transport loads for energy provision, there is a payoff between size-linked efficiency increase and the ecological impact of this transport. The optimal sustainable size of these processes may be considerable and comparable to that of current fossil-based processes.

Dedication

This chapter is dedicated to Gernot Gwehenberger, whose contribution to the thoughts and results presented here is tremendous. He died on February 7, 2008. We lost in him a very thoughtful and resourceful scientist and a wonderful colleague.

REFERENCES

Brunner, P., and H. Rechberger. 2004. *Practical Handbook of Material Flow Analysis.* Boca Raton, FL: Lewis Publishers.

Eurostat. 2004. *Europa in Zahlen: Eurostat Jahrbuch 2004.* Accessed Aug. 20, 2007, at http://epp.eurostat.ec.europa.eu/.

Friedl, A. 2005. *Production of Bioethanol in Addition with Heat, Power and Valuable Byproducts.* Final report of project 807764. Vienna, Austria: Program Energy Systems of Tomorrow, Vienna University of Technology.

———. 2007. *Economic and Ecological Feasibility of Small Scale Bioethanol Plants.* Final report of project 811264. Vienna, Austria: Program Energy Systems of Tomorrow, Vienna University of Technology.

Friedler, F., K. Tarjan, Y. W. Huang, and L. T. Fan. 1992a. Graph-theoretic approach to process synthesis: axioms and theorems. *Chem. Eng. Sci.*, 47:1973–1988.

———. 1992b. Combinatorial algorithms for process synthesis. *Comput. Chem. Eng.*, 16:S313–S320.

———. 1993. Graph-theoretic approach to process synthesis: polynomial algorithm for maximal structure generation. *Comput. Chem. Eng.*, 17:929–942.

Friedler, F., J. B. Varga, and L. T. Fan. 1995. Decision-mapping: a tool for consistent and complete decisions in process synthesis. *Chem. Eng. Sci.*, 50:1755–1768.

Gwehenberger, G., M. Narodoslawsky, B. Liebmann, and A. Friedl. 2007. Ecology of scale versus economy of scale for bioethanol production. *Biofuels Bioprod. Biorefin.* 1(4):264–269.

Kemp, I. C. 2006. *Pinch Analysis and Process Integration: A User Guide on Process Integration for the Efficient Use of Energy*, 2nd ed. Woburn, MA: Butterworth–Heinemann.

Krotscheck, C., and M. Narodoslawsky. 1996. The sustainable process index: a new dimension in ecological evaluation. *Ecol. Eng.*, 6:241–258.

Niederl, A., and M. Narodoslawsky. 2004. Ecological evaluation of processes based on by-products or waste from agriculture: life cycle assessment of biodiesel from tallow and used vegetable oil. Chapter 18 in *Feedstocks for the Future*, ed. J. Bozell and M. Patel. ACS Symposium Series, Vol. 921. Washington, DC: American Chemical Society.

Schnitzer, H. 1991. *Grundlagen der Stoff- und Energiebilanzen.* Wiesbaden, Germany: Vieweg.

Siirola, J. J. 2007. Sustainability in the chemical and energy industries, plenary lecture, NASCRE-2, Feb. 4–8, Houston, TX.

5

ECO-INDUSTRIAL PARKS IN THE NETHERLANDS: THE ROTTERDAM HARBOR AND INDUSTRY COMPLEX

L. W. Baas

Erasmus Centre for Sustainability and Management, Erasmus University, Rotterdam, The Netherlands; Linköping University, Linköping, Sweden

G. Korevaar

Delft University of Technology, Delft, The Netherlands; Institute of Environmental Sciences, Leiden University, Leiden, The Netherlands

5.1 INTRODUCTION

In the last decade, organizations have undergone fundamental changes as a result of outsourcing, focusing on core activities and the increasing importance of strategic partnerships. As a result, the organizational boundary has become fuzzy, and organizations need to develop capabilities to deal with their organizational environment in a new way, combining organizational and technological innovations in an interactive way.

Industrial ecology (IE) is a relatively new field of research that is emerging rapidly on a global scale and that results in the initiation and development of industrial ecosystems (Korevaar et al. 2006). IE aims at the sustainable coexistence of technological systems, the technosphere, and environmental systems, the biosphere (Frosch 1992). The analogy between natural and technical systems and processes is a core concept. Processes in nature, where cycles are closed and waste from one process is input for another, are models for sociotechnological processes. Frosch and Gallopoulos (1989) introduced the term *industrial ecology* together with the concept of industrial ecosystems, referring to the design of production sites in analogy with natural ecosystems (Korevaar et al. 2006).

In the practice of sustainable development, environmental management, and policymaking, concepts such as industrial ecology, eco-industrial parks, and product chain management have been studied increasingly. The development of industrial symbiosis in the Netherlands began in the mid-1990s with initiatives in the Rotterdam Harbor and Industry Complex that were inspired by the Kalundborg industrial symbiosis project in Denmark.

In this chapter, the historical background and development of these industrial ecosystems in the Rotterdam area are sketched. From this history it can be learned how organizations and individuals act in such a complex system. Further, in this chapter we describe and analyze how engineers and organizational managers learn from each other in developing a connection between the technological and social systems.

5.2 INDUSTRIAL ECOSYSTEM PROGRAMS IN ROTTERDAM[1]

5.2.1 Introduction

Due to its geographical location at the end of the river Rhine and near the North Sea, the Rotterdam harbor was developed as the largest port in the world during the period 1960–2000. The harbor and its surrounding industrial area occupy a region that is 1 to 2 km wide on the northern and southern banks of the river Rhine and about 40 km long from east to west (starting in the Rotterdam urban area and ending at the edge of the North Sea). The harbor area occupies a transit position on the way to Germany, with many transport and storage facilities for both fuel resources (e.g., coal and crude oil) and other goods that are transported by inland waterway shipping and rail and road haulage. Value-adding activities also take place, based primarily on crude oil (four refineries and many petrochemical facilities).

The industrial ecosystem (INES) program in the Rotterdam Harbor and Industry Complex (1994–1997) was inspired by the Kalundborg industrial symbiosis project, which was introduced in a two-hour presentation by two company managers at the Kalundborg site in April 1994. The INES projects began in September 1994 with two events: a two-hour introduction of the industrial ecology concept to the plant managers, and a 1.5-day workshop to familiarize and educate environmental managers with industrial ecology.

The first four-year industrial symbiosis program generated the basis for 15 projects that were developed further in a second four-year industrial symbiosis program that started in 1999 and merged into an eight-year sustainable enterprises program in 2003. In Section 5.2.2 we overview these develop-

---

[1]Sections 5.2.1 to 5.2.3 are based on the Ph.D. dissertation of L. W. Baas (2005).

ments, in Section 5.2.3 describe and order by themes a number of projects that recurred during these program and in Section 5.2.4 review an application. In Section 5.3 we present conclusions on the lessons learned in more than a decade of Industrial ecology projects in the Rotterdam Harbor and Industry Complex.

5.2.2   The Industrial Ecosystem Programs

The Rotterdam Harbor and Industry Complex (HIC) has been an environmental sanitation area operating in the period 1968 to 1998. The regional environmental protection agency and water authority regulates all companies in the area. Many companies are involved in various covenants[2] concerning environmental performance targets, such as covenants on the reduction of hydrocarbons and chlorine fluorocarbon, the implementation of environmental management systems, and the four-year environmental management plan of a company. The INES project in the Rotterdam harbor industrial area began in 1994 with the participation of 69 industrial firms (Boons and Baas 1995). The project was initiated by an industrial association, Deltalinqs, active in the joint interests of industrial companies in the Europoort/Botlek harbor area near Rotterdam.

Originally, the Deltalinqs approach to environmental problems was very defensive. Later, a more constructive attitude was developed through the stimulation of environmental management in companies. Subsidies for the development and implementation of environmental management systems were used for the supervision of this implementation process in the period 1991 to 1994. Deltalinqs stimulated the acquisition of knowledge about environmental management and the feeling of responsibility of the companies through a communication structure involving meetings of environmental coordinators in six similar sectors of industry.

Activities Leading Up to the INES Project   Following the national trend toward self-regulation, in 1989 Deltalinqs began development of an approach to promote environmental management systems in 70 member companies. During the period 1991 to 1994, it stimulated the companies' own responsibility through separate meeting groups for six branches of industry. Facilitated by a consultant, companies exchanged information and experiences on the implementation of environmental management systems. In a coordinating group, experiences were exchanged among the companies. This structure was evaluated positively by the participating environmental coordinators of the firms. In their final group meeting on environmental management systems, a university researcher introduced the upcoming INES project.

In 1992, Deltalinqs asked Erasmus University Rotterdam and Delft University of Technology to organize a workshop to discuss possibilities of building on the positive collaborative experiences. The workshop provided

---

[2]Voluntary agreements between the government and industry.

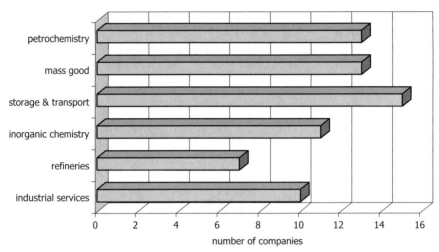

Figure 5.1 Number of companies by industrial category in the communication structure of environmental management systems in the Europoort/Botlek area.

the concept of industrial ecology, wherein the interrelations between companies would become a focus. The Kalundborg site provided a real-life example that was studied for its possibilities to emulate. Deltalinqs began a search for funds, which led to the start of the INES program with 69 companies in 1994 (see Figure 5.1). Funding was provided by various regional and national governmental bodies.

Phase I: INES (1994–1997)   INES was initiated by Deltalinqs in April 1994 by means of an awareness-raising and educational workshop for environmental managers and co-coordinators, as well as local plant managers of member companies. At the workshop, two representatives of the Kalundborg industrial symbiosis project presented data on industrial ecology. During their orientation visit in the area, they saw many challenges for industrial ecology approaches (Figure 5.2).

Although several bilateral arrangements already existed, the systematic holistic search for the possibilities of sharing resources across firms—symbiotic linkages to use the language of industrial ecology—was new in the region. Also, cooperation between industry and universities in development and experimentation of the use of applied science for environmental purposes was a new experience.

The two universities organized a second workshop in September 1994, aimed at educating the environmental coordinators. To assess their needs, a survey (with a response of 80%) was held which gave a general image of the 69 companies participating in INES. At the workshop, participants expressed the desire to make a project statement. They formulated the INES Declaration, which was never formalized but, nevertheless, expressed the view of environmental

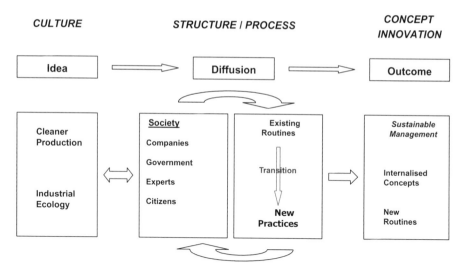

Figure 5.2 Transition processes: from idea to new routines.

coordinators and managers. It captured the development of companies from environmental management systems toward an approach that considers the life cycle of their products (thus including the product chain), as well as the need to look for possible exchanges within the region (regional industrial ecology).

In general it can be stated that process intensification has a sustainability advantage in the process industry (Harmsen et al. 2003). Following the workshop, the resources, products, and waste streams of companies were assessed to define possible projects. In all, 15 projects were defined, which had a limited scope in terms of parts of the product chain and a preventive approach. Nevertheless, sharing of utilities was found to be a first possibility for developing alliances within the region. It is obvious that in terms of interconnection between the technosphere and the social systems, the technosphere background dominated in the decision-making processes (Korevaar 2004).

Before a further selection was made, a pre-feasibility study was done on all 15 ideas by researchers from the participating universities. Then, after a complex garbage-can model (Michael et al. 1972) decision-making process within the INES-project team [consisting of the two university researchers, the Deltalinqs project leader, the consultant (already involved with environmental health and safety), and a company representative], three projects were selected for further development. They were seen as good prospects for development within the INES framework due to their economic potential, environmental relevance, and company participation potential. The projects were:

- *Joint systems for compressed air.* The use of compressed-air systems constituted a significant (7 to 15%) portion of the electricity use of companies.

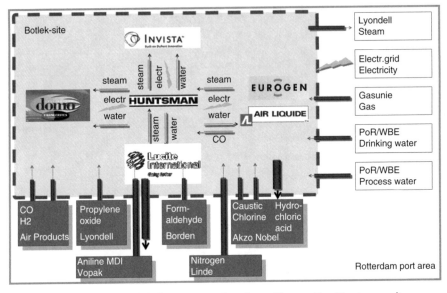

Figure 5.3   Industrial cluster around and co-siting on the Huntsman site.

- *Wastewater circulation.* The reduction of diffuse sources had a high priority for the water authority and was consequently of interest to companies.
- *Biosludge reduction system.* Biosludge represents a significant amount of waste, with large treatment costs.

Concluding Remarks on Phase I   In this phase, these projects did not result in immediate innovations; the projects mirrored the political demands of the industry association and were to a great extent end-of-pipe oriented. But they created awareness of the need for efficiency improvements at the company level (wastewater cascading, compressed air). In the latter case, this actually decreased the necessary economies of scale for a collaborative system. In at least one case, an identified project was commercialized. This concerned the flaring of natural gas that occurred as a by-product of oil drilling in Rotterdam harbor. Through the INES project, a contract for utilizing this natural gas was made with the Lyondell company within a week. See Figure 5.3 for an example of interconnections around the Huntsman site.

Phase II: INES Mainport Project (1999–2000)   From the end of 1997 to 1999, results from the INES program were evaluated by the full board of Deltalinqs. This took time, given that they met only twice a year (Baas 2001). In addition, one project with great potential—waste heat utilization—was considered by the Deltalinqs project leader to be beyond the scope of the university researchers. He decided to work on this himself. This led to some frustration by the researchers, who were critical about the results thus far. The ideas were simple and showed little innovation, not the cleaner technological results they had hoped to obtain. In this period of evaluation of the 1994–1997 INES program, their involvement was minimal. Nevertheless, the Deltalinqs board evaluated the INES program positively and used this period to acquire new funding, and thus the insights from the first INES program and the reflexive learning process that arose from it, and the institutional context of the ROM–Rijnmond program, led to a second INES program, the INES Mainport project (1999–2002).

The Mainport project was a four-year program focused on initiating and supporting industrial ecology initiatives, again coordinated by Deltalinqs. The project was developed within the framework of the ROM–Rijnmond covenant. This covenant was signed on December 9, 1993 by national and regional governments and industry to develop and implement a vision for 2010 on physical planning and environmental issues in the Rijnmond–Rotterdam region. Its aim was to provide "a responsible balance between the strengthening of the Mainport Rotterdam and the improvement of living conditions." The Mainport project took the feasibility studies of the INES 1994–1997 program and focused on the following themes: water, CO_2/energy, utility sharing, waste products/management, soil, and logistics. At the same time, a more strategic process was initiated. The project initiated a strategic decision-making platform in which the following societal actors were involved:

- *Industry:* Deltalinqs (supervising the projects); representatives from major companies in the area; national industry association
- *Government:* national Ministries of Economic Affairs (EZ) and Environment and Spatial Planning (VROM): province of Zuid-Holland; municipal port authority; regional environmental agency (DCMR); and regional water management agency (RWS/directory Zuid-Holland)
- *Environmental advocacy organization:* provincial environmental association (MFZH)
- *University:* Erasmus University, Rotterdam

National departments for spatial planning and environment, such as VROM, were interested in seeing the development of initiatives beyond the scope of regulation, while the department of Economic Affairs was interested primarily in regional development. Their activities did not go beyond these information interests. Deltalinqs involved the environmental association for legitimacy purposes, while the university could provide the input of knowledge from other industrial ecology initiatives throughout the world. In short, the members of the platform were selected from Deltalinqs for specific purposes.

The platform did meet occasionally, but it was not used to bring in new incentives. Members saw themselves as part of a sounding board and were willing to think along during meetings with project reports as they were presented by Deltalinqs. In 2000, the functioning of the platform was evaluated. It was found that each member had a different view as to the platform and what could be derived from it. The evaluation resulted in giving the platform the task to write a sustainability vision for the region. Although a trajectory for discussion was initiated (see below), a vision was never formally adopted in this phase. The chairman of the strategic decision-making platform thought that the project was too focused on the short term and wanted to formulate a renewed medium- to long-term strategy. The following main issues were discussed: the necessity for an eco-park management structure that can steer sustainable area policies, a process development path for use of the surplus energy currently wasted, the development of membrane and nanotechnology, and the implementation of a backcasting approach (Weaver et al. 2000) in the region.

In the Deltalinqs workshop "New Chances for Industrial Ecosystems,"[3] industrial representatives discussed the relevance of industrial ecology. The outcome of the discussion can be summarized in the following issues:

- What is the optimal use of existing pipeline infrastructure?
- Should investment in the industrial ecology infrastructure be done by government and/or by the provider?
- How should we proceed to develop a database for spare parts, second-hand compounds, resources, semimanufactured articles, energy, residues or by-products, personnel, pipelines, end products, and knowledge?
- Should we consider a pilot project on cold storage?
- How can the slowness of regulation be overcome?
- How should we go about enrolling energy-demanding companies (new and removal), cold-demanding companies and projects, metallurgic companies, and an asbestos treatment facility?
- How can the surplus electricity be utilized in the region?
- How can we cluster steered synergy via the optimization of intensity (e.g., through the measurement of space intensity)?[4]
- Should Deltalinqs provide an overview of surplus and lack of energy and residues?
- Can EON[5] capture and bind CO_2 from flue gases?
- Can pyrolysis products from biomass be utilized in refineries?
- Could DSM's tar incineration be combined with AVR's[6] process to achieve more efficient generation and delivery of steam?

---

[3]The workshop, held on June 9, 1999, was attended by 46 participants in total: 36 from industry and consulting firms (among them eight guest speakers), five participants from government (among them, one guest speaker) and five participants from specialized institutes (among them, two guest speakers).

[4]In metric tons per square meter per year.

[5]An electricity supplier with a production facility in the area.

[6]An incinerator for regional chemical waste in the Rijnmond industry area.

As an overall conclusion about the discussions, it can be stated that general initiatives such as the organization of a database, a web site, and a newsletter were supported. The workshop was strongly dominated by technical solutions. Social issues such as carpooling and cooperation on, and organization of, joint emission of water and air, for example, were barely discussed.

Twenty-seven officials[7] attended a workshop for government about the Mainport project. The objective of developing policy for the project was elaborated in two working groups, one on the development of a database, the other on the issue of residues. Their conclusions were that as regards the database, government has an insufficiently detailed knowledge of database input but does have an understanding of residues. This can have a positive effect on an enrollment policy for new companies. Furthermore, it was concluded that continuous information exchange between industry and government is very important.

Concluding Remarks on Phase II   The overall conclusions and ideas behind the government workshop were that for the organization of industrial ecology, one must not look at environmental permits, that hydrocarbons can be used as a cost accounting balance in an area bubble construction, and that the possibility of generating cold out of waste heat was worth exploring. It could save 10% of the energy utilized and result in an annual emissions reduction of approximately 9 million metric tons of CO_2 in the Rijnmond area.

It can also be reported that there was a gap between the two conceptual approaches expressed in the two workshops. The government officials were less optimistic than the industry representatives regarding the pollution reduction possibilities. There was also a divergent appreciation of the database: government officials had limited expectations about its potential value, whereas the industry representatives had great expectations. Finally, government officials considered that the current regulatory procedure was also suited to fostering industrial ecology. This was in contrast to the industry representatives, who experienced much paperwork, time-consuming procedures, uncertainty, and sometimes the rejection of requests for financial support.

Phase III: Inclusion in the Sustainable Rijnmond Program (2003–2010)

Starting on January 1, 2003, industrial ecology programs were included in the Sustainable Rijnmond and Energy 2010 programs under the label of R3 sustainable enterprises in the Rotterdam Harbor and Industry Complex under the umbrella of the Rom–Rijnmond project. It can be observed that on the whole, the initial institutional framework of the ROM–Rijnmond project was traditional. Up until 2003, no new actors at higher levels became involved.

---

[7]The INES Mainport project government workshop on September 2, 1999 was attended by representatives of the province of Zuid-Holland (5), the regional EPA: DCMR (10), ROM–Rijnmond (1), the Engineering Department of Rotterdam (4), the Ministry of Environment (3), the Ministry of Water Management, directory Zuid-Holland (2), the municipality region Rotterdam (1), and the environmental advocacy organization of North Holland (1).

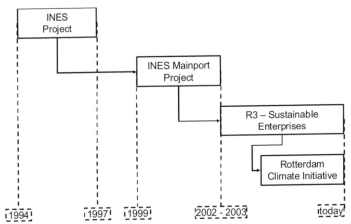

Figure 5.4 Time line of INES developments in the Rotterdam Harbor Industrial Complex.

The initial INES program also had a traditional approach, in which stakeholders were kept at a distance. The INES Mainport Rotterdam project had the potential of constituting a new step in industrial ecology. Although in the Mainport project the economy dominated the bottom line, space was created for new activities, such as the establishment of an intermediary organization for management of the project; new actors from the highest levels of industry, government, academia, and nongovernmental organizations; and the start of a dialogue about regional developments in a sustainability perspective. Although the Mainport project was explored under the umbrella of the ROM–Rijnmond project, it was hardly known to ROM–Rijnmond management (Baas, 2002).

Concluding Remarks on Historic Developments in INES   Earlier we gave an overview of the developments in the Rotterdam Harbor Industrial Complex within INES projects. In Figure 5.4, the time line is sketched schematically. From this history it can be learned how organizations and individuals act in such a complex system. We analyzed how engineers and organizational managers learn from each other in developing a connection between technological and social systems (Hoffman 2003). The lessons learned apply to other locations as well (Baas 2005). Although development such as that within INES projects cannot be transferred as imply a blueprint for other developments, its structure and organization can be of inspiration for other smaller- or larger-scale initiatives.

5.2.3 Technological Development in Projects and Clusters

The possible projects as they were identified in the starting workshop of the INES project proved to provide a basis for innovative initiatives throughout the research period. For this reason, in this section we describe the themes chronologically throughout the various phases. As has been described, the projects came out of an initial list of 15, for which prefeasibility studies were performed by the two participating universities. Three of these were selected in phase II. Each of these was assessed further under the coordination of one or both universities, whose personnel interviewed potential companies that could implement these innovations (based on geographical proximity and willingness to participate), and sought advice from experts to quantify economic and technical parameters. The results of these three studies were reported to the project manager of Deltalinqs and a representative of industry, the chairman of the still operational industrial sector structure of communication groups.

Compressed-Air Systems Before the start of the INES project, every company had its own compressed-air system with much backup capacity, often in standby operation. The maintenance engineering staff always managed the compressed-air systems, which were seldom seen in an environmental perspective. Environmental managers were unaware that the use of compressed-air systems by companies in Rotterdam harbor had significant environmental consequences and that the energy requirement for compressed air represented 7 to 15% of the total electricity use of those companies. After the identification of the opportunities represented by the compressed-air subproject, it took five years before implementation.

The companies participating in the pilot project were an air supplier, an organic chemical company, an inorganic chemical company, an aluminum-processing company, and a cement company. It was assumed that the companies in the pilot project could achieve the following results in the economic and environmental spheres: the price of compressed air could be lowered by approximately 30%, and energy consumption could be reduced by approximately 20%. When the real use of compressed air was measured, it was found that it was much lower than expected ($7000\,N\cdot m^3/h$ instead of the anticipated 12,000 to $15,000\,N\cdot m^3/h$).

Another finding was that the total energy consumption could be reduced in two ways. First, by lowering pressure, preventing or reducing leaks, and by redesign of the existing pipeline system, companies could save approximately 20%. Second, by installing a central supply through a ring pipeline system, companies could save approximately another 20%. The results meant at the same time that the economies of scale for price reduction became too low. The partners decided to explore the expansion of the number of companies to restore the original price effect (Silvester 1997).

Compounding the problem of diminishing economies of scale, the supplier was very busy with the installation of a larger system for the delivery of compressed air to the largest refinery in the region. As a result, it gave less priority to the INES compressed-air subproject. In addition, not all of the potential users were enthusiastic about the INES subproject, although they did not reject participation completely. The commercial implementation should have been completed in 1998, the period between the first and second INES programs. That period was a hiatus, lacking the active participation of an intermediary organization. As a result of these factors, both the supplier and the companies using compressed air decided to avoid the risks of a new system.

Another compressed-air supplier, HoekLoos, learned about this subproject (it saw the concept report, with confidential company information omitted). This company was able to start a new project by building the trust required for the exchange of knowledge with four other firms and by reducing the scale of the investment needed for the installation. The supplier invested in the installation and the pipelines, and now runs the process, maintains the system, and is responsible for a continuous supply. This central installation for four companies has been in operation since January 2000. HoekLoos invested in the installation and the pipelines; they ran the process, maintained the system, and were responsible for ensuring a continuous supply of compressed air. They delivered compressed air to Cytec, DSM Special Products, AVR, and Kemira Pigments. Preliminary results showed 20% costs and energy savings and an annual CO_2 saving of 4150 metric tons (see also Figure 5.5). In 2002, the delivery was extended to a total of seven plants. In 2002, eight companies participated in the joint compressed-air system. The system extended to the participation of 14 companies in 2003.

This project provided new business opportunities for the utility provider. They designed a new utility infrastructure for compressed air and nitrogen for 10 companies in the Delfzijl industrial park in the north of the Netherlands (aluminum, chemical, and metal-working companies) that opened under the management of the utility provider in 2004 (Voermans 2004). In addition, the utility provider is exploring the concept in several countries in Europe.

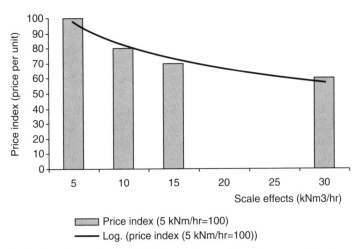

Figure 5.5 Scale effects of the linked capacity on the price per unit of compressed air.

Surplus Steam Capacity and Waste Heat Application   Another subproject, concerning the use of surplus steam capacity and CO_2 by other companies, residential areas, and greenhouse horticulture, was considered by the project leader to be beyond the scope of the universities, and he therefore undertook investigation of this theme by himself. The industrial association and an energy distributor discussed jointly how to utilize approximately 2200 MW of heat that was emitted into the air. A pipeline system to connect suppliers and buyers in the region was a first option for further study. It was calculated that such a pipeline system would cost €112,700,000 and would require government funding for the new infrastructure needed for energy distribution in the region. This steam project was further elaborated in the follow-up Mainport project.

After it was determined that the establishment of a pipeline infrastructure for the entire area was not feasible, smaller-scale projects were initiated in phase II. The BIR (utilization of industrial waste heat) project involved eight partner projects in the Botlek and Pernis industry clusters. The total estimated investment was €83.6 million. The Dutch National Project Office for CO_2 reduction plans was asked to provide a 30% subsidy in March 1998. A 27% subsidy was reserved in November 1998. A partnership of seven Deltalinqs companies tested the technical, operational, and economic feasibility of the eight partners' subprojects during 1999. They decided to reject four subprojects, three for economic reasons and one on grounds of discontinuity of supply (Table 5.1). The four projects represented 63% of the estimated investments for the eight subprojects, which meant that 63% of the subsidy was rejected. One of the two largest remaining subprojects was dropped because of closure of the Kemira Agro plant in Pernis.

At the beginning, despite the enormous steam surplus, nearly all managers of large plants had reasons to prefer their own facilities for economic (the costs of the required infrastructure) or strategic (the perceived loss of independence) reasons. That is why during the period 1997–2001, the steam supply subproject had to be downsized from a holistic regional approach to a number of small cluster subprojects. After this approach, too, appeared to be economically unsuccessful, a feasibility study for warmth delivery through a private company was performed. One of the drivers of the continuing effort to implement this theme was pressure from the water authority, which made it clear that they would no longer accept emission of heat on the surface water.

TABLE 5.1 Steam Supply Subprojects and the Reasons for Their Rejection

Project from:	Reason for Rejection
Air Products to Shell Chemistry	Economic (payback time is longer than 30 years)
AVR to Dapemo	Discontinuity in steam demand of Dapemo
Lyondell to Climax	Economic (not feasible)
Esso to ORC	Economic (not feasible)

Another large project was under study under the condition that coupling the waste industrial heat of Shell Pernis (and later of Esso/Exxon) to the Rotterdam city district heating system should be feasible economically and that responsibility for the coupling between industry and city should be organized clearly. In 2002, the Rotterdam municipality decided to provide a guarantee for the extra funds that had to be invested in a heating system with temporary equipment in a new residential area near the Shell industrial site in Pernis. When all conditions for realization were finally met in 2004 (including liberalization of the Dutch energy market and reductions in CO_2 demanded by the national government), the coupling of the 6 MW of Shell's waste industrial heat with the city's district heating system would make the temporary equipment redundant; 3000 houses would benefit in the Hoogvliet residential area in 2007. The heat supply system could be extended to 100 MW for application to 50,000 houses[8] (ROM–Rijnmond 2003). The aim of the project is to use waste heat (70 to 120 °C) from industrial processes in the Rotterdam harbor region for heating of the built environment and the greenhouse sector (ROM–Rijnmond 2005).

The project has a long history; it was designed as a waste-heat application in the Rotterdam harbor region in the first INES project in 1994 (see Section 5.2.2). Several modifications of the project—from large- to small-scale application—failed. However, the challenge for the allocation of large volumes of waste heat meant that the project had periodically attracted attention for exploration. When the policy and economic conditions were met in 2004, a heat company was established to connect 50,000 dwellings in Rotterdam to a waste-heat infrastructure.[9] In addition, activities are set up to connect 500,000 dwellings and companies in the southern part of the province of Zuid-Holland by 2020 (ROM–Rijnmond 2006). Also, CO_2 is part of the project; the delivery of CO_2 from the Shell plant in Pernis to 400 greenhouse companies in northern Rotterdam was begun in July 2005.

The "Industrial Ecology in Chemistry" Study   This subproject[10] was conducted as part of the second phase in 1999, in partnership with the Rotterdam municipality port authority. The project's two objectives were to find a solution for the lack of space for new companies—to strengthen the gateway function of Rotterdam—and at the same time to improve living conditions in the Rijnmond area. Within the project, 43 existing industrial clusters were analyzed with the help of an industrial ecological cluster instrument[11] (IECIN), which functions as an assessment and steering instrument for the optimization of industrial ecology clusters. The 43 clusters identified were classified with

[8]This is the part of the Hoogvliet/Rotterdam South river border delivery.

[9]The first heat pipe was officially placed by the Dutch Minister of Environment and the Alderman of Environment of the municipality of Rotterdam in November 2005.

[10]Project Maasvlakte Rotterdam: PMR ECO-015 research project.

[11]The IECIN model, developed by INES Mainport, Grontmij, and SMV2.

the IECIN model according to the type of complexity of cooperation in the industrial park. For 12 of the clusters, the type of cooperation, the types of companies, and the impact on employment were also described.

Analysis of the clusters identified the industrial ecology aspects that influenced the settlement needs for new companies. The industrial ecology aspects were divided into 10 categories of settlement requirements, such as settlement locations, infrastructure and logistics, and residential and living conditions. Furthermore, the success and failure factors for industrial ecology clusters were divided into three phases of the appraisal–implementation cycle within the industrial ecology cluster: feasibility, selection, and implementation.

The chemistry trends in the twenty-first century were translated into two illustrative clusters of the presumed basic products, such as the (strong) growth of ethylene and derivatives production in the future. The following conclusions were drawn from these studies:

1. Industrial ecology is current practice in some chemical companies and has been supported and initiated primarily by a small number of companies.
2. Industrial ecology is important for the Rotterdam Maasvlakte phase 2 project for a number of reasons:
   a. Space saving through more efficient production in clusters with higher productivity per square meter, co-siting, rationalization of logistics, and the transition of petrochemistry to biomass chemistry.
   b. Improving the efficiency of land use, thanks to upscaling and better physical planning.
   c. The fact that existing environmental laws and regulations are not yet appropriately fine-tuned to support or facilitate optimal applications of industrial ecology activities.
   d. Because the integration of policy instruments is a potentially important further step in the development of industrial ecology activities in this region.
   e. The fact that Mainport Rotterdam has built a good name in the sphere of cooperation between companies (via Deltalinqs), and industrial ecology is a fine-tuning of that activity.
   f. Because any company in the Mainport Rotterdam area can become a member of one or more clusters in the future.
   g. Because cooperation inside clusters makes it easier to obtain external financing.

Fuel Scenarios for Fossil and Biomass Integration   The potential to realize substantial reductions in operational business costs was one of the key drivers for companies cooperating within clusters. Companies can reduce material input costs and lower waste treatment disposal and environmental charges through greater recycling and waste reduction within clusters. Currently, crude oil and natural gas are the principal energy sources for refineries and chemical industries within the Mainport. Combustion of these fossil fuels contributes significantly to the greenhouse effect and exacerbation of global warming. It has been recommended that non-fossil-fuel sources replace crude oil and natural gas in order to achieve greater sustainability in the petrochemical sector.

The DTO program (a Dutch interdepartmental research program on sustainable technological development; Weaver et al. 2000) had set future sustainability objectives to promote the use of biomass as a substitute for the use of crude oil and natural gas as fuels and raw materials. This was considered by stakeholders to be an important development in attempts to improve the sustainability of industrial production within the Rotterdam Mainport. At the beginning of the project in 2000, it was necessary to determine the current availability of biomass that can substitute existing fossil-fuel-based energy and raw materials before beginning detailed research that leads to implementation of long-term developments within the Mainport. The actual production and market potential within the Mainport needed to be determined critically, with particular emphasis on the quantitative and qualitative analysis of potential available biomass streams (the reproduction of a fossil-fuel balance), the market demand for biomass substitution, the existing level of local knowledge, the current locally developed technological concepts for biomass utilization, and the indicative analysis of technical and economic feasibility with respect to the input of these streams in the current situation (fossil-fuel scenarios).

5.2.4 Happy Shrimp Farm

A spontaneous industrial ecology application of the INES project was constructed as the Happy Shrimp Farm. Two young professionals at the Rotterdam port authority were inspired by the INES Mainport program as well as the concept of *Agroparks*, clusters of food production and industrial activities in an ecological symbiosis (Weterings 2000) that was launched by the Dutch Innovation Network in 2000. They developed the blueprint for the Happy Shrimp Farm (HSF): producing king-sized shrimps in a harbor area using waste heat from a company at the same site, which should be regarded as a first step in the formation of a symbiosis of food and other industries in the Rotterdam harbor area.

The HSF feasibility study in 2004 was facilitated by the port of Rotterdam. The initial setup was as an incubator directed by two young professionals who could use the existing infrastructure and network of the port of Rotterdam organization. The feasibility study in 2004 had a very down-to-earth entrepreneurial character, and described the benefits and risks of co-siting two or more companies in an ecological symbiosis on one site. On the basis of criteria such as access to energy and utilities, waste treatment, efficient spatial use, and last but not least, the perception of the location by the

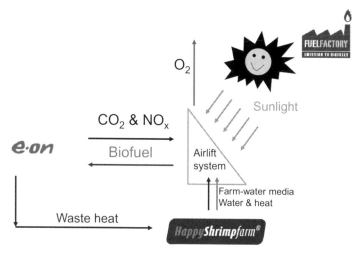

O_2

FUELFACTORY
EMISSION TO BIOFUELS

Sunlight

CO_2 & NO_x

e·on

Biofuel

Airlift
system

Farm-water media
Water & heat

Waste heat

HappyShrimpfarm®

Figure 5.6 Interconnections between the Happy Shrimp Farm and surrounding activities.

public, a choice was made for a location and a host company (an electricity plant) for the HSF. The final concept for the HSF is as an integrated shrimp and algae farm (Figure 5.6).

The first stage is to develop a shrimp farm in the port of Rotterdam and to utilize the co-site benefits. In the second stage, an algae reactor is to be incorporated within the shrimp farm. The various processes in the HSF were explained in the business plan report in 2005 (Greiner and Curtessi 2005) and funded by the ROM–Rijnmond program. The HSF business plan attracted the interest of many public and private parties. The HSF has certain unique selling points: the freshness and quality, and the socially responsible way of farming will create its own niche market. A new production chain has been established with outlets to high-quality markets. In addition, HSF has become a popular symbol of IE activities in the Rotterdam region.

During the building of the shrimp farm, the directors started a joint venture with another company to also grow sea vegetables in the farm, combining the shrimp production with the production of cress on the top of the water basins, thereby benefiting from the warmth and humidity present within the HSF. The first shrimp batch within the HSF was begun in March 2007, with first production brought to market in December 2007. The experiments with the sea vegetable *cress* have been successful; the production of cress for the market was begun in 2008. Another experiment was to grow orchids in the top layer in the greenhouse construction. The year 2007 was thus the beginning of the original idea to farm king-sized shrimp with additional activities in sea vegetable and flower growing in the same industrial ecology system. Furthermore, an algae production plant to produce biofuels on an industrial ecology basis is in the process of a feasibility study.

5.3 CONCLUSIONS

The Rotterdam HIC is a conglomerate of many operational production units of multinational corporations. This means that hardly any R&D staff was available for exploring new concepts, such as industrial ecology. The INES project management had to put much energy into overcoming the issue of in-the-box thinking to break the routines of finding optimized solutions only within one's own company. When managers are not intimately familiar with the industrial symbiosis process, they may conclude that there are no industrial symbiosis opportunities because they cannot see them (the "you cannot find when you do not know where to look" theorem; Cebon 1993).

The industry association Deltalinqs had to spend much information and communication effort, followed by demonstration projects, to overcome this barrier. Deltalinqs' vision developed to more self-responsibility for improving its environmental performance instead of merely meeting the governmental requirements in the 1990s. Organizations operating within the Rotterdam harbor have been able to question existing routines and sometimes replace them by new ones that are better suited to the increasingly strategic nature of their development toward sustainability. Most important of all, the routines that lead to a focus solely on the individual firm have been partially unlearned. However, this process was complicated by the fact that the cluster consists primarily of existing firms that are worldwide competitors. They held different perspectives on implementing new regional ideas, and Deltalinqs needed to develop a strategy to focus on how to break open these different perspectives. Moreover, as firms in the cluster often are subsidiaries of multinational companies and pressure from headquarters to deliver on ever-stricter financial or production goals has increased, less room for experimentation with regional collaboration remains.

HIC is very large, which means that linking actors and organizations within the development of industrial ecology is more complex than it is in smaller industrial areas. Nevertheless, it can be concluded that knowledge of three issues is portable to other locations:

1. *Sustainable region development*, especially partnerships of the regional industry, government, and knowledge institutes, are providing a platform for knowledge exchange, sustainability input, and commitment for new initiatives.
2. *Utility sharing*, entailing optimization of the application of utilities beyond plant boundaries, is challenging.
3. *Sensibility processes*, communication about industrial ecology projects, provides a sensibility basis for spontaneous ideas for new applications. There are several illustrations in the HIC, of which the Happy Shrimp Farm is the most famous.

Of course, each industrial location that decides to start industrial symbiosis initiatives must modify these findings to its specific situation. The applicability of the INES projects in other locations has also been made clear extensively by publications on these projects in the scientific world and in close cooperation with other projects worldwide (Baas 2005). The implementation and organization may differ because of the location-specific stakeholders, industrial facilities, infrastructure, and governmental power.

The separate INES projects and the follow-up ROM–Rijnmond program created a basis for long-term development for complex projects such as the application of waste heat. Continuity in knowledge application and exploration became a basis for new approaches such as the start of a heat company for the application of waste heat in a district heating system. The first INES project and evaluation halfway for the INES Mainport projects also learned to rely on industrial ecology as the interconnection of the technosphere with social systems. With a monodisciplinary approach in the INES project, the results had a limited technical scope. The Mainport and ROM–Rijnmond projects connected the representatives of organizations from national and regional levels in a strategic decision-making platform that was responsible for research and reflexive evaluation of projects in the techno- and organizational management spheres. The elaboration of sustainability approaches is still dominantly techno-centered, although learning processes and sustainability aspects are beyond an emerging approach (Korevaar 2004). Sensitivity for industrial ecology has grown for new business initiatives such as a regional compressed-air supplier, outsourcing of utilities, and the Happy Shrimp Farm.

The description of events in the Rotterdam harbor area shows the development of a region of sustainability from projects based on the principle of regional efficiency toward activities that show elements of the inclusion of a broader scope of actors, more intensive relationships, an increase in the depth of issues, and a more strategic vision that has been developed for the system as a whole. Developments at the system level can only be understood through their emergence from actions of individual organizations (Boons 2004). The process in the complex evolution of a sustainability region such as in the Rotterdam harbor shows that it is not individual organizations per se that hold the key to progress but rather their embeddedness in a receptive techno-, eco-, and socio-centered encouragement situation and their embodiment of crucial sustainability capabilities (Figure 5.7).

The management level of the projects was upgraded and linked to an array of relevant organizations in such a way that the dialogues led to innovative thinking and dissemination, such as the application of waste heat and CO_2 in greenhouses. Although communication about the results in the area was always a point of attention (see the web site of the projects), special arrangements such as the Symbiosis Institute in Kalundborg have never been established. The focus has been on "doing things" on the basis of a joint vision that was the result of insights obtained in continuous dialogues, and trust building in the INES and ROM–Rijnmond projects. That situation became the basis for a structured approach in which engineers and managers work together toward industrial ecology development in the Rotterdam Harbor and Industry Complex.

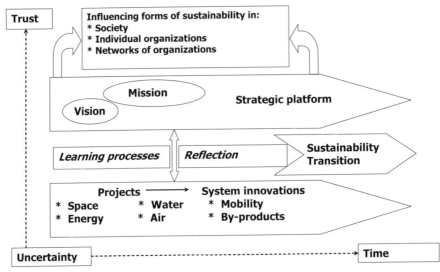

Figure 5.7   Reflexive learning processes during INES phase II and beyond.

Acknowledgment, commitment, vision, trust, and a long-term program are necessary and essential to make it happen; these issues can only be addressed if the people in the network share their goals and have the means to take actions on the right system levels. From the INES projects described, on the one hand it can be learned that it is crucial for sustainable development to focus on the industrial organization, not on the individual plant manager. On the other hand, it is necessary that the managers of the individual plants have the chance to get acquainted with each other and the possibility to share their visions.

REFERENCES

Baas, L. 2001. Developing an industrial ecosystem in Rotterdam: learning by   what? *J. Ind. Ecol.*, 4(2):4–6.

———. 2002. *Woorden en Daden: Evaluatierapport INES Mainport Project, 1999–2002* [Words and Actions: Evaluation Report of the Mainport Project, 1999–2002]. Rotterdam, The Netherlands: Erasmus Universiteit.

———. 2005. *Cleaner Production and Industrial Ecology: Dynamic Aspects of the Introduction and Dissemination of New Concepts in Industrial Practice*. Delft, The Netherlands: Eburon.

Boons, F. A. 2004. Connecting levels: a systems view on stakeholder dialogue for sustainability. *Prog. Ind. Ecol.*, 1(4):385–396.

Boons, F. A. A., and L. W. Baas. 1995. The organisation of industrial ecology: the importance of regions. In *Proceedings of the 2nd European Roundtable on Cleaner Production*. Rotterdam, The Netherlands.

Cebon, P. 1993. Corporate obstacles to pollution prevention: the sociology of the workplace is just as important as technical solutions. *EPA J.*, 19(3):20–22.

Frosch R. A. 1992. Industrial ecology: a philosophical introduction. *Proc. Nat. Acad. Sci. USA*, 89:800–803.

Frosch, R. A., and N. E. Gallopoulos. 1989. Strategies for manufacturing. In: *Managing Planet Earth, Scientific American Special Issue*, Sept., pp. 144–152.

Greiner, B., and G. Curtessi. 2005. *The Happy Shrimp Farm*. Rotterdam, The Netherlands: ROM–Rijnmond.

Harmsen, G. J., G. Korevaar, and S. M. Lemkowitz. 2003. Process intensification contributions to sustainable development. In *Re-engineering the Chemical Processing Plant*, ed. A. Stankiewicz and J. A. Moulijn. New York: Marcel Dekker, pp. 495–522.

Hoffman, A. 2003. Linking social systems analysis to the industrial ecology network. *Organ. Environ.*, 16(1):66–86.

Korevaar, G. 2004. *Sustainable Chemical Processes and Products: New Design Methodology and Design Tools*. Delft, The Netherlands: Eburon.

Korevaar, G., L. W. Baas, R. Kleijn, K. F. Mulder, and E. Voet. 2006. Industrial ecology as outline for sustainability education. In C. Subaï, D. Ferrer, and K. F. Mulder, *EESD 2006 Engineering Education in Sustainable Development*, ed. Lyon, France: EESD.

Michael, D., M. D. Cohen, J. G. March, and J. P. Olsen. 1972. A garbage can model of organizational choice. *Admin. Sci. Q.*, 17(1):1–25.

ROM–Rijnmond. 2003. *To C or Not to C*. Rotterdam, The Netherlands: ROM–Rijnmond.

———. 2005. *Rijnmondse Routes*. Rotterdam, The Netherlands: ROM–Rijnmond.

———. 2006. *Grand Design: Warmte voor Zuidvleugel Randstad* [Heat for the Southern Part of Zuid-Holland]. Rotterdam, The Netherlands: ROM–Rijnmond.

Silvester, S. 1997. *Air-Sharing*. End report INES project phase 3a. Rotterdam, The Netherlands: Erasmus Studiecentrum voor Milieukunde.

Voermans, F. 2004. Delfzijl krijgt persluchtnet [Delfzijl starts a compressed-air network]. *Petrochem*, 6:22.

Weaver, P., L. Jansen, G. van Grootveld, E. van Spiegel, and P. Vergragt. 2000. *Sustainable Technology Development*. Sheffield, UK: Greenleaf Publishing.

Weterings, R. A. P. M. 2000. *Agroproductieparken: Perspectieven en Dilemmas*. Rapportage in Opdracht van Innovatie Netwerk Groene Ruimte en Agrocluster. The Hague, The Netherlands.

6

BY-PRODUCT SYNERGY NETWORKS: DRIVING INNOVATION THROUGH WASTE REDUCTION AND CARBON MITIGATION

ANDREW MANGAN

U.S. Business Council for Sustainable Development, Austin, Texas

ELSA OLIVETTI

Massachusetts Institute of Technology, Cambridge, Massachusetts

6.1 INTRODUCTION

By-product synergy (BPS) is the matching of undervalued waste or by-product streams from one facility with potential users at another facility, to create new revenues or savings with potential social and environmental benefits. The process may involve the physical exchange of materials, energy, water, and/or by-products. The premise is that turning waste output from one company into a product stream for another company can generate revenue while reducing both emissions and the need for virgin-stream materials. Most exchanges take place between nearby companies and therefore capitalize on regional opportunities.

The BPS process provides manufacturing facilities with opportunities to reduce pollution and save energy and money by working with other plants, companies, and communities to reuse and recycle wastes. The process brings

Sustainable Development in the Process Industries: Cases and Impact, Edited by Jan Harmsen and Joseph B. Powell

clusters of facilities together to create closed-loop systems in which one facility's wastes become another's raw materials. These synergies reduce waste, promote the efficient use of natural resources, and create a legally protected forum of enterprises in which process-knowledgeable experts can safely explore reuse opportunities. Organizations involved in by-product synergies form a network. Along with reducing waste and avoiding pollution, BPS reduces climate-changing emissions. As companies prepare to confront challenges resulting from climate change both in the United States and around the world, in this chapter we offer descriptions and examples of by-product synergy's use as a proven cross-industry and community-wide approach to meeting emission reduction goals.

6.1.1 Terminology

Several terms are used in discussing concepts similar to by-product synergy. A *waste exchange* is a static process, whereas by-product synergy is an active process that may involve process changes that allow synergies that would otherwise not be feasible. By-product synergies involve communication and implementation as business agreements, and therefore incorporate quality control and supply issues. Unlike eco-industrial parks, BPS networks do not depend on co-locating industries but, rather, take advantage of existing industries in heavily industrialized areas.

The term *by-product synergy* has been used synonymously in the literature with green twinning and industrial symbiosis (BCSD 1997). *Green twinning* refers to the waste product of one industry being used as a product for a second industry (US EPA 1995). However, in the academic literature, *industrial symbiosis* (IS) has acquired a more precise meaning: defined as "traditionally separate industries in a collective approach to competitive advantage involving physical exchange of materials, energy, water and/or by-products together with collaboration on the shared use of assets, logistics and expertise" (Chertow 2000). Chertow has defined minimum criteria for industrial symbiosis as requiring three different organizations involved in exchanging at least two resources, where resources can be either materials, utility/infrastructure sharing, or joint services (Chertow 2007b). This distinguishes these networks from traditional linear waste exchanges. The process can involve regionally delivered programs with national links. In the United Kingdom, the term *industrial symbiosis* is used in place of *by-product synergy*. The U.S. Environmental Protection Agency (EPA) has developed a series of programs based on the phrase "beneficial use of industrial by-products" to refer to a similar set of initiatives.

What all synergies have in common is the potential to cut costs and/or increase sales for the companies involved, as well as to create significant environmental benefits, such as a reduction in landfill needs and greenhouse gases. The economic activity that is generated creates new businesses and jobs. Each network develops a distinctive terminology that resonates with its stakeholders. For the purposes of this chapter, the term *by-product synergy* will be used most often.

The primary examples are drawn from the U.S. Business Council for Sustainable Development (U.S. BCSD), a nonprofit association of businesses engaged in collaborative projects that advance sustainable development. Other examples are included as well. In this chapter we provide the background and origins of by-product synergy through two seminal examples. We then detail the process of synergy network development and outline potential barriers and benefits. Specific examples are scattered throughout the text, and the chapter ends with a closer examination of a few by-product synergy networks.

6.2 BPS ORIGINS

Industrial symbiosis and by-product synergy have been cited as tangible and applied examples of *industrial ecology*, a term defined in 1989 by Frosch and Gallopoulos that described industrial ecosystems (Frosch and Gallopoulos 1989). No conversation about BPS is complete without mention of the project at Kalundborg, Denmark. This oft-cited example began in the late 1980s as a series of independent by-product exchanges that developed into a complex network among six processing companies, one waste-handling facility, and the local municipality. The Kalundborg case, depicted in Figure 6.1, was not centrally planned but evolved over a series of decades through contractual arrangements among firms.

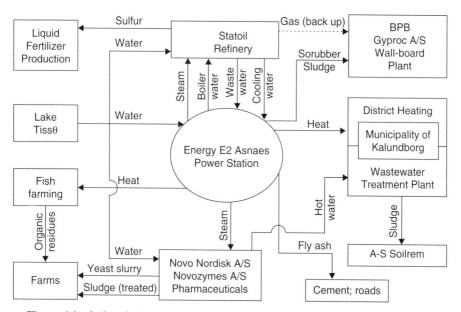

Figure 6.1 Industrial symbiosis Kalundborg, Denmark. (From Chertow 2007b.)

These companies engage in approximately 20 energy, water, and materials exchanges, including an oil refinery, providing cooling water and wastewater to a power plant whose cogeneration provides heat for the town and steam for the oil refinery and a local pharmaceutical company. The power plant uses the water from the refinery as feedwater for its boilers and input for the desulfurization process. This process, in turn, produces gypsum used by a local plasterboard company. Cooling water from the power station is also used by a nearby fish farm. Sludge from the Kalundborg wastewater treatment plant provides a nutrient stream for a local soil remediation company and other solid by-products, including fly ash used in the cement industry and biomass used by local farmers as fertilizer (Ehrenfeld and Chertow 2002; Jacobsen 2006). This example is frequently cited as a network that developed organically and proved that industrial symbiosis provides an economically feasible way to exchange materials and energy streams. The program reports that water consumption has dropped by 25% and oil consumption has been reduced by 20,000 tons per year through steam exchanges. The process also produces enough gypsum to offset 200,000 tons of natural gypsum mining per year.

Benefits have been realized through energy and water cascading, direct substitution, and utility sharing. The water and steam exchanges are driven by the search for a diversified water supply in the face of water shortages. These shortages, caused by insufficient groundwater, pose a supply security issue. Equally important are cost savings from energy-efficiency gains (Jacobsen 2006). Regulation has played a role in the Kalundborg case because of water shortages. The national ban in Denmark on placing organic waste streams into landfills caused the pharmaceutical company to seek arrangements to apply its sludge on agricultural lands.

Rather than a static system of locked-in firms and technologies, these networks evolve over time as the needs of companies change and the ecosystem adapts. For example, over the past several years, Kalundborg's Statoil refinery doubled its capacity based on North Sea claims, while the Asnaes power station switched from coal to bitumen-based fuels to comply with mandated CO_2 reduction and later switched back to coal (Jacobsen 2006). The pharmaceutical plant split into two ventures and eliminated some product lines (including penicillin) while expanding others. Rather than tie themselves to a single supplier, the participants try to insulate themselves from supplier interruptions by diversifying sources.

An example of industrial symbiosis investigated by Chertow and co-workers at the Yale School of Forestry is located in Guayama, Puerto Rico. Companies involved in this exchange include a Phillips/Chevron-owned petrochemical refinery, along with several pharmaceutical companies, light manufacturers of aluminum cans and plastic bottles, heavy machine repair, and a fossil-fuel-powered generation plant (Chertow and Lombardi 2005). The power plant uses reclaimed water from the wastewater treatment plant. Coal ash is used to stabilize liquid waste while providing steam to the oil refinery.

Benefits include reductions in SO_x and NO_x emissions of approximately 99% and 84%, respectively, as well as avoiding 4 million gallons a day of freshwater consumption (Chertow and Lombardi 2005).

As a follow-up to the United Nations Conference on Environment and Development in Rio de Janeiro, the Business Council for Sustainable Development of Latin America (BCSD-LA) was founded in 1992. The Business Council for Sustainable Development for the Gulf of Mexico (BCSD-GM) was subsequently established in 1993, comprising a nonprofit organization of business leaders sharing the belief that businesses' success is measured increasingly by their contribution to economic, social, and environmental sustainability.

In 1995, EPA, working with industry to promote incentives for green twinning, established grants to promote joint commercial development of one economic sector with a related environmental sector. Alan Hecht, the principal deputy assistant administrator for international activities, was involved at this stage and saw the role of the EPA as helping remove barriers for moving "waste" from one facility to another (Hecht 2007). Later that year, BCSD-GM received an EPA grant to identify case studies and opportunities in green twinning, which the BCSD-GM called *by-product synergy*. This venture stemmed from the efforts of Gordon Forward, then president of two neighboring companies, Chaparral Steel and Texas Industries, a cement company (BCSD 1997).

6.2.1 Chaparral Steel and CemStar

One of the first companies to adopt the by-product synergy concept was the Chaparral Steel Company (now Gerdau Ameristeel), a steel product manufacturer based in Midlothian, Texas. Its parent company, Texas Industries, produced construction materials from sand, aggregates, cement, and concrete. In the early 1990s, managers of Chaparral Steel began exploring synergies between the company's operations and the operations of its parent company, Texas Industries, a manufacturer of Portland cement. Chaparral Steel had established a history of continuous learning and a forward-thinking approach to building competition in the steel market. Its goals included driving production down from 4 to 2 labor-hours per ton of steel. Gordon Forward, president of both companies at that time, pursued a "zero waste, 100 percent product" approach to steelmaking. Forward called a meeting between managers of the two companies to see if there were any redundancies between the two company's processes. Forward described the early meetings as "awkward," but after the cement managers came to understand the steel managers, and vice versa, they agreed to work together toward potential product overlap. They called this effort STAR (systems and technologies for advanced recycling) (Forward 2007). The first idea that came from those meetings was to stop running flatbed trucks empty on return runs from deliveries. From that first example, the ideas spiraled to take employees out of their "silos" and

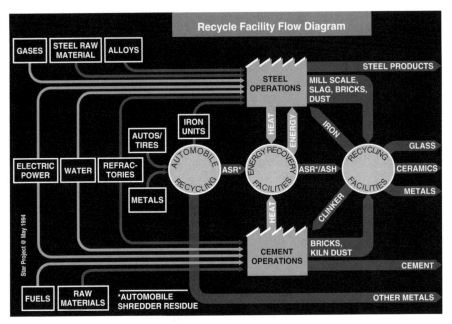

Figure 6.2   Proposed facility flow diagram at Chaparral Steel.

transform their thinking beyond the "fence lines" of the processes and systems with which they were accustomed (Figure 6.2) (Forward 2007).

Managers of the two jointly owned businesses determined that steel slag (a residual of the steelmaking process) could be converted to a raw material in Portland cement, thereby patenting the CemStar process. Steel slag contains dicalcium silicate (calcined lime), which constitutes a building block of portland cement. By using lime that has already been calcined, cement manufacturers are able to skip a step that would have expended considerable energy and generated CO_2 (Forward and Mangan 1999). Previously, slag was cooled, crushed, and sold to the road construction industry. By using steel slag instead of purchased lime (which requires heating), Texas Industries significantly reduced the energy requirements and related emissions of its cement-making process. The CemStar concept has resulted in 10 to 15% overall energy savings, 10% CO_2 reductions, 25 to 45% NO_x reductions, and a 5 to 15% production increase. In addition, the slag is worth 20 times as much as it was when it was used as road construction fill.

Chaparral discovered further potential synergies by importing a density separation process that was originally developed to sort carrots in Belgium. With an auto shredder working through 1 million automobiles per year (one every 9 seconds), Chaparral was producing approximately 120,000 tons of shredder residue. *Auto shredder residue* (ASR), also called *fluff*, consists of about 25% of an automobile by mass (IHS Automotive 2004) and includes materials not removed by standard steps in the shredding process, such as plastics, oxides, fluids, and foams. The float–sink technology imported from the food industry enabled high throughput and inexpensive separation of these materials. It generated 15% more metals (aluminum, copper, and tin) over what was obtained in the shredder. In addition, this separation generated a stream of concentrated nonchlorinated plastics, a potential synergy in which the plastics could be used as a highly efficient fuel source rather than being landfilled. This potential new ASR-derived fuel source has a calorific value of 14,000 Btu/lb, the equivalent of a light bituminous coal. A version of this synergy is being pursued by Gerdau Ameristeel and Lafarge Cement as part of the Kansas City BPS project, in direct collaboration with EPA Region 7 (Mangan 2007). The regulatory hurdle still preventing implementation involves the 50 ppm of polychlorinated biphenyl (PCB) that is present in the fluff. If the incineration process used in high-temperature kilns proves to be as effective as current approved methods for destroying PCBs, this synergy would represent an economic windfall for the companies and municipalities involved (Mangan 2001; Forward 2007).

Based on this foundational example of by-product synergy, the US BCSD developed and applied a replicable process that has enabled the establishment of expanding networks in locations including Chicago, the U.S. Gulf coast, Kansas City, New Jersey, and the Pacific Northwest. In addition, a national network has been developed in the United Kingdom, motivated by the work of the U.S. BCSD, called the National Industrial Symbiosis Program. Furthermore, these networks have begun in other countries, including burgeoning work in China, through its circular economy concept (Anon. 2007); Mexico, including the opportunity to design new waste policies; and Japan, an example of which is provided below. Details on these networks are presented as the chapter continues, but first, the process of developing BPS networks is described in more detail.

6.3 THE BPS PROCESS

BPS can offer true business opportunities beyond cost reduction if wastes are viewed not as wastes but as raw materials for other industries. As by-product synergy networks develop, industry goals may shift from reducing waste generation toward producing zero waste and finally to producing 100% product, all while lowering emissions and reducing energy use.

Maintaining a *life-cycle perspective* allows for analysis that extends beyond one facility or industry and considers all the economic and environmental impacts along a product or service's trajectory. Synergies are often uncovered by examining the entire supply chain and life cycle of a product to determine where a by-product might be used or reused. *Cascading* refers to the use of a resource several times over a series of applications, with each subsequent use decreasing in value or quality (Graedel and Allenby 2003). By ordering the use of a resource based on the need for decreasing purity, savings can be realized compared with the use of virgin materials. Cascading is often seen with energy, water, or other solvents. For example, industries such as pharmaceutical, semiconductor, and food processing require very pure raw materials and clean processes. By-product streams from these activities may be only slightly contaminated and therefore could be used by industries with less stringent requirements. Typical materials considered for by-product synergy include alkaline spent solvents for wastewater treatment, fuel sources such as auto shredder residue, heat exchanger fluids, materials for paint additives, additives for enhancing filtration, and spent caustics as replacements in paper production.

6.3.1 Workings of BPS

The underlying concept relevant to industrial ecology is that everything used by a member of an ecosystem has a potential use elsewhere in the network. Rather than simply announcing potential exchanges, the BPS process fosters relationships among companies and municipalities. The process is about information gathering and facilitation, but also about trust and bridge building.

The business council's BPS methodology involves establishing a forum in which companies, regulators, and municipalities explore reuse opportunities through information collected and interactions facilitated. Participants sign an agreement that spells out deliverables, confidentiality issues, and intellectual property rights. The methodology introduces local public- and private-sector partners to the synergy process and its values and enables them to take ownership of the network as an ongoing collaborative program. Teaming with a local coordinating body, often a local nonprofit agency such as the Chicago Manufacturing Center in Chicago or Bridging the Gap in Kansas City, is an important first step. Making use of an independent facilitator eases the difficulties in bringing together companies of all shapes and sizes across traditional sector and industry boundaries (Mangan 2000).

Several additional components need to be in place for a potential synergy network, including project champions, a researched and justifiable location, and several interested stakeholders. Potential network participants have several responsibilities. A company staff member needs to attend several working meetings during the first year of the project. The company is asked to provide resources for coordination of data collection and implementation. Company staffs also need to participate in task groups formed around company-relevant synergy opportunities. Companies discuss specific goals as well as waste disposal or raw materials problems they may face. Action plans are created and strategies for overcoming barriers are crafted for synergies that are judged to be workable. This interaction allows companies to create mutually beneficial relationships that enable better resource use and reduce costs.

Adequate funding is also necessary to staff the network, search for synergies, and perform ongoing evaluation and measurement. Implementation requires broad-based support from local, state, and federal government agencies (such as the EPA) as well as network participants. The government's role in developing synergy networks has been to provide technical expertise and funded grants, coordinate learning and resource sharing across regions (both in the United States and abroad), and ensure that appropriate regulations are in place. However, there are limits to what the government can enforce. By-product synergy networks need to evolve synergistically, with the support of agencies but without mandates.

6.3.2 Approaches to BPS

A series of methods are used in implementing by-product synergy. A few steps from the U.S. BCSD model will be described in detail here (Mangan 2000). The U.S. BCSD approach involves locating a region for a potential network, recruiting participants, and facilitating a series of meetings to discuss synergies. Although this model may change from location to location, a basic framework is outlined in the following paragraphs.

U.S. BCSD Approach   To begin with, a project location will be selected based on a series of evaluations or expressed interest by local stakeholders. The availability of project partners and participants is vital to the potential of a specific location. Often, heavily industrialized areas serve as fertile grounds for network development. Also, if companies are involved in a synergy network at one facility, they may seek to extend realistic synergies to other locations to leverage the opportunities. This can also lead to the establishment of additional networks.

Project champions and a project manager must then be identified. This may be coordinated at the regional level or provided by the U.S. BCSD. Strong partnerships with the local government are cultivated to align with city and state initiatives and goals. Technical advisors form an integral part of the team, which should also establish relationships with regulatory, financial, and academic partners to address barriers along the way. After developing a team of coordinators and advisors, the project team will perform market research to target relevant companies.

A kick-off recruiting meeting allows facilitators to describe the benefits of by-product synergy to potential partners. These meetings introduce participants to the process and provide a forum for understanding the benefits, expectations, commitments, and potential stumbling blocks. Under the U.S. BCSD model, participating companies will pay a membership fee to the network. This provides support for the staff and the resources necessary to develop the network. The investment also demonstrates a company's commitment to the process. Smaller companies may have more difficulty with the payments, so they have been recruited through different mechanisms (see Section 6.3.4). As mentioned previously, funding can be sought from local and federal agencies as well.

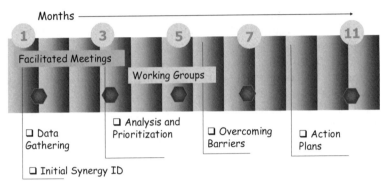

Figure 6.3 Steps in the U.S. BCSD BPS process.

Once a first round of participants has been identified, the core of the process begins. Key to establishing potential synergies is the tracking of material, water, and energy flows. *Materials budgeting* focuses on tracking stocks and flows in a system, including reservoirs. It details where a material is stored, the flows of materials entering or leaving a reservoir per unit time; and finally, sources and sinks, which are rates of input and loss of specific materials entering or leaving a system (Graedel and Allenby 2003). This can be done formally through tools such as material flow analysis or substance flow analysis. Some tools that have been used are discussed in the next section. The analysis of these stocks and flows uncovers opportunities to exchange materials, energy, or water and to use resources more efficiently.

Figure 6.3 outlines these next stages of the process according to the U.S. BCSD model. The companies and project team participate in a series of facilitated working meetings using data collection templates to capture raw materials, by-products, and potential synergy ideas. These structured brainstorming and inventory-gathering sessions provide material balance information and a confidential database that is analyzed by the project team and other participants. Information is needed to characterize input and output streams. This includes physical and chemical compositions, concentrations of primary and trace components, including any potential regulated components, and estimates of energy content, throughput, and physical properties such as density, compressive strength, or tensile strength. Other useful information includes the specific geographic location and transportation pathways and alternatives.

Firm deadlines move the process along and help prioritize conversation among the many issues competing for staff time. Once the data are transferred to a database, they are analyzed for synergies. Participants are provided with results of the database analysis. Teams are convened, sometimes along similar product lines, such as organics, metals, or wood products, to brainstorm potential synergies. For each stream in and out of a particular company, a question can be asked: Could the physical, chemical, or energy requirements be met by a waste or product from another process? The brainstorming process should involve as many plant representatives as possible to evaluate potential synergies and establish teams to define and prioritize synergies on the basis of environmental, technical, and cost criteria. This leads to a report of potential synergies and business plans for implementing them. Throughout the process, barriers are encountered and addressed (more on barriers in the next section). Individual businesses decide the best action to take. Close matching of compositions and appropriate volumes must be made if streams are aggregating from various suppliers, and supplies must be secure.

Participants must establish baselines from which to measure benefits and to use in monitoring and reporting. An initial results report might be created to test potential measuring techniques and to troubleshoot metrics. The coordinating body must document the process to highlight results and opportunities specific to each participant, along with the network as a whole.

After the first year, meetings are convened at least quarterly to bring in new companies and to continue to implement action plans. As a network progresses and grows, a coordinating body informs the entire group of successes that participants have had with their synergies, keeps participants connected to the growing global BPS network, and educates them about similar synergies elsewhere.

6.3.3 Tools for BPS

Several tools can facilitate the process described above. They relate to data collection and analysis, metrics gathering, and communication, and must address challenges in usability, the need for training and expertise, and high startup costs. In a particular region considering by-product synergy, having an inventory of local businesses, utilities, and relevant government institutions can be useful. Confidentiality may require that initially, this information be collected generically.

A systematic matching of inputs and outputs increases the probability that synergies may arise. The tools developed for input/output matching by the EPA in the mid-1990s included FaST (Facility Synergy Tool), a large materials and energy flow database of industry profiles that describes typical inputs and outputs with data input and searching capabilities. Other tools include DIET (Designing Industrial Ecosystems Tool), a scenario analysis tool with a linear programming model that optimized environmental, economic, or other objectives based on FaST output, and REaLiTy (Regulatory, Economic, and Logistics Tool), which addresses regulatory, economic, and logistical obstacles (US EPA 1999). These tools never caught on, due to their complexity and emphasis on idealized scenarios and the fact that they did not capture the time-intensive process of developing the necessary relationships among companies. More successful tools capture knowledge throughout the process to document lessons that can be applied to future projects.

U.S. BCSD Process Tools   Some of the tools necessary for the BPS approach have been alluded to in the discussion above. These include survey forms about production processes, raw material needs, and waste streams. Forms are designed to collect information in a standard format to facilitate matchmaking. Other forms gather general narrative information such as BPS project charters. These charters describe potential synergy and project impacts, along with descriptions of the opportunities, project scope, time line, and drivers. Describing the project impact will help align the project with a particular company's strategic goals. Defining the scope identifies the division, business unit, or site in which the project will take place within a company.

A project database includes information on the concentration, description, source, cost, quantity, and priority to the company for each input. Outputs are delineated with a description, a list of primary components and their concentrations, quantities, current disposal methods, as well as costs and priority to the facility. For networks to be most effective, metrics must be gathered at the outset of a project. Therefore, tools are necessary to quantify potential financial impacts and environmental benefits. Data may be compiled in a central database accessible to all team members, and potential synergies may be prioritized by establishing weighted criteria for each potential activity. Business or project plans are developed and described in project templates. In addition, the ongoing status of synergies is documented with tools that rank the necessary steps for synergy progress as well as logging the barriers and benefits for each potential exchange.

The Center for Resilience at Ohio State University, under the direction of Joseph Fiksel, has developed a decision support model called EcoFlow that enables design and reconfiguration of industrial ecology networks to maximize profitability and waste reduction (Fiksel 2006). The model, based on a mathematical approach called *integer programming* that is used for complex logistical problems, can be customized to represent a multicompany production and distribution network. This provides a tool for sustainable and cost-effective management of material flows. Coordination of flows across a changing set of facilities in varying industries may be facilitated by a tool that rapidly and repeatedly calculates the optimum pathways for material utilization. It can be used to maximize profitability for one or more companies, to minimize environmental impacts such as waste generation and fossil-fuel combustion, or to combine these strategies. By matching resource inputs and outputs continuously, businesses can create synergistic relationships that improve resource productivity and enhance shareholder value (Fiksel 2006).

6.3.4 Hybrid BPS

The U.S. BCSD, in conjunction with the Chicago BPS network, designed a slightly modified approach to network development that has been employed in a few locations. The hybrid strategy is a combination of the U.S. BCSD approach (co-funded by public and private participants) and the NISP approach, which is entirely government funded. This hybrid strategy may encourage greater participation of small and medium-sized companies that may be unable to pay the fees required in the process described above. The jury is still out on this approach, which is in its early stages, but preliminary indications are promising.

The first sphere, made up of fee-paying companies, is similar to the network process described above. A second sphere, free of charge, involves 50 to 100 small and midsized entities organized separately but concurrent with the large-company sphere. By careful screening and selection of participants, the coordinating body seeks to align the interests of the region and the needs of large companies to increase the number and potential for synergies. A third sphere, coordinated by the project team, bridges the first two. This hybrid network can be a means of involving more companies and facilitating communication between larger firms and smaller ones that may be more nimble in process transformation. It also requires a source of funding to pay the operational costs of the free network, which could change its focus somewhat from a market-driven to a government-driven effort.

There is ongoing dialogue in the academic literature related to the difference between uncovering and fostering *existing* exchanges versus *planned* industrial parks that are built from scratch. A recent study by Chertow and co-workers found that fostering existing symbiosis and synergies had longer lasting effects than designing and building industrial parks (Chertow 2007b). This report compared 15 projects proposed under the U.S. President's Council on Sustainable Development beginning in the early 1990s. Twelve of the projects arose from self-organization. The report, as well as several others, found that the planned industrial parks often encountered difficulty in sticking with the program or emerging beyond the planning stages.

Therefore, a more robust model of this network-building approach to resource conservation is required. There are several reasons that exchanges might arise organically, stemming from resource scarcity or regulatory drivers. As mentioned above in the Kalundborg case, groundwater shortages and resource scarcity gave rise to materials streamlining and reuse. Regulatory mechanisms can also provide incentives such as the Public Utilities Regulatory Policy Act (PURPA) in the United States, which provide cost benefits to industries pursuing cogeneration of steam and electricity. Another example can be found in regulations for flue gas desulfurization or scrubbing that prompt companies to seek other options for waste handling (Chertow and Lombardi 2005). In Japan, scarcity of landfill space motivated alternatives for waste disposal such as the Japanese cement industry's use of 6% of the country's waste, including half of the fly ash produced by power plants (Chertow 2007a). A Japanese industrial project led by companies including the Mitsubishi Chemical Corporation began in 2000. The initial project involved the development of synergies among several chemical companies, oil refineries, several steel companies, and a power company. The Japanese government played a key support role for the project, known as the Mizushima Regional Cooperation

Complex. All recognized that the aging industrial infrastructure required a dramatic increase in productivity if they were to remain competitive at a time when newer plants were coming on line (Mangan 2005). Resource scarcity or regulations are two reasons that drive companies to create exchanges. These exchanges, which are further motivated by the desire to cut costs and enhance revenues, gradually grow to more complex interactions. In the Mizushima case, the collaborations have expanded to include a growing number of industries and service firms within a geographic "ring." This ring has grown progressively over the years to include more territory and a broad range of industries.

Policies can be prescribed to encourage the uncovering of existing symbioses. These may involve forming reconnaissance groups to identify industrial areas likely to have a baseline of exchanges, and mapping their flows accordingly. Other strategies include offering technical or financial assistance to increase the number of interactions, and pursuing locations that already have common synergetic precursors, such as cogeneration, landfill gas mining, and wastewater reuse (Chertow 2007b).

The BPS process coordinated by the U.S. BCSD provides an approach that spans these two techniques. Facilitating a proactive but private conversation among existing businesses can lead to the discovery and development of naturally occurring synergies. Rather than arising from direct governmental regulation, these efforts are supported by government funding and technical expertise. Projects may develop slowly at first because of the need to prove themselves in the marketplace, but initial successes create momentum to explore additional, often greater, synergistic opportunities. By engaging companies while providing a supportive coordinating structure, the BPS process fosters growth of this collaboration.

6.4 BARRIERS AND CHALLENGES

The BPS process provides many opportunities for businesses and municipalities, but for networks to be implemented successfully, participants must overcome substantial challenges and barriers. This section outlines a few of the difficulties that organizations may encounter when undertaking the BPS process. These challenges include regulatory, economic, technical, and organizational barriers. Only with determination, commitment, and an open-minded view of the opportunities can they be overcome. For each challenge described below, we consider potential solutions or approaches to addressing the problem.

6.4.1 Legal and Regulatory Challenges

By-product synergies and industrial symbiosis may be at odds with local and national environmental regulatory requirements. This may limit the possible by-product exchanges or at least create disincentives for network development. Barriers may include regulations on the transport and reuse of waste.

In the United States the Resource Conservation and Recovery Act (RCRA), passed by Congress in 1976, regulates the treatment, storage, and disposal of hazardous wastes. The law requires that by-products be dealt with using specific mandatory protocols through a set of precise rules. There may be specific restrictions on transport and transfer of a particular substance. A change in a process or use of waste in the process could lead to increased liability. New regulations may need to be implemented as a result of new processes. All of these factors may contribute to legal and regulatory challenges for organizations pursuing by-product synergy.

In 2003, the EPA began a national effort called the Resource Conservation Challenge, designed to provide new incentives for reuse and recycling. The effort encourages the reuse of industrial materials, specifically coal ash, construction debris, and foundry sands (US EPA 2007). In addition, the EPA developed a discussion paper to motivate a vision of how the RCRA program may evolve over the longer term. This vision, commonly referred to as RCRA Vision 2020 (US EPA 2002), predicts a system that promotes sustainability and more efficient use of resources. These steps may help reduce regulatory barriers, but there is still progress to be made (Morriss and Mangan 2005).

Proponents of by-product synergy and industrial symbiosis recommend that relevant stakeholders be involved in the process from the beginning. When networks view regulators as partners rather than obstacles, they can respond to regulations along the way, not simply when a process is ready to be changed. Companies' time is valuable, and spending resources developing potential synergies only to have them blocked by regulation or delayed by unexpected permitting requirements creates disincentives to continue. Regulators have been willing to consider permitting reuse options when projects produce environmentally beneficial results (BCSD 1997). By-product synergy offers a cooperative, rather than a confrontational approach in which business can take the lead on environmental remediation.

In some cases, regulation provides incentive for by-product synergy development through mechanisms such as landfill bans and disposal fees. Synergies offer innovative ways to comply with regulations. In the United Kingdom, for example, the waste industry has undergone a rapid transformation in the last five years, due to diminishing landfill space, European Union directives on reuse, climate change initiatives, and rising energy costs.

6.4.2 Technical Challenges

Concerns about the technical feasibility of exchanges could provide another barrier to execution. From the outset, tracking and characterizing material flows requires a level of technical expertise within a company. It is possible that technologies from other industries could be employed if the proper patent permissions were obtained. In the case of Chaparral Steel, modifications were a necessary part of the synergy development, and technologies were borrowed from the food industry to make plastic recycling possible (Mangan 2001). In some cases, research and development may be necessary before a particular synergy can be pursued. As new processes are added to a company's repertory, employees must receive appropriate training.

Networks must involve people or groups that can help them work through technical challenges. They might include a governmental agency such as the regional EPA or a facilitating organization. Some solutions emerge as companies work with networks to implement strategies and create databases of feasible exchanges. Investing in innovation and providing support for training, education, and research provides the necessary expertise to overcome technical obstacles. Companies may create new product lines or approaches as they tackle obstacles standing in the way of synergies.

6.4.3   Economic Challenges

Economic barriers can also block successful synergies. Businesses are in business to be profitable. Companies will do what is in their economic interest and if possible, through incremental improvements or through broader-scale process redesign, they will eliminate waste in a cost-effective manner. Companies are less likely to pursue synergies if the potential savings are not documented and clearly demonstrated.

Companies seeking investment support for synergies may lose out to more traditional business investment opportunities unless consideration is given to the true project economics. This can be determined using life-cycle cost analysis and full-cost accounting tools. All appropriate externalities should be included, and environmental and societal benefits appropriately credited, using sound and reliable metrics as part of the BPS process. As environmental impacts become integrated into process costs, incentives may align more toward developing synergies or interorganization collaboration.

Some critics of the synergy process contrast the environmental benefit of BPS networks with the benefit of eliminating waste at the front end. They argue that BPS and IS may favor older, dying industries rather than investing in a new generation of technologies. However, the larger consensus from those involved in the networks is that when synergies succeed, companies are inspired to look elsewhere in their process and further improve their approach to business, sometimes leading to new and unexpected business opportunities.

6.4.4   Communication or Informational Challenges

Synergies require sufficient communication among interested parties. Companies must freely exchange waste and by-product characteristics, resource requirements, conversion technologies, economic information, and other factors that affect project feasibility. Communication and trust are especially important because of potential liabilities when materials are being exchanged or infrastructure is being shared. Participating industries may use different terms to describe their products and processes, which can create confusion and inhibit collaboration. Companies must be willing to work with and trust managers from another industry or from within their own industry. Strong social networks can facilitate the discovery and implementation of synergies (Howard-Greenville and Paquin 2006).

6.4.5 Time Challenges and Competing Priorities

Although crucial for BPS networks, developing social networks based on trust and understanding takes time. Relationships have to be developed, and participants have to be committed. However, most businesses are expending so much energy keeping up with the competition within their own industries that they do not have the time to consider cross-industry synergies. Since successful synergies cannot be guaranteed at the beginning of a network development, companies may be reluctant to get involved. Companies that are comfortable with the status quo may be uncomfortable with a process that requires shifting organizational cultures and crossing boundaries.

6.4.6 Geographic Challenges

Most BPS networks involve industries and organizations that are close geographically. Transportation costs are lower and substances can be transported from generator to consumer safely and economically with less stringent regulation. Networks can, however, develop among companies that are farther apart if the potential benefits are great enough.

6.4.7 Perception Challenges

In addition, companies may be reluctant to engage in BPS networks because they don't want to draw attention to "waste," which often has negative connotations. Educating stakeholders and the general public about reuse opportunities is crucial. The keys to by-product synergy are collaboration, motivation, innovation, and participation. All levels of an organization should be involved in identifying, evaluating, and implementing a project to ensure that all potential barriers to success are identified and overcome. Successful networks include a diverse range of industries and organizations. Communication and a safe forum to share ideas without fear of threats are vital. Successful companies embody the creativity to look beyond their own missions to develop efficient partnerships with other companies, technical consultants, regulatory agencies, and research organizations.

6.5 BENEFITS AND OPPORTUNITIES

By-product synergy creates economic, environmental, and social benefits. BPS networks can create new business opportunities by identifying new markets.

Manufacturing innovations may improve efficiency and productivity, boosting revenue. BPS can eliminate or reduce disposal and treatment costs, and can cut the costs of energy, transportation, and materials while improving internal processes. One way to cut costs is by avoiding landfilling, thereby saving landfill taxes and site charges as well as transportation costs. Under ideal conditions, the waste produces new revenue through connection to new markets.

These same savings also help the environment. The network and region, as a whole, benefit from these reductions in pollution, emission, and waste streams. Overall reduced resource use can result in savings of energy, water, petroleum, or other natural resources. Another benefit is the reduced carbon emissions resulting from the reuse of existing materials rather than the use of new materials with carbon-intensive extraction or production impacts. Companies that communicate and share inventories may discover opportunities to obtain materials locally rather than importing them from other regions.

Participating in by-product synergy creates opportunities for regional and national leadership in sustainability. The relationships established by these networks can improve a company's reputation and network of contacts. They also provide a means to showcase sustainable practices and processes. Opportunities arise to address regulatory issues and thereby reduce barriers in materials-exchange processes. Industrial areas may be made more attractive to incoming companies interested in clustering around synergistic opportunities. Another important social impact would be the creation of new jobs and businesses.

The strength of a by-product synergy network often hinges on the development of accurate measuring protocols and metrics. The need for quantifiable results in showing environmental benefits has increased in recent years, due to concerns about CO_2 emissions and climate change. Recently, the implementation of by-product synergy networks has spurred the measurement of inputs and outputs, along with quantification of benefits, in an unprecedented fashion. Staff from both the national headquarters and regional EPA offices expressed interest in increased use of metrics for energy use and CO_2 emissions (Sherman 2007). Economic benefits are quantified by determining the extent to which companies cycling by-products can capture revenue streams or avoid disposal costs. Those businesses receiving by-products benefit by avoiding transport fees or obtaining inputs at a discount.

One example inspired and encouraged by the networks developed by the U.S. BCSD is the United Kingdom's National Industrial Symbiosis Program (NISP). This program shows how metrics have allowed the expansion of a regional project to a national level and how networks can be scaled nationally, especially with extensive government funding.

NISP has more than 10,000 industrial member companies through the UK, including internationals such as Lafarge Cement and Corus, as well as small to midsized companies and single operators (Laybourn 2007). The program consists of a network of 12 regionally based office partnerships in England, Ireland, Wales, and Scotland that deliver a centrally coordinated national strategy. By having a regionally delivered but linked national program, business problems identified in one region can often benefit from solutions developed in other regions. Having a national office allows for the dissemination of information and best practices and provides a structure for consistent metrics reporting. It also enables negotiation with nationally focused trade associations and government agencies, engages companies with national scope, and frees regional networks to focus on delivery (Laybourn 2007). Peter Laybourn, founder of NISP, credits its creation to hearing about the BCSD–Gulf of Mexico programs through the U.S. BCSD.

Membership in the NISP program is free, due to public funding from sources such as the Department for Environment Food and Rural Affairs through its Business Resource Efficiency and Waste program. This program uses money derived from increases in the UK landfill tax. NISP also works closely with the Resource Efficiency Knowledge Transfer Network, Environment Agency, and the Local Government Association (LGA). Individual regions also receive support from regional development agencies charged with promoting economic well-being and sustainable practices within their regions. By supporting NISP, they are able to achieve both of these goals. Through this support, the national and local governments have found in NISP and the opportunities provided by BPS, a demonstrable and relatively inexpensive approach to carbon mitigation (Laybourn 2007; NISP 2007).

Much of NISP's success stems from the program's ability to demonstrate to participants and government agencies the value of industrial symbiosis. The numbers that NISP uses to benchmark companies' performances have been verified by research firm Databuild Ltd., acting as an independent auditor. An example of these metrics is shown in Table 6.1, which details seven key outputs across environmental and economic categories. These include reduction in CO_2 (direct fuel savings or reduction in electricity use), diversion of landfill waste, elimination of hazardous waste, virgin materials saved, reduction in use of potable water, additional sales to industry, and cost savings. Additional metrics within the program include the number of jobs saved and created, the number of people trained, and the private investment level each year in reprocessing and recycling (Agarwal and Strachan 2006).

TABLE 6.1   NISP Metrics for a Two-Year Period

Value of new markets to UK industry	£85.9 m
Private-sector investment	£66.7 m
Cost savings to UK industry	£53.5 m
Landfill diverted (tons)	1.2 m
CO_2 reduction (tons)	1.44 m
Hazardous waste eliminated (tons)	245 k
Virgin material saved (tons)	4.2 m
Water saved (tons)	2.3 m

Source: Scott Wilson (2007).

NISP, in collaboration with the Robert Gordon University (UK), identified several challenges in consistent reporting norms and methods throughout all the regions within the network. It has committed to maintaining up-to-date information for each project while continuing to investigate the most effective ways to present and normalize metrics (Agarwal and Strachan 2006). By creating a consistent and verified set of quantified successes along with a nationally used database of IS information, NISP has begun to demonstrate the strength of a national program. In addition, as the NISP regional networks expand, they may become more involved in proactive synergy propositions. To develop such "intelligence-based" IS, the value of metrics and documentation consistency increase in importance (Laybourn 2007). The BPS networks in the United States have built relationships and collaborations with NISP to learn from past experience with metrics and to share future improvements. The U.S. BCSD and U.S.-based networks have developed projects to determine the applicability of the NISP metrics approach for use in the United States.

6.6   EXAMPLES

In this final section we describe three networks in more detail. The first, along the Gulf coast of the United States, emphasizes opportunities within several divisions of one large company. Then two burgeoning multicompany efforts in Chicago and Kansas City are described.

6.6.1   Gulf Coast BPS Project

A recent BPS project, the Gulf Coast By-Product Synergy Initiative, was launched in August 2003 with the support of the U.S. EPA and the U.S. BCSD. In addition, the U.S. Department of Energy cofunded the project as part of its Industries of the Future program, aimed at identifying energy-efficient production and manufacturing techniques to be leveraged across U.S. industries. Agency representatives have helped ease roadblocks to sound material reuse, and view BPS as a way of moving beyond case-by-case regulatory flexibility into categorical reuse opportunities.

The early phases of the Gulf coast project involved 40 Dow Chemical business units from six Gulf coast manufacturing facilities in Texas and Louisiana: Freeport, La Porte, Seadrift, and Texas City in Texas and Plaquemine and St. Charles in Louisiana (Figure 6.4). These businesses sought both internal and external synergies and discovered 27 possibilities involving six different Dow technologies. Dow, which provides chemical, plastic, and agricultural products and services to a variety of consumer markets, became interested in the business opportunities that might emerge from seeking out reuse options internally and externally in the Gulf region. Dow leadership describes BPS as a way for the company to actively demonstrate its commitment to sustainable development. The network involved 40 manufacturing plants representing

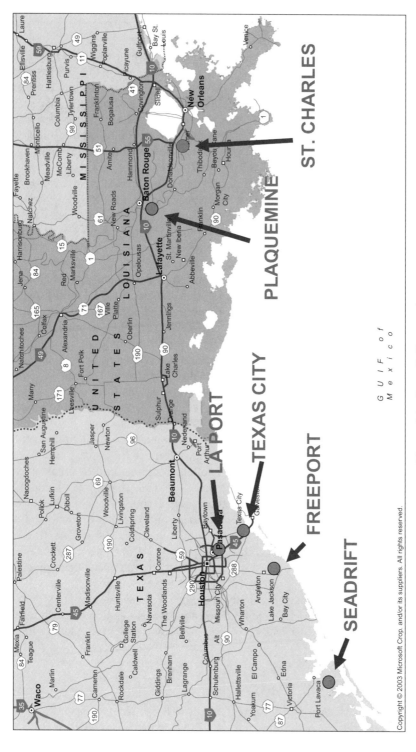

Figure 6.4 Dow Gulf coast sites.

101

various businesses supported by 14 business technology centers. Each plant produces more than 1 million pounds of waste per year.

The objective of the first phase was to identify opportunities within Dow to reuse nonchlorinated wastes and gain experience in using the process. Since the first phase of the project involved different divisions within the same parent company, certain regulatory barriers otherwise present in BPS networks were avoided. Processes within the company catalog more easily, and similarities are relatively easy to identify within the same product lines. As external companies are added to this network, they learn from the experiences within Dow.

The project resulted in $15 million in potential annual cost savings, fuel reductions of 900,000 MMBtu/yr, total waste reduction of 155 MMlb/yr, and CO_2 emission reductions of 108 MMlb/yr. Some specifics of the projects are described below to provide information on the many possibilities for nonchlorinated process wastes. Wastes diverted included volatile materials such as spent solvents and hydrocarbons, sodium hydroxide by-products, sulfuric acid wastes, hydrogen by-products, and other materials. Several million pounds per year of low-concentration (1 to 5%) sodium hydroxide (NaOH) solution generated in these plants are currently discarded, after neutralization with hydrogen chloride. By increasing the concentration of NaOH to make it more usable, or converting the soluble NaOH in the dilute aqueous stream into more usable insoluble salts, waste is reduced. This results from decreasing the use of hydrogen chloride to neutralize NaOH for disposal. Ideas were proposed that involve new on-site or external applications for medium-strength (ca. 50%) sulfuric acid waste to control pH in the wastewater treatment unit, or converting it to ammonium sulfate for use in manufacturing fertilizer.

Dow identified other spent solvents that underwent costly incineration for disposal, such as highly concentrated cellulose ethers (trademark: Methocel) and *ortho*-toluenediamine (oTDA). Methocel opportunities involved the potential recovery of the crude cellulose ether, while spent oTDA could be used to manufactured polyols (polyethers, glycols, polyesters, and castor oil) or sold as raw material for use in manufacturing antioxidants, corrosion inhibitors, rubber chemicals, and dyes. Finally, the Dow Gulf coast efforts revealed that some plants produce by-product hydrogen of various qualities, including "ultrapure," which could be used as a pure hydrogen feedstock for other companies.

Several crucial components of the network have been supported by the company's top leadership. As the Gulf coast partnership among Dow business units continues, the effort seeks to broaden the network by engaging outside companies.

6.6.2   Kansas City BPS Project

The Kansas City Project is a direct result of one event sponsored by the Mid-America Regional Council and the Environmental Excellence Business

Network (EEBN): the program "Bridging the Gap." The event brought the U.S. BCSD and the BPS concept to the Kansas City metropolitan area, which generated great interest from the local business community.

The project was officially launched on July 20, 2004. EEBN led the effort to recruit 11 diverse companies as fee-paying participants and secured public financial support from U.S. Environmental Protection Agency Region 7, as well as the Environmental Improvement Energy Resources Authority and the Mid-America Regional Council Solid Waste Management District. The initiative brought neighboring industrial companies and organizations together to discover innovative ways to integrate their operations to cut pollution, reduce material costs, and improve internal processes. This network has led to shared energy purchasing among several companies and has launched partnerships in which multiple companies consolidated shipping routes to save costs on long-distance trucking, with obvious environmental benefits.

The story of the company Cook Composites and Polymers (CCP), a member company of the Kansas City BPS network, illustrates one path toward embracing BPS as adding value to the company. CCP's core business involves the production and distribution of gel coats, unsaturated polyester resins, coatings resins, and emulsions. CCP had a long history of waste reduction and reuse within its own company, but it had reached a point where everything within its fence line had been combined or reduced as much as possible without affecting the bottom line. The company was looking for a new strategy to use its by-products outside the walls of its own facilities. One of its most important products is the polyester gel coat on fiberglass boats. This coating must be entirely blemish-free and clean of any contaminants. To ensure this perfection in the coating, CCP used a rinse step between coatings that involves a non-aqueous organic styrene that was typically incinerated after use. Seeking a less expensive disposal technique, the company had tried using alternative rinse chemicals, but that caused problems in their coatings. So alternatives to incineration were sought so that CCP would not have to accept the disposal of styrene as a cost of doing business (Gromacki 2007).

At first, the company had options with a few small singly owned companies that approached it to use the styrene by-product in curbstones. However, whenever one of these companies went out of business, CCP was left with a disposal nightmare. After a few difficult experiences with these smaller operators, the company became wary of any by-product network possibilities, until Bridging the Gap and Hallmark invited it to join the Kansas City network. With EPA involvement and the participation of strong and respectable companies, the concept became much more palatable. Now in its fourth year of membership in the network, CCP explains that its involvement is not about the "quick hit" but about the longer-term benefits of building trust among companies and piloting potential synergies. The Kansas City project as a whole is in its fourth year, and companies trust each other enough to have begun developing new and innovative strategies for by-product synergies. CCP sees an opportunity for use of its spent rinse material as resurfacing material for factory floors, municipal polymer concrete, and protective coatings. This creates the potential for profitable solutions for a material they used to pay to incinerate. As a subsidiary of Total, a European company, it also had international developments, including important upstream synergies involving alternative polyester feedstocks and use of glycerin from biodiesel as a coating resin (Gromacki 2007).

6.6.3 Chicago BPS Project

In the fall of 2005, the Department of Environment for the city of Chicago was looking for a proven but exciting process for developing ecoindustrial activities in the Chicago region. Coincidentally, the Chicago Manufacturing Center (CMC) had begun collaborating with the U.S. BCSD to create a BPS process toward business resiliency (CMC 2007). Through this partnership, with assistance from EPA Region 5, the city of Chicago could leverage both groups' expertise to develop the type of network that the city had hoped to develop. The Chicago Waste to Profit Network (CWTPN) was launched in October 2006 by Mayor Richard M. Daley, who has been a strong proponent of collaboration among local businesses to cut costs through innovation. As many as 80 companies have become a part of this network and have discussed more than 100 synergies. Around 50 of the projects have been implemented in this partnership mentored by the city of Chicago, US BCSD, and the CMC (CWTPN 2007).

Through city of Chicago leadership, additional investments were provided through the state of Illinois' Department of Commerce and Economic Opportunity Recycling Expansion and Modernization Program, and the National Institute of Standards and Technology's Manufacturing Extension Partnership. Company participants paid fees to be part of the network. Project partners crucial to the network include the Chicago Department of Planning and Development, NISP in the UK, and the Waste Management and Research Center of Chicago. Using the hybrid approach of *innovation networks* among fee-paying companies as well as smaller *community networks,* the CWTPN has enabled involvement by smaller companies and entrepreneurial firms. These two networks are combined by a collaboration bridge network. The innovation network, based on the U.S. BCSD BPS model, forms the core of the CWTPN and is coordinated by a team providing communication, technical expertise, and facilitation. This network is designed for 10 to 25 organizations that have signed an agreement spelling out deliverables, confidentiality, intellectual property, and other necessary elements to foster interaction and collaboration (Wan 2007).

To illustrate the breadth of companies involved in the network and the variety of products that lend themselves to by-product synergy development, the founding members of the CWTPN are listed here along with a brief phrase describing their core businesses. These include Abbott Laboratories (health care), Acme Refining (scrap metal processing), Akzo Nobel (supplier of paints and coatings), ArcelorMittal (steel), Baxter International (health care), Christy Webber Landscaping, Cloverhill Bakery, Computers for Schools, Cook Composites and Polymers, Curb Appeal, East Balt Commissary, Engineered Glass Products, General Iron Industries, Lafarge Cement, Kraft Foods, M1 Energy, Midwest Generation, Naylor Pipe, Kimball International (office furniture), Goose Island Brewery, S&C Electric (provider of electrical power), Sara Lee, Schulze and Burch Biscuit Company, Sherwin Williams (coatings), Smurfit Stone (paper product manufacturers), and USG (gypsum) (CWTPN 2007). The great variety of companies involved in this network has allowed for a diversity of potential materials streams. This increases the probability of synergistic exchanges, including food waste, plastics, solvents, chemicals, paper, construction materials, soils, and metals.

An important structural element in the Chicago network that is typical of BPS projects is a series of working or affinity groups divided along types of potential synergies. These subcommittees of the larger network focus on individual opportunities within one type of by-product stream. For example, the organics group involves 12 companies and two city departments that are collaborating on 11 synergies, with a current estimated total waste diversion from landfill of 4400 tons. This group focuses on long-term projects involving alternative fuels, composting, anaerobic digestion, and changing regulations to reflect changing resources. One company that has benefited significantly from its involvement with the network was the Schulze and Burch Biscuit Company. Before joining the network, this company was using small recyclers that could only handle one type of material. Since it is a food-handling facility, it could not have materials waiting to accumulate and was therefore limited in the amount it could recycle. Since joining the network, it has gained access to full-service recyclers that handle more diverse materials. Another affinity group, the chemicals group, which is focusing on transforming hazardous waste into revenue streams, involves 10 companies and five city departments. They are collaborating on 14 synergies, with a current estimated total waste diversion from landfill of 1117.5 tons. Two other active groups are the metals group and a building and construction group. In the future, these affinity groups will expand to include water and energy sections (Wan 2007).

The CWTPN has framed itself as a metrics-driven network from the beginning and focused on Chicago area manufacturing sectors in a ratio aligned proportionately with its prominence in the area. As of this date, the CWTPN has completed its pilot year and has diverted approximately 22,118 tons of landfill-bound waste, generated $4.5 million in cost savings and new revenue creation, and reduced CO_2 emissions by almost 50,000 tons (CWTPN 2007). Recently, the CWTPN was awarded Mayor Daley's Green Works Award for Market Transformation in Green Practices. This network will continue to expand, taking on more companies in both the innovation and community networks. It will continue to implement product synergies while developing the capacity within firms to increase their sustainability.

6.7 CONCLUSIONS

The by-product synergy process offers a wealth of opportunities to companies and regions in the economic, environmental, and social arenas. Developing these networks requires significant investment on the part of companies and governments, but the return on investment is high. BPS has enabled companies to interact across fence lines where they wouldn't have before. Benefits continue to accrue from this relationship building.

Those who have BPS network experience report that it takes time and effort to map out companies' processes and develop the necessary trust among participants. The development of consistent, indicative metrics is key to a successful network. In addition, pricing new products presents both a challenge and an opportunity for new developments in business planning. Because so many of these by-product synergies are new to these businesses, there is little precedent for setting or testing prices in the marketplace. As networks become more mature, there will be opportunities to learn how price structures should be negotiated within these networks.

What will enable BPS to advance even further and discover more opportunities to achieve 100% product? As our world becomes more carbon-constrained, it will become increasingly important to find ways to reduce wastes by reusing by-product streams. We will need to define the balance between the public and private sectors in these networks. The UK has developed a fully funded governmental program. Will that be the model cultivated in the United States, or will it leverage our public agencies to facilitate national communication while relying on the private sector to continue taking advantage of business opportunities that these synergies create? These opportunities present the potential for important economic development through increased product revenues and jobs. The gold at the end of the rainbow is product redesign that comes about because of by-product synergy and sustained networks that engage and benefit their communities.

REFERENCES

Agarwal, A., and P. Strachan. 2006. NISP: towards developing a new and integrative methodology to evaluate industrial symbiosis networks. In *Industrial Symbiosis Research Symposium*, ed. D. R. Lombardi and P. Laybourn. Birmingham, UK: Yale School of Forestry and Environmental Studies.

Anon. 2007. Circular (recycling) economy in China. Accessed Dec. 2007 at http://www.chinacp.com/eng/cppolicystrategy/circular_economy.html.

BCSD (Business Council for Sustainable Development, Gulf of Mexico). 1997. *By-Product Synergy: A Strategy for Sustainable Development—A Primer*. Austin, TX: BCSD-GM.

Chertow, M. R. 2000. Industrial symbiosis: literature and taxonomy. *Annu. Rev. Energy Environ.*, 25:313–337.

————. 2007a. Industrial symbiosis. Accessed Nov. 18, 2007 at http://www.eoearth.org/article/Industrial_Symbiosis.

————. 2007b. "Uncovering" industrial symbiosis. *J. Ind. Ecol.*, 11(1):11–30.

Chertow, M. R., and D. R. Lombardi. 2005. Quantifying economic and environmental benefits of co-located firms. *Environ. Sci. Technol.*, 39(17):6535.

CMC (Chicago Manufacturing Center). 2007. Accessed at http://www.cmcusa.org/index2.cfm.

CWTPN (Chicago Waste to Product Network), 2007. Accessed at Dec. 2007 at http://www.wastetoprofit.org/.

Ehrenfeld, J., and M. R. Chertow. 2002. Industrial symbiosis: the legacy of Kalundborg. In *A Handbook of Industrial Ecology*, ed. R. Ayers. Northampton, UK: Edward Elgar; pp. 334–350.

Fiksel, J. 2006. Eco-Flow Industrial Ecology Network Model. Accessed at http://www.resilience.osu.edu/EcoFlow.pdf.

Forward, G. 2007. Former President Chaparral Steel, personal communication.

Forward, G., and A. Mangan. 1999. By-product synergy. *The Bridge*, 29:12–15.

Frosch, R. A., and N. E. Gallopoulos. 1989. Strategies for manufacturing. *Sci. Am.*, 261(3):144–152.

Graedel, T. E., and B. Allenby. 2003. *Industrial Ecology*. Uppor Saddle River, NJ: Prentice Hall.

Gromacki, M. 2007. Vice President for Engineering and Loss Control, personal communication.

Hecht, A. 2007. Director of Sustainability, Office of Research and Development, personal communication.

Howard-Greenville, J. A., and R. Paquin. 2006. Facilitated industrial symbiosis: network forms and evolution in NISP. In *Industrial Symbiosis Research Symposium*, ed. D. R. Lombardi and P. Laybourn. Birmingham, UK: Yale School of Forestry and Environmental Studies.

IHS Automotive. 2004. Automotive Shredder Residue: The Final Mile in Automotive Recycling. Accessed at http://auto.ihs.com/news/newsletters/automar04-shredder.jsp.

Jacobsen, N. B. 2006. Industrial symbiosis in Kalundborg, Denmark. *J. Ind. Ecol.*, 10(1–2):239–255.

Laybourn, P. 2007. Director, NISP, personal communication.

Mangan, A. 2000. *By-Product Synergy Manual*, U.S. Business Council on Sustainable Development.

————. 2001. *Case Study: ASR*. Austin, TX: U.S. Business Council on Sustainable Development www.usbcsd.org.

————. 2005. Meeting with Japanese team.

————. 2007. Executive Director, US BCSD, personal communication.

Morriss, J., and A. Mangan. 2005. *Comments on EPA's Proposed Revision to the Definition of "Solid Waste."* RCRA-2002-0031. Austin, TX: US BCSD.

NISP (National Industrial Symbiosis Programme). 2007. Accessed Dec. 2007 at http://www.nisp.org.uk/.

Scott Wilson. 2007. *NISP Strategy Executive Summary*. Scott Wilson Business Consultancy, London, UK.

Sherman, S.. 2007. Associate Administrator, Office of Solid Waste, personal communication.

US DoE (U.S. Department of Energy). 2008. *Best Practices Plant-Wide Assessment Case Study*. I.T. Program Washington, DC: US DoE.

US EPA (U.S. Environmental Protection Agency). 1995. *Initiative on Commercial Diplomacy and Sustainable Development*, Green Twinning Concept Paper, 3rd draft. Washington, DC: US EPA.

————. 1999. *Tools for Eco-industrial Development Planning*. Version 1.3. Washington, DC: US EPA.

————. 2007a. Resource Conservation Challenge. Accessed at http://www.epa.gov/ epaoswer/osw/conserve/index.htm.

————. 2007b. *Beyond RCRA: Waste and Materials Management in the Year 2020*. Washington, DC: US EPA.

Wan, K. 2007. Director of Sustainability and Competitiveness, Chicago Manufacturing Center, personal communication.

7

FAST PYROLYSIS OF BIOMASS FOR ENERGY AND CHEMICALS: TECHNOLOGIES AT VARIOUS SCALES

R. H. VENDERBOSCH

Biomass Technology Group, Enschede, The Netherlands

W. PRINS

Biomass Technology Group, Enschede, The Netherlands; Ghent University, Ghent, Belgium

7.1 INTRODUCTION

Environmental concerns and possible future shortages have boosted research on alternatives for fossil-derived products. Biomass is generally considered as such: It is abundantly available worldwide and considered to be renewable. Despite its complexity, the use of biomass is expanding rapidly. Agriculture and petrochemical industries have developed production of first-generation biofuels from vegetable oils (biodiesel), sugar, or starch (bioethanol). The scale of production of the first-generation fuels ($<100\,MW_{th}$) appears to be significantly lower than that of unit operations in traditional petroleum refineries (several gigawatts thermal). Obviously, the production of first-generation biofuels is in competition with the food and feed industry, a nonethical situation that is accepted to get started while developing the techniques for second-generation biofuels derived from lignocellulosic biomass (residues such as

Sustainable Development in the Process Industries: Cases and Impact, Edited by Jan Harmsen and Joseph B. Powell
Copyright © 2010 John Wiley & Sons, Inc.

wood thinnings, bagasse, rice husks, and straw). Second-generation biofuels can be made by (1) fermentation of cellulosic materials (and then mainly its sugar fractions) to sugars and ethanol, (2) gasification of lignocelluloses to syngas and further conversion to, for example, methanol or gasoline/diesel, and (3) liquefaction of lignocelluloses with further upgrading, either by gasification [see (2)] or by hydro-deoxygenation (CO_2 and H_2O removal).

Large-scale implementation of biomass technologies is hindered by a number of adverse biomass properties causing difficulties or excessive costs in its processing. Such problems are in the highly distributed occurrence of biomass and its low annual yields (generally less than 10 tons per hectare (dry and ash free), as well as in the wide variety in biomass structure and energy density (compare, e.g., wood logs with rice husks). To overcome these general disadvantages for biomass, a more indirect approach could be followed, based on including a pretreatment process for the biomass as a first step. Fast pyrolysis as such a pretreatment process creates a uniform liquid intermediate that is virtually ash free and has a significantly increased energy density. It can be produced at a scale matching the size of cost-efficient biomass collection, stored until transport to the nearest harbor, and finally, shipped together with the production of many other pyrolysis plants to a central site (e.g., a refinery or a power station) for further conversion to heat, electricity, chemicals, or fuels at any time desired. On top of this distributed-model approach, it is also important to note that the handling and processing of liquids has many advantages over the treatment of solid or gaseous feedstreams.

Interest in the production of pyrolysis liquids from biomass has grown rapidly in recent years, due to a number of possibilities:

- Decoupling liquid fuel production (scale, time, and location) from its utilization
- Minerals separation on the site of liquid fuel production (to be recycled to the soil as a nutrient)
- Producing a renewable fuel for boilers, engines, and turbines, power stations, and gasifiers
- Secondary conversion to motor fuels, additives, or special chemicals (biomass refinery)
- Primary separation of the sugar and lignin fractions in biomass (biomass refinery)

Many reviews on pyrolysis can be found in literature [e.g., Bridgwater (1999a, 2007) or Mohan et al. 2006)]. Much information can also be found in the three handbooks edited by Bridgwater (1999a, 2002, 2005), and on the PyNe web site (www.pyne.co.uk), established by a network of researchers in, and developers of, fast pyrolysis.

Pyrolysis processes are carried out in the absence of oxygen, at atmospheric pressure and temperatures ranging from 300 to 600 °C. Charcoal is the main product of the traditional slow pyrolysis process in which the biomass (usually wood) is heated slowly to temperatures between 300 and 400 °C. In contrast, fast pyrolysis processes are characterized by a high rate of particle heating to temperatures around 500 °C, and rapid cooling of the vapors produced to condense the liquids. This yields a maximum quantity of dark-brown mobile liquid with a heating value roughly equal to that of wood, which is approximately half the heating value of fossil-fuel oil. The earliest recorded use of this technique was in Egypt, where the product was used for sealing boats. In more recent times a number of chemicals have been derived from the liquids as well (e.g., methanol, acetic acids, liquid smoke).

Whereas the function of slow pyrolysis is primarily to produce charcoal and gas, fast pyrolysis is meant to convert biomass into a maximum quantity of liquids. The processes have in common that the biomass feedstock is densified to reduce the transport costs and storage space to obtain a more stable (and cleaner) product and/or to provide a uniform well-defined feedstock for further processing. In this chapter the principles of fast pyrolysis are discussed to some detail, followed by a review of the major technologies available and a discussion of possible product applications.

7.1.1 Principles of Pyrolysis

Thermal decomposition of biomass results in the production of char and noncondensable gas (the main slow pyrolysis products) and condensable vapors (the liquid product aimed at in fast pyrolysis). It is realized by rapid heat transfer to the surface of the particle and subsequent heat penetration into the particle by conduction. For fast pyrolysis conditions meant to maximize the oil yield, the temperature development inside the particle and the corresponding intrinsic reaction kinetics dominate the decomposition rate and product distribution. Principally, biomass is decomposed to a mixture of defragmented lignin and (hemi)cellulose plus material from the extractives (if present). The intention of *fast* pyrolysis is to prevent the primary decomposition products (1) to be cracked thermally or catalytically (over char formed already) to small noncondensable gas molecules, on the one hand, or (2) to be recombined or polymerized to char (precursors) on the other. Such conditions would then lead to a maximum yield of condensable vapors and include the rapid heating of small biomass feed particles. It is also essential to create a short residence time for the primary products, both inside the decomposing particle and in the equipment before the condenser. First reactor developers adopted the concept of *flash* pyrolysis, in which extremely small particles (<1 mm) were used to achieve high oil yields. Later research (Wang et al. 2005; Wang 2006) showed, however, that the oil yield is much less dependent on biomass particle size and vapor residence times than assumed originally. The composition of the oil is still sensitive to these parameters, however.

An extensive external heat transfer to the biomass particles can be realized by mixing the cold biomass feedstream intensively with an excess of preheated sand (as an inert heat carrier). A number of reactor designs, such as fluidized beds and mechanical mixing devices, have been explored that may be capable of achieving high heat transfer rates. For efficient heat transfer *through* the biomass particle, though, a relatively small heat penetration depth is required, which limits the size of biomass particles to, typically, 3 mm. For such particles the decomposition rate is controlled by a combination of intraparticle heat conduction and the decomposition kinetics.

Oil yield values observed in continuously operated laboratory reactors and pilot plants, for wood as a feedstock material, are usually in the range 60 to 70 wt% (dry-feed basis). It should be noticed, however, that for biomass types with high ash content, the oil yield may drop to values even below 50 wt% (Fahmi et al. 2008). In an industrial process, the by-products char or gas (both 10 to 20 wt%) would be used primarily as a fuel for the generation of the process heat required (including feedstock drying). Any by-product left could be used otherwise. Active carbon, carbon black, or a pelletized fuel could be produced from the char. For specific purposes such as entrained flow gasification (syngas production), recombination to a char–oil slurry is sometimes considered. If cleaned properly, the gaseous by-product could also be used in an engine for electricity production. Basically, there are no waste streams. The ash in the original biomass will be concentrated largely in the char product and is separated when the char is combusted in the process for drying and heating of the biomass feedstream. It allows recycling of the minerals as a natural fertilizer to the site where the biomass was grown originally.

If the objective is to derive chemicals from the pyrolysis liquid, it is essential to operate the process at the proper conditions (temperature, residence time, feedstock type, and feedstock pretreatment) to maximize the yield of the specific component targeted. When fuels are required, less stringent criteria must be met; the conversion of as much biomass energy as possible to the liquid product is then decisive. Until recently, most research and technology development (RTD) work has been focused on maximizing the overall oil yield without paying sufficient attention to product composition and quality.

The major components of biomass are:

- Cellulose (mostly glucans), with a composition roughly according to $(C_6H_{10}O_5)_n$, with $n = 500$ to 4000
- Hemicellulose (mostly xylans), with an average composition according to $(C_5H_8O_4)_n$, with $n = 50$ to 200
- Lignin, consisting of highly branched substituted mononuclear aromatic polymers, often bound to adjacent cellulose and hemicellulose fibers to form a lignocellulosic complex

Cellulose, hemicellulose, and lignin all have a different thermal decomposition behavior, also depending on heating rates (e.g., Gupta and Lilley 2003). A typical temperature dependence of the decomposition through thermogravimetric analysis (TGA) for reed is given in Figure 7.1. TGA data are plotted versus the temperature on the left-hand side (solid line), while on the right-

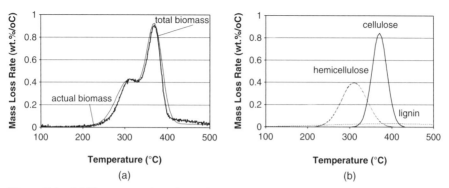

Figure 7.1 (a) Thermogravimetric analysis curve for reeds; (b) differential plot interpreted in terms of hemicellulose, cellulose, and lignin.

hand side the TGA data are interpreted in terms of cellulose (38%), hemicellulose (30%), and lignin (12%). The differential plot for these fractions is plotted on the left-hand side against the original biomass data. Hemicellulose is the first to decompose, starting at about 220°C and completed around 400°C. Cellulose appears to be stable up to approximately 310°C, whereafter almost all cellulose is converted to noncondensable gas and condensable organic vapors at 320 to 420°C. Although lignin may already begin to decompose at 160°C, it appears to be a slow, steady process extending up to 800 to 900°C. At fast pyrolysis temperatures of around 500°C, a limited conversion is likely (up to 40%). In general, solid residues remain (char, not shown in Figure 7.1), derived primarily from lignin and some hemicellulose: 40 and 20 wt% of the original sample, respectively (see also Yang et al. 2007).

The pyrolysis of biomass may be endothermic or exothermic, depending on the temperature of the reactions. For (holo)cellulosic materials, the pyrolysis is endothermic at temperature below about 450°C and exothermic at higher temperatures. As argued already, vapors formed inside the pores of a decomposing biomass particle are subject to further cracking, leading to the formation of additional gas and/or (stabilized) tars. Also, the sugarlike fractions can readily be repolymerized, thus increasing the char yield in the pyrolysis process itself. This may be the purpose of slow pyrolysis, but should be avoided in fast pyrolysis. For the small particles used in fast pyrolysis, the secondary cracking reaction inside the particles is relatively unimportant, due to a lack of residence time. However, when the vapor products enter the surrounding gas phase, they can still decompose further if they are not condensed rapidly enough.

Although other mechanisms have been proposed as well, Figure 7.2 shows a reaction pathway for biomass pyrolysis. Schemes such as these, including three lumped product classes, were originally proposed by Shafizadeh and co-workers (Shafizadeh and Chin 1977; Shafizadeh 1985) and start with a reaction that is first order in the decomposing component. Unfortunately, there is a wide variety in results of reaction-rate measurements, even for a "single"

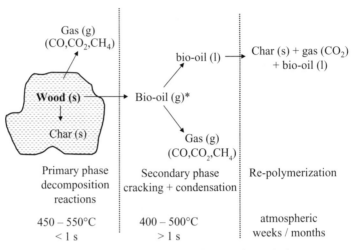

Figure 7.2   Reaction paths for wood pyrolysis.

biomass type such as wood. Published rate and selectivity expressions (see, e.g., Wagenaar 1994; Wagenaar et al. 1994; Di Blasi 1997; Di Blasi 2008) may be useful in describing trends, but they can hardly be used for reliable quantitative predictions (Wang et al. 2005). It should be realized here that biomass is a natural material with widely varying structural and compositional properties. Despite all such uncertainties in the input data required, many scientists still propose single-particle models based on fundamental chemical and physical phenomena taking place inside the particles. The reader is referred to a recent review by Di Blasi (2008). Although the predictive power is limited, modeling is still useful to create better understanding.

7.2   OIL PROPERTIES

Representative values for wood-derived pyrolysis oil properties are summarized from various resources and listed in Table 7.1. It is a liquid, typically dark red-brown to almost black, a color that depends on the chemical composition and the presence of microcarbon (see Figure 7.3). The density of the liquid is about 1200 kg/m^3, which is significantly higher than that of fuel oil. It has a distinctive acid smell and can irritate the eyes. The viscosity of the oil varies from 25 up to 1000 cP, depending on the water content and the amount of light components in the oil. It is important to note that oil properties may change during storage, a process indicated as "aging," which (by lack of definition) is usually noted by an increased viscosity in time and potentially a phase separation of the oil into a watery phase and a viscous organic phase.

Due to the presence of large amounts of oxygenated components, the oil has a polar nature and does not mix readily with hydrocarbons. In general, it

TABLE 7.1 Range of Elemental Composition and Properties for Wood-Derived Pyrolysis Oil

Physical Properties		Pyrolysis Conditions	
Water content (wt%)	15–30	Temperature (K)	750–825
pH	2.8–3.8	Gas residence time (s)	0.5–2
Density (kg/m³)	10,500–1250	Particle size (μm)	200–2000
Elemental analysis		Moisture (wt%)	2–12
(wt% moisture-free)		Cellulose (wt%)	45–55
C	55–65	Ash (wt%)	0.5–3
H	5–7	Yields (wt%)	
N	0.1–0.4	Organic liquid	60–75
S	0.00–0.05	Water	10–15
O	Balance	Char	10–15
Ash	0.01–0.30	Gas	10–20
Higher heating value	16–19	Solubility (wt%)	
(MJ/kg)		Hexane	~1
Viscosity (315 K, cP)	25–1000	Toluene	15–20
ASTM vacuum distillation (wt%)		Acetone	>95
430 K	~10	Acetic acid	>95
466 K	~20		
492 K	~40		
Distillate	~50		

Source: Data from Piskorz et al. (1988), Freel et al. (1993), Bridgwater (1996).

Figure 7.3 Flash pyrolysis oil.

contains less nitrogen than petroleum products and almost no metal and sulfur components. However, nitrogen is transferred to the oil product as well: Feed materials with high nitrogen contents yield oil with higher pH values and larger amounts of nitrogen in the oil. Degradation products from the biomass constituents include organic acids (e.g., formic and acetic acids), giving the oil its low pH value of about 2 to almost 4. The oil attacks mild steel, and storage of the oils should be in containers made of acid-proof materials such as stainless steel or polyolefins.

Water is an integral part of the single-phase chemical solution. The (hydrophilic) bio-oils typically have water contents of 15 to 35 wt%, which cannot be removed by conventional methods such as distillation. This high water content is a serious drawback when considering the heating values: The higher heating value (HHV) is below 19 MJ/kg (compared to 42 to 44 MJ/kg for conventional fuel oils). Above a certain water-content level (i.e., in the range 30 to 45 wt%), phase separation may occur. The presence of two phases can complicate the oil's use. In many cases sufficient drying of the biomass feedstock material prior to pyrolysis prevents phase separation, but the choice of the feedstock and process (characteristics) will usually determine the "oil" quality and possible phases.

Beneficial effects of the water contents have also been reported: for example, in the case of combustion. It causes a decrease in viscosity of the oil (facilitating transport, pumping, and atomization); it reportedly improves stability; it lowers the combustion temperature and, as a consequence, it may cause a reduction in the NO_x emission (Diebold and Bridgwater 1997).

Generally speaking, the oil yield achieved in fast pyrolysis should be as high as possible. Besides, the oil should have a much higher (volumetric) energy content than the original biomass. As discussed above, the maximum possible oil yield depends on various parameters, including temperature and vapor residence time. Experiments also indicate that the ash present in the oil has a dominant effect on the oil yield and composition (Figure 7.4), with sodium and potassium having the greater impact. Although it is reasonable to assume that ash and metals can have a catalytic effect on the thermal degradation of biomass during pyrolysis, such data should be taken with some care, as the data points in Figure 7.4 are derived for different types of biomass as well. It has been suggested by both Fahmi et al. and Chiaramonti et al. that alkali metals have the potential to lower the optimal pyrolysis temperature as well.

7.2.1 Composition and Stability

Pyrolysis oil is produced by the rapid quenching of fragmented biomass, these fragments being derived from the biomass constituents cellulose, hemicellulose, and lignin. The largest fragments, although being conveyed to the condenser in the vapor phase, have a molecular mass that is far too high to be a gas component at temperatures around 500 °C. They may be present in the

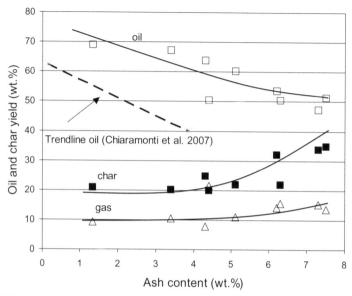

Figure 7.4 Relationship between oil yield and ash content in the biomass. The solid lines represent trend lines taken from Table 4 in Fahmi et al. (2008) for various feedstocks. The dashed line is a trend line based on more than 20 data points presented by Chiaramonti et al. (2007) for wood.

vapor phase as aerosols or are produced upon "freezing" the vapors. This liquid product collected in the condenser includes the complete spectrum of oxygenated components, with molecular weight ranging from 18 to over 10,000 g/mol, some probably produced by repolymerization of the biomass fragments. Whereas some researchers believe that the oil is a (micro-) emulsion of these components, there is also reason to believe the oil is a mixture of soluble components, probably with water as the solvent and polar sugar constituents behaving as bridging agents in the dissolution of hydrophilic lignin material (Diebold 2002).

Gas chromatographic (GC) analysis (including two-dimensional GC and GC–mass spectrometry) appears, to a certain extent, valuable in the interpretation of oil quality. However, the usefulness of GC data is limited, due to the (unknown) destructive effect of the technique on the oil composition. GC injection includes vaporization of the feed, which is known to be very difficult for pyrolysis oils and yields quite some coking in the injection part of the system. Moreover, chemical reactions occurring in the GC column cannot be excluded as well, and it is questionable whether the components actually detected are really present in the feed oil as well. Other techniques of which the potentials for pyrolysis oil analysis are being investigated are GPC and high-performance liquid chromatography (HPLC), methods to be handled with great care as well. Fortunately, development of new techniques to foot-

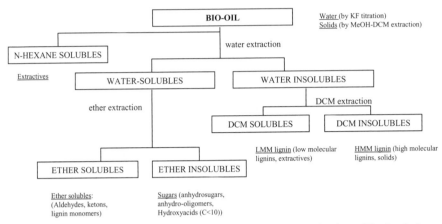

Figure 7.5 Fractionation scheme for chemical characterization. [Derived from Oasmaa et al. (2003).]

print the oils is ongoing as well: As the oil cannot be distilled very well, a solvent fractionation technique, illustrated in Figure 7.5, has been developed (Oasmaa et al. 2003) to analyze the oil in an alternative way and reveal the presence of certain fractions present in the oil:

- Water solubles (acids, alcohols, diethyl ethers)
- Ether solubles (aldehydes, ketones, lignin monomers, etc.)
- Ether insolubles [(anhydo)sugars, hydroxyl acids]
- *n*-Hexane solubles (fatty acids, extractives, etc.)
- Dichloromethane (DCM) solubles (low-molecular-mass lignin fragment, extractives)
- DCM insolubles (degraded lignins, high-molecular-mass lignin fragments, including solids)

The ether insolubles especially (the sugar components, a syruplike fraction) appear to have high oxygen contents (up to 50%) compared to, for example, the DCM solubles and insolubles (25 to 30% oxygen). Research ongoing is aimed at revealing the various components in each fraction and the effects of them on storage, stability, upgrading, and so on. The results from solvent fractionation and GC-MS can be combined (Oasmaa 1999, 2003). The main part of GC-eluted compounds is the ether-soluble fraction in the solvent fractionation scheme. Table 7.2 shows the combined results of solvent extraction, GC/MSD, and CHN analyses for a reference pine liquid. Although this method may not be the future standard for bio-oil analysis, it could be an important technique relevant to understand the oil's oxygen functionalities.

An important property of pyrolysis oil is its change in characteristics over time. The "instability" is then indicated by a viscosity increase during storage,

TABLE 7.2   Chemical Composition (nt%) of Reference Pine Oil and Its Fractions

Reference Pine Oil	Wet	Dry	C	H	N	O
Water	**23.9**	**0**				
Acids	**4.3**	**5.6**	40.0	6.7	0	53.3
Formic acid		1.5				
Acetic acid		3.4				
Propionic acid		0.2				
Glycolic acid		0.6				
Alcohols	**2.23**	**2.9**	60.0	13.3	0	26.7
Ethylene glycol		0.3				
Isopropanol		2.6				
Aldehydes and ketones	**15.41**	**20.3**	59.9	6.5	0.1	33.5
Nonaromatic aldehydes		9.72				
Aromatic aldehydes		0.009				
Nonaromatic ketones		5.36				
Furans		3.37				
Pyrans		1.10				
Sugars	**34.44**	**45.3**	44.1	6.6	0.1	49.2
Anhydro-β-D-arabinofuranose, 1,5-		0.27				
Anhydro-β-D-glucopyranose (levoglucosan)		4.01				
Dianhydro-a-D-glucopyranose, 1,4:3,6-		0.17				
LMM lignin	**13.44**	**17.7**	68	6.7	0.1	25.2
Catechols		0.06				
Lignin-derived phenols		0.09				
Guaiacols (methoxyphenols)		3.82				
HMM lignin	**1.950**	**2.6**	63.5	5.9	0.3	30.3
Extractives	**4.35**	**5.7**	75.4	9.0	0.2	15.4

some formation of carbon dioxide, and increased water content. The detailed mechanism of this "aging," its causes, and the consequences for further use, are still unclear and will depend heavily on the various oxygen functionalities in the oil (and thus the feedstock, operating conditions, initial quality, storage temperatures, etc.). At room temperature the aging of bio-oil occurs over periods of months or years, depending on the type of feedstock and its initial quality. However, at elevated temperatures the polymerization reactions are enhanced significantly, and it is therefore recommended that lengthy storage at temperatures above 50 °C be avoided.

Recent work indicates that recombination and polymerization of oil fragments, accompanied by separation and evaporation of small molecules, could be an important cause (Oasmaa et al. 2003). Although the reasons for instability may not be clear, Oasmaa et al. showed that the major chemical change in wood-derived oil is due to an increase in the DCM-insoluble fraction and a significant decrease in the ether-insoluble constituents. The average molecular weight, the viscosity (of the organic fraction) and pour point increase in time, and changes in the molecular structure cause phase separation.

The instability of the oil and the varying quality of oils produced worldwide may be hurdles to further development of oil applications, but does not have to be. Much depends on the eventual end application: Although technologies are already being demonstrated at a significant scale (up to a 100-ton biomass throughput per day), standards and specifications are still underdeveloped. Some progress has, however, been made in recent years; various physical and chemical methods for the characterization and analysis of pyrolysis liquids in relation to their future applications have now been identified. This applies to properties such as the viscosity, water content, pH, density, elemental composition, lower heating value (LHV), ash content, char content, surface tension, solubility in various solvents, aging characteristics, and pour and flash points.

7.2.2   Health and Safety Aspects

Some remarks should be made regarding health and safety aspects in relation to bio-oils. As far as the toxicity of the oil is concerned, Diebold (1999) concluded that it is a function of feedstock, process, and operating conditions. The projected acute oral toxicity is estimated to be around 700 mg/kg of body weight. Chronic toxicity is unclear, with one study indicating no tumor activity and another showing mutagenicity. Based on acute exposure tests, it was recommended that fast pyrolysis oils are a hazardous substance to eye and to inhalation exposure, but not to dermal exposure. It can be handled safely using personnel protective gear (rubber gloves, goggles, and protective clothing). The biodegradability of oils was examined further by Blin et al. (2007) and classified as inherently biodegradable.

7.3   FAST PYROLYSIS PROCESS TECHNOLOGIES

The aim of the slow pyrolysis process is to produce mainly charcoal, whereas the fast pyrolysis process should convert the biomass into a maximum quantity of liquid. As mentioned in the introduction, both processes have in common that the energy in the biomass feedstock is concentrated in a smaller volume by which transport costs and storage space can be reduced. Also beneficial is the fact that a more uniform, stable, and cleaner-burning product is obtained which could serve as an intermediate energy carrier and feedstock for subsequent processing.

The by-products gas and char can be used (partially) within the fast pyrolysis system itself: that is, to deliver energy for the drying and heating of the biomass feed material, to deliver energy for the (presumed) endothermic pyrolysis reactions, and to compensate for heat losses from the system. To maintain good process efficiencies, any surplus of by-product should be considered carefully for other useful applications. Because there are good opportunities in most cases, undesired waste streams can be avoided in practice.

The essential characteristics of a fast pyrolysis reactor for maximal oil production are the very rapid heating of the biomass, an operating temperature around 500 °C, and rapid quenching of the vapors produced. Crucial in the pyrolysis reactor is the ability to have high heat transfer rates to (and preferably also inside) the solid particles. On an average basis, it can be estimated that 1.5 MJ/kg is required (which is two-thirds that of water evaporation). Moreover, the time and temperature profiles of the gases produced affect the composition of the oil as well. In small laboratory reactors, where very rapid transfer rates are achieved and vapor residence times of only a few tenths of a second can be realized, oil yield can be maximized. For heat transfer–limited systems and longer residence times of the pyrolysis vapors at higher temperatures, occurring especially in real scale installations, the consequences of secondary cracking can become quite significant. As a practical figure, high external medium-to-solid heat transfer rates are required (say, $>500 W/m^2 \cdot K$), internal biomass heat transfer rates limitation should be avoided (requiring particles below 5 mm in size for the heat penetration depth), and gas-phase residence times of 2 seconds maximum may be tolerated without too much loss in oil yield. In case a pyrolysis plant is meant to produce a liquid fuel for combustion or gasification, the process could be designed so as to maximize energy conversion to this liquid product. However, when the bio-oil product is meant to derive chemicals from (see one of the next paragraphs), factors other than simply the vapor residence time should be considered as well. The composition of the oil can be steered by process conditions, equipped dimensions, and perhaps the application of catalysts.

Although laboratory studies regarding the thermal decomposition of various organic substances have been carried for a much longer period, the technology development of "flash" and "fast" pyrolysis started only some 20 years ago when the advantages of liquefying biomass in such a simple way were gradually recognized. During the 1980s and the early 1990s, research focused on the development of special reactors, such as the vortex reactor, rotating blade reactor, rotating cone reactor, cyclone reactor, transported bed reactor, vacuum reactor, and fluid-bed reactor. Since the late 1990s, process realization emerged, resulting in the construction of pilot plants in Spain (Union Fenosa), Italy (Enel), the UK (Wellman), Canada (Pyrovac, DynaMotive), Finland (Fortum), and the Netherlands (BTG). In the United States and Canada, Ensyn's entrained flow bed process is applied at a scale of around 1 ton/h for commercial production of a food flavor called "liquid smoke." DynaMotive (www.dynamotive.com) and BTG (www.btgworld.com) designed and operate demonstration installations of 2 to 4 tons of biomass throughput per hour for utilization of bio-oil in energy production primarily. Meanwhile, many pilot-plant projects have stopped at some time following the initial testing. At the time of writing, the plants of Union Fenosa, Enel, Wellman, Fortum, and Pyrovac's large-scale installation in Jonquière, Canada, are no longer in operation. This may be caused by a lack of confidence in economic prospects and markets at that time, or by legislative limitations.

By reflection, the state of the art in the development of pyrolysis is somewhat comparable to the situation in 1936 in the petrochemical industry, when the Houdry (FCC) process was first demonstrated on a scale of 2000 barrels per day. Nevertheless, today, fast pyrolysis is attracting increased interest. Fields of science other than engineering (e.g., agriculture, organic chemistry, catalysis, separation technology) are getting involved, together accelerating the developments in bio-oil applications. Oil companies and the food and feed industries are building biofuel departments and looking for existing knowledge matching their strategies and targets regarding renewable resources. Also, new developers of fast pyrolysis technology are showing their intentions with the construction of pilot plants based on proprietary technology. Forschungs Zentrum Karlsruhe is constructing a plant of 5 tons/day in their laboratories based on a twin-screw reactor technology (Dahmen et al. 2007). Since 2006, Pytec has been testing a small pilot plant based on ablative pyrolysis technology near Hamburg and plans to construct a 50-ton/day installation in Mecklenburg–Vorpommern (Schöll et al. 2004; Meier 2007). TNO is operating a 30-kg/h pilot plant at the University of Twente in the Netherlands, based on cyclone reactor technology with integrated particle separation (PyRos). Last but not least, VTT (Finland) has a well-equipped circulating fluid-bed pilot plant in operation (30 kg/h) for research purposes; it was erected in the mid-1990s on the basis of the technology developed by Ensyn (Canada). A selection of historical developments is discussed hereafter, with emphasis on the rotating cone technology of BTG.

7.3.1 Entrained Downflow

Early attempts at fast pyrolysis have been carried out in entrained flow reactors, where biomass particles (1 to 5 mm) were fed to a hot, down-flow reactor. The reaction was supposed complete within a residence time of less than 1 s when the reactor tube was held at temperatures between 700 and 800 °C. Unlike many other fast pyrolysis reactors, no extra hot solid material was used to transport and heat the biomass particles. An early process was developed at the Georgia Tech Research Institute (United States) and a first unit transferred to Egemin (Belgium) for further development and scale-up in a project funded partly by the EC. The plant was dismantled in 1993. It appeared that the feedstock was incompletely pyrolyzed in the reactor, particularly at high feeding rates. Insufficient heat transfer to the solid biomass particles during their short travel in the reactor was the probable cause.

7.3.2 Ablative Reactor

Ablative pyrolysis was then considered as a possible alternative to entrained flow reactors. The principle of ablative pyrolysis is demonstrated in Figure 7.6.

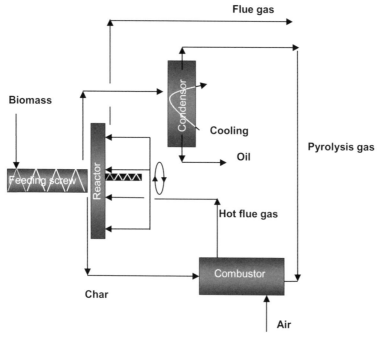

Figure 7.6 Principle of ablative pyrolysis.

The surface, heated by hot flue gas, is rotating, and biomass is pressed onto the hot surface (approximately 600 °C). The flue gas is produced by combustion of pyrolysis gases and/or produced char. In the 1990s, BBC (Canada) demonstrated an ablative flash pyrolysis technique for the disposal of tires at a capacity of 10 to 25 kg/h. The process was licensed to Castle Capital (a holding company of several companies involved in the fabrication of pressure vessels, military vehicle modification, etc.) for the erection of a 50-ton/day plant in Halifax, Nova Scotia, using solid wastes. What happened to these plans is not known to the present authors.

Much of the pioneering work on ablative pyrolysis was carried out by NREL (Golden, Colorado). In their approach, the forces to press the biomass to a hot surface are by centrifugal forces in a vortex reactor (Johnson et al. 1994). The biomass, though, appeared to be insufficiently converted, requiring the solids to be redirected back to the entrance. In 1989, NREL entered a consortium with Interchem Industries Inc. in the United States to develop and exploit NREL's ablative pyrolysis for the production of phenol adhesives and alternative fuels. However, the construction of a demonstration plant was never completed. NREL is no longer contractually involved with this firm and abandoned the vortex design concept in 1997.

In the 1990s, Aston University (Birmingham, UK) built and tested a prototype rotating blade reactor for ablative pyrolysis on the small scale of 3 kg/h.

Oil samples were produced in yields of up to 80 wt%. At present, the German company Pytec is the only company developing ablative pyrolysis technology, with a pilot plant of 250 kg/h in operation near Hamburg (Meier 2004; Schöll et al. 2004) and plans for demonstration of a 2-t/h unit in Mecklenburg–Vorpommern (Meier 2007).

In general, the following limitations for this technology can be mentioned:

- Limited heat transfer rates due to the indirect heating principle, the limited temperature difference between hot flue gas (ca. 800 °C) and pyrolysis reactor (ca. 500 °C), and a low heat transfer coefficient
- Restriction on the particle size and its free-flowing characteristics, as the material needs to be pressed against a heated surface

7.3.3   Fluid Bed

The preferred method for the rapid heating of biomass particles is to mix them with the moving sand particles of a high-temperature fluid bed. The principle of fluid-bed pyrolysis is shown in Figure 7.7. High heat transfer rates can be achieved, as the bed usually contains small sand particles. The heat required eventually is generated by combustion of the pyrolysis gases and/or char, which is eventually transferred to the fluid bed by heating coils. The sand-to-

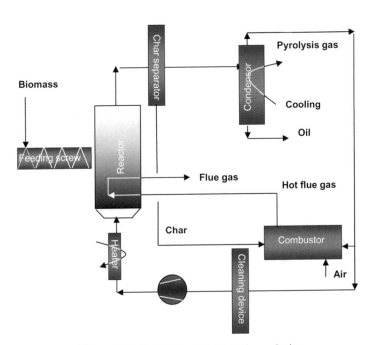

Figure 7.7   Principle of fluid-bed pyrolysis.

biomass heat transfer may not be limiting here (over $500 W/m^2 \cdot K$), but the heat transfer rates from the heating coils to the fluid bed itself will be low, due to the small overall heat transfer coefficient from gas to fluid bed (estimated at 100 to $200 W/m^2 \cdot K$), and the limiting driving force (800 down to $600 °C$ in coils versus 500 to $550 °C$ in the fluid bed). In an optimistic case, a surface area of about 10 to $20 m^2$ is required per ton of biomass fed per hour.

The University of Waterloo in Canada reported early work at the beginning of the 1980s on fluid-bed pyrolysis. In 1990, a 200-kg/h demonstration plant was built by Union Fenosa, a utility company in Spain for generation, transmission, and distribution of electricity (Cuevas et al. 1995). Meanwhile, this plant is dismantled. The Canadian company Ensyn Technologies Inc. (ETI) developed industrial applications for their RTM (rapid thermal processing), in which woody biomass is converted to pyrolysis liquids as a source of valuable chemical and fuel products. Commercialization was enabled through the granting of an exclusive license to Red Arrow Food Products Company Ltd. of Wisconsin for certain product applications in the food industry. Ensyn and Red Arrow have been producing large quantities of bio-oil for the production of specialty products since 1990 (Graham et al. 1994). By 1996 there were four RTP plants in commercial operation. In 2001, a RTP biomass refining plant was built and commissioned to produce annually over 1800 tons of natural resin products from the existing bio-oil plants. In 2002, Ensyn increased its total capacity to 100 tons/day by taking into operation another RTP plant. A sixth commercial RTP biomass plant, designed to produce specialty chemical products, was built and put into service in 2003. Ensyn's largest RTP biomass refinery was established in Renfrew, Ontario, converting up to 200 tons of wood per day into natural resin products, copolymers, other chemicals, liquid fuel, and green electricity. Details of the operation (or operational performance) are unknown [see Freel (2002) for a photograph of an Ensyn plant].

Another fluid-bed project was started in the UK by the end of the 1990s. It was a fluid-bed system of 150 to 200 kg/h, to be designed, constructed, and operated by Wellman Process Engineering in a European Union project coordinated by Aston University in Birmingham. Construction of the pilot plant was completed in early 1999, but due to permit problems it could never be started.

Vapo Oil and Fortum Oil together undertook another initiative from 2001 onward (Nieminen et al. 2003), and developed a newly patented principle for fluid-bed pyrolysis. Pictures of the plant are shown in Figure 7.8. The project was abandoned, presumably for economic reasons.

A Canadian company, Dynamotive Corporation, is commercializing further the fluid-bed technology at the University of Waterloo. The design and development of the first commercial plant at West Lorne began in 2002. The plant started operations in early February 2005 with a design capacity of 100 tons/day of waste sawdust. At the beginning of 2008 the plant was not in full production and did not reach the designed bio-oil production capacity, presumably due to mechanical and design difficulties. The company did not wait for

Figure 7.8 Forestera pilot: reactor and product storage area. (From Nieminen et al. 2003.)

the West Lorne plant and in 2006 started to build a second plant in Guelph with a design capacity of 200 tons/day. Operational performances for neither plant can be found in the open literature.

The oil of the West Lorne facility was meant originally for combustion in Orenda's GT 2500 gas turbine to produce electricity. A project description and update can be found in a PyNe newsletter (DynaMotive 2005b). Figure 7.9 is a photograph of the West Lorne plant. The Orenda turbine is an industrial Mashproekt-designed engine, with nine axial and one radial stage compressor. Due to variations in the oil quality (perhaps off-spec) and a limited supply of oil, the turbine has been little used. Fluid-bed operation is a pretty well understood technology for pyrolysis (see, e.g., Bridgwater 2007 and Di Blasi 2008), but experimental experiences in fluid-bed pyrolysis still indicate a number of serious technical problems to overcome. While referring to Figure 7.7 the following remarks can be made:

1. Heat is to be transferred to the bed particles by submerged heating coils. Depending on the type of heating, it is questionable if at larger scales all the necessary heat can be provided in this way. Heat transfer from hot flue gas to the fluid bed is limited, and perhaps hot oil or molten salts are to be applied at temperatures above 550 to 600 °C. Application of hot oil at these temperatures would be a demonstration purpose in itself.

2. Separation of char and sand is to be achieved by entrainment of char from the fluid bed. This requires delicate control of fluidization gas velocity and operating temperatures in relation to the fluidized-bed particles and char

Figure 7.9 DynaMotive's West Lorne plant: wood feed hopper on left, char product hopper on right.

(thus feed) characteristics. It will put serious constraints on the biomass characteristics.

3. Char may act as a catalyst in the pyrolysis reaction. Because pyrolysis gas is used to entrain the char particles, the catalytic effect on any further cracking of the pyrolysis vapors may be considerable, reducing the oil yields. Char accumulation in the fluid-bed reactor will contribute to this phenomenon as well.

4. Due to the entrainment of all char fines by the pyrolysis vapors, the solids loading of fine char in the gas is significant. This requires high-performance, gas (!) solids separators, cyclones, and so on, to avoid large quantities of char ending up in the bio-oil. Char fines in the oil cause increased instability, problems in pumping, and more important, difficulties in the end-use applications (turbines, engines, boilers). Perhaps because of the difficulties in char separation, and because of its pyrophobic properties, Dynamotive now deliberately leaves the char in the oil, calling it intermediate bio-oil (BioOil Plus; see www.dynamotive.com).

5. The gas used for fluidization of the reactor bed logically is the noncondensable part of the pyrolysis gas. This gas needs to be reheated and compressed, which requires careful cleaning to avoid blockage of heat exchangers, blowers, and so on. For comparison, gas cleaning appears to be one of the main hurdles in "conventional" gasification.

7.3.4   Circulating Fluid Bed

The first circulating fluid-bed (CFB) process was developed at the University of Western Ontario in the late 1970s and early 1980s. Biomass could be converted to bio-oil at yields of over 70 wt%. The principle is shown in Figure 7.10: Biomass is screwed into a (riser or fast fluidization) reactor, where extensive contacting between inert particles (sand) and biomass takes place. Together with the char, sand is entrained out of the reactor and sent to a combustor chamber where the char is combusted. The main advantage of the CFB system compared to fluid bed and ablative is the direct heat supply to the biomass by recirculation of hot sand, generated by combustion of the char from the pyrolysis.

In the beginning of the 1990s, Ensyn Technologies in Ottawa, Canada offered the technology indicated as rapid thermal processing, or RTP-III, and a fairly large circulating fluid-bed pilot plant of 625 kg/h throughput capacity has been built in Bastardo, Italy (Rossi and Graham 1997). The plant is stated "running on demand," which is never in practice or hardly ever. A 100-, a 40-, and a 10-kg/h R&D unit were available at Ensyn's site in Ottawa, while a 20-kg/h PDU unit was built for research purposes at VTT in Finland. Large-scale facilities of biomass capacities of up to 350 tons/day are said to be in the design or construction stage (see, e.g., Graham 1998), but to date none of these has actually been built. Just as for fluid-bed technology, CFB technology is said

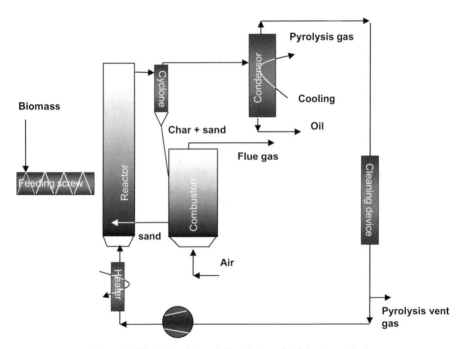

Figure 7.10   Principle of circulating fluid-bed pyrolysis.

to be well understood (Bridgwater 2003), but actual operation in pyrolysis appears problematic, with substantial erosion problems and complications due to operational parameters such as the use of dip legs. This is a problem solved in the chemical industry (e.g., in fluid catalytic cracking processes). Nevertheless, and similar to fluid-bed technology, the large amounts of gas used for fluidization of the reactor should be the noncondensable part of the pyrolysis gas. This gas needs to be reheated and compressed, which requires careful cleaning to avoid blockage of heat exchangers, blowers, and so on. For comparison, gas cleaning appears to be one of the main hurdles in conventional gasification. Finally, to realize the rather low solids hold-up in riser systems at solid fluxes of $G_s = 100$ to $200 \, kg/m^2 \cdot s$, the gas flow rate in the riser is high, on the order of $1000 \, m^3/h$ (tons/h biomass).

7.3.5 Vacuum Moving Bed

The Université de Sherbrooke during 1981 to 1985, and the Université Laval, both in Canada, developed vacuum pyrolysis. The process includes a combination of slow and fast pyrolysis conditions. Course solids are heated relatively slowly to temperatures higher than that of slow pyrolysis, while the gas is removed from the hot-temperature zone relatively quickly by applying a reduced pressure of 2 to 20 kPa in the process. An attempt to commercialize it was carried out by Pyrovac International by the end of the 1990s. In the concept, biomass material was conveyed over horizontal plates, which were heated indirectly by a mixture of molten salts composed of potassium nitrate, sodium nitrite, and sodium nitrate [Roy et al. (1997); see also Figure 7.11]. The salt itself was heated by a gas burner fed with the noncondensable gases produced by the pyrolysis process. Limitations in heat transfer required the bed of particles to be agitated. A 3.5-ton/h demonstration plant for bark pyrolysis was erected in Jonquiere, Quebec, Canada, and placed into operation in 1998. For operational reasons, including limitations of heat transfer from a molten salt bath to the biomass, plant operation was discontinued in 2002.

7.3.6 BTG's Technology: Rotating Cone Reactor

Fast pyrolysis has been a continuous research item at Twente University in the Netherlands for a few decades. The researchers started with the principle that intense mixing of biomass and hot inert particles is the most effective way to transfer heat to the biomass, but that fluid-bed mixing requires too much ineffective inert carrier gas. Consequently, a high-intensity reactor for the pyrolysis of biomass was developed that did not require inert gases, simplifying the reactor and peripheral equipment as oil condenser, gas cleaning, and so on. The original idea in 1989 to rely on a merely ablative principle without inert sand was later modified to a sand transported-bed rotating cone reactor (RCR). The concept is depicted in Figure 7.12. Instead of mixing the biomass in hot sand

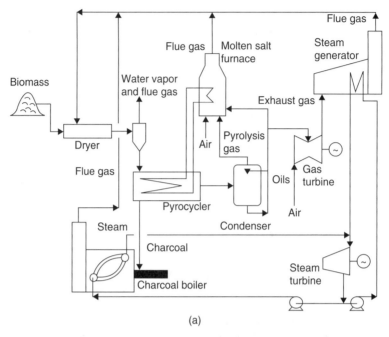

(a)

(b)

Figure 7.11 (a) Flow sheet of the Pyrocycler and the IPCC process (from Roy et al. 1997); (b) Pyrovac installation in Jonquière, Canada (source: Christian Roy).

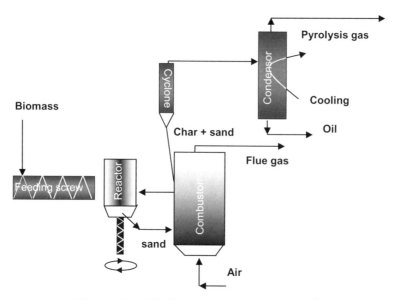

Figure 7.12 Principle of rotating cone pyrolysis.

driven by inert gas, the pyrolysis reactions take place by mechanical mixing of biomass and sand. Similar to CFB operation, the sand and char are transported further to a separate fluid bed, where the combustion of char takes place. The RCR enables a high solids throughput and short vapor residence times.

RTD work was continued in two groups, one at the University of Twente (research) and the other at BTG (Biomass Technology Group) (scale-up and commercialization) (Venderbosch et al. 1999, 2000). Figure 7.13 shows the process scheme of a first prototype installation built by BTG and Royal Schelde in Vlissingen as a test unit for Shenyang Agricultural University. It was shipped to China in 1994. Biomass particles are fed near the bottom of the rotating cone together with an excess flow of heat carrier material such as sand, and then transported upward along the cone wall in a spiral trajectory by the centrifugal forces (up to 600 rpm). An electrical oven in which the sand and char are trapped surrounds the RCR. The vapors produced pass through a cyclone before entering the condenser, in which the vapors are quenched by recirculated oil.

Subsequently, a novel reactor system (throughput capacity of up to 20 kg/h) was developed and built again by Royal Schelde in Vlissingen for the University of Twente (Venderbosch et al. 1997). In contrast with Wagenaar's original reactor, this rotating cone had a number of holes near the bottom, through which the sand enters the cone. To compensate for heat losses and provide both the energy for heating of the biomass particles and, consequently, the overall endothermic pyrolysis reactions, the char produced during pyrolysis was burned in this second fluid bed (the "combustion chamber"). Experiments

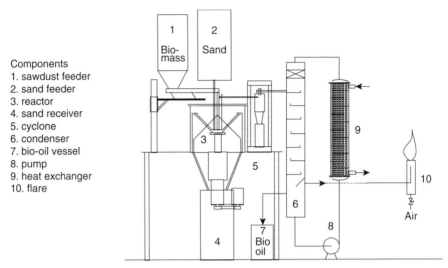

Components
1. sawdust feeder
2. sand feeder
3. reactor
4. sand receiver
5. cyclone
6. condenser
7. bio-oil vessel
8. pump
9. heat exchanger
10. flare

Figure 7.13   Flow sheet of the 50-kg/h RCR prototype developed for China in 1994.

with sand and catalysts demonstrated that autothermal operation can indeed be achieved with this system, but unfortunately, the operational flexibility of this advanced concept appeared to be poor, and therefore the concept was no longer considered for further scale-up.

BTG scaled up the RCR technology, first to about 50 kg/h. Figures 7.13 and 7.14 show the process scheme and some pictures of this first version of BTG's pilot plant. A cone reactor was integrated in a circulating sand system composed of a riser, a fluid-bed char combustor, the RCR reactor, and a downcomer. Char is burned in the combustor to generate the heat required for the pyrolysis process: by (re-)heating the inert sand that is recirculated to the reactor. Oil is the only product of this lab facility, and gases were flared. In 2001 the system was scaled-up further, to 250 kg/h. Through the past decade, about 100 tons of bio-oil have been produced from over 50 different materials. Oil is partially sent out to universities, institutes, and industrial companies for application research. In addition to this pilot-plan installation, a smaller (5 kg/h) test unit has been erected in BTG's laboratories, for quick screening of potential feedstock materials in a continuously operated system.

Initially, researchers reported that the RCR principle would be limited to particles less than 1 mm in diameter. Over the years, however, the way of mixing in the cone and the pyrolysis system were improved considerably. The overall efficiency of the process is increased, the acceptable particle diameter demonstrated to be up to 10 mm, and product quality and consistency for different feedstocks are improved considerably. This led to the world's first unit sold commercially, producing 50 tons/day and running on "empty fruit bunch" (EFB), a leftover from palm oil mills. In the Malaysian plant, EFB is taken

Figure 7.14 The 200-kg/h rotating cone process.

directly from a nearby palm mill, pressed, shredded, dried, and converted to bio-oil. From reception to oil delivery takes about 1 hour, time that is consumed almost entirely by the pretreating process. The overall (simplified) scheme is given in Figure 7.15, which includes the complete chain from EFB reception, storage, pretreatment (pressing, shredding and drying), storage (approximately 4 tons), and conversion. The heat required to dry the EFB (up to 70 wt% moisture upon reception) is taken from the pyrolysis unit, and a steam production system is fully integrated in the production unit.

EFB and the pyrolysis plant are shown in Figure 7.16. From mid-2005 the plant ran on a daily basis, showing the potentials but also the shortcomings. The main achievements over recent years are as follows:

- Over 1000 tons of bio-oil have been produced from more than 5000 tons of wet (up to 70% moisture) EFB.
- Oil is co-fired, replacing conventional diesel in a system located 300 km from the site.
- Drying of dewatered EFB from around 50 wt% moisture content down to 5 wt% is possible using the excess heat from the pyrolysis process.
- Oil quality can be controlled by tuning operation conditions.

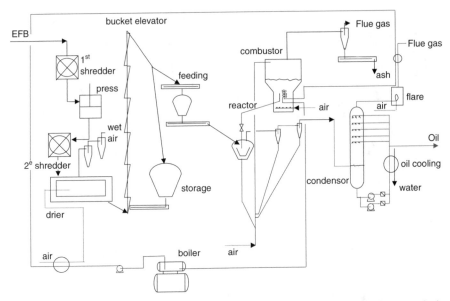

Figure 7.15 Process scheme of the Malaysian plant for fast pyrolysis of empty fruit bunches (EFBs), including the complete chain from EFB reception, storage, pretreatment, and conversion.

- Any excess energy recovered from the process after drying of the (very) wet EFB is potentially available to generate electricity for on-site use.
- The maximum capacity of the plant achieved is about 1.7 tons/h (the design capacity was 2 tons/h).
- No problems were observed in the actual reactor system. Technical problems related to erosion due to high-velocity sand in riser parts, cyclones, and other equipment could easily be overcome.

Some shortcomings of the system should also be noted:

- Fluid-bed combustion of the char from EFB creates a high risk of blockages, but this appeared to be due specifically to the nature of the EFB ash (e.g., low melting point).
- Considerable pretreatment of EFB is necessary, and wear and tear in pretreatment equipment is significant (e.g., in presses and shredders).
- By average, the bio-oil yield on the basis of good-quality dried EFB is 50 to 60 wt%; the oil yield is lower than for wood (typically, 70 wt%), while the water content is higher.
- The supply rate of wet EFB from the palm mill and the quality vary considerably: from 2 to 2.5 tons/h during daylight, and 1 to 1.5 tons/h at night, with moisture contents up to 70%. Large amounts of EFB cannot be stored easily.

Figure 7.16 BTG's Malaysian plant feed and production process: (a) fresh fruit bunch (FFB); (b) empty fruit bunch (EFB); (c) pyrolysis unit; (d) pyrolysis plant; (e) oil storage tanks.

- As a first-of-a-kind installation, the reliability of the plant was limited; much effort and resources were spent to improve and optimize the plant.
- Efficient heat integration, together with an improved reliability of the total system, will be the challenge for the coming years.

Considering the status of the pyrolysis process at the beginning of the plant design in 2004, the progress made in Malaysia is significant. From an initial set of experiments in 2003 (8 hours and maximum 100 kg/h feeding), the system has been scaled up to a factory running 24 hours per day, where a direct link has been established between the palm mill and the pyrolysis plant. In addition, the process is applied here for a difficult type of biomass feedstock, as, next to being fluffy and wet, the ash of the mineral rich feed has a very low melting point (below 650 °C). At the time of writing the plant is operational.

7.4 MASS AND ENERGY BALANCE FOR PRODUCTION OF BIO-OIL AND CHAR IN A 2-TON/H WOOD PLANT

Here the fluid-bed concept (Figure 7.17) is adopted to get an indication of the mass and energy streams in a pyrolysis process. In this theoretical case, wood logs are chunked ($70 \times 70 \times 70$ mm, 30 wt% moisture), dried (10 wt%), down-sized to 10 mm, and introduced subsequently (1) through a series of screws into the fluid bed, which is operated at 530 °C. The fluidizing gas is derived from the noncondensable pyrolysis vapors, which are scrubbed and cleaned

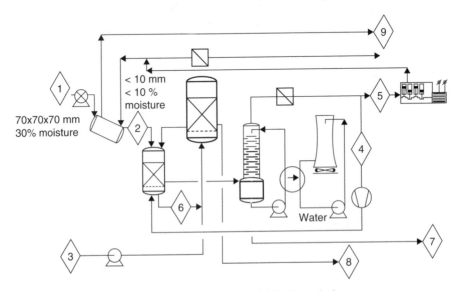

Figure 7.17 Flow sheet for the fluid-bed pyrolysis process.

to meet the requirements of the compressor, heat exchangers, and the fluid-bed distributor design. For this particular case, the ratio between the fluidizing gas flow rate at 530 °C and the biomass feed rate is taken to be 1:2.2. The pyrolysis vapors are produced by rapid heating of the biomass and fed to one or more condensing towers (one is shown). The noncondensable vapors, consisting of CO, CO_2, and CH_4 but also some aerosols, are transferred to an electrostatic precipitator, after which part of these gases are recycled through a compressor (4). The char produced upon pyrolysis is (theoretically) divided in two fractions. One part is separated and collected as such. The remainder is transported from the fluid-bed pyrolysis reactor to a second fluid bed where air is used to burn the char (570 °C). The ratio between the sand circulation flow and the biomass flow rate is taken 30:1 (kg sand:kg biomass) to allow a maximum temperature decrease of the sand of less than 50 °C. The heat of combustion from the char is used to reheat the sand and to heat the biomass to the required pyrolysis temperature.

The mass and energy balance can be constructed for this process. The data are shown in Table 7.3. The overall reaction equation for the pyrolysis system (without any application of the pyrolysis gas) is based on product composition data obtained experimentally:

(wood [DAF]) + (water) + (oxygen in air) →
  (bio-oil incl. water) + (flue gases) + (char) + (pyrolysis gas)

or

$$CH_{1.60}O_{0.68} + 0.136H_2O + 0.230O_2 \rightarrow 0.624CH_{2.59}O_{1.05} +$$
$$(0.0250H_2O + 0.095O_2 + 0.131CO_2) +$$
$$0.185CH_{0.72}O_{0.22} + 0.0735CH_{0.54}O_{1.30}$$

The RCR process differs from the hypothetical fluid-bed process described above in the sense that recycle gas flow is absent. This leads to higher thermal efficiency for the RCR process because heating of the recycle gas requires a thermal duty. No compressing, heating, and gas cleaning equipment for the recycle gas is required, and 65% (instead of just 60% in case of the fluid bed) of the char is available for uses other than internal process heating. For the RCR process, a single condenser is sufficient to collect more than 98% of the liquid product. In the literature on fluid-bed pyrolysis, two or more vessels are recommended.

In summary, 2.9 tons/h of biomass (as received, 30 wt% moisture) yields as main products 1.6 tons/h of bio-oil (6.6 MW_{th}), 200 kg/h of pyrolysis gas (0.42 MW_{th}) and 400 kg/h of charcoal (3.5 MW_{th}). Part of the charcoal (40%) is combusted for heating the biomass and providing the heat of pyrolysis (slightly endothermic reaction). In principal, there are two possibilities to retain the char: by separation from the bio-oil (liquid filtering) in the form of millimeter-sized char particles, or collected and emulsified in the bio-oil in a

TABLE 7.3 Mass and Energy Balances for 2000-kg/h (Dry, Ash-Free) Fluid-Bed Pyrolysis

Stream no.:	1	2	3	4	5	6	7	8	9
	Input	Reactor Feed	Air	Inert Carrier Gas	Pyrolysis Vapors	Heat Carrier	Bio-oil	Surplus Char	Flue Gas
Organics	2000	2000	—	—	—	—	1200	—	—
Water	900	200	—	—	—	—	400	—	740
O_2	—	—	600	—	—	—	—	—	250
N_2	—	—	2400	—	—	—	—	—	2400
CO_2	—	—	—	—	—	—	—	—	470
Pyrolysis gas	—	—	—	1000	200	—	—	—	—
Char	—	—	—	—	—	155	—	245	—
Ash	20	20	—	—	—	—	—	12	8
Sand	—	—	—	—	—	66,600	—	—	—
Total	2920	2220	3000	1000	304	—	1600	257	3868
Temp. (K)	291	291	291	326	—	804	317	804	400
Pressure (bar)	1	1	1	1.2	1	1	1	1	1
Chem. heat (MW)	10.4	10.4	—	2.1	0.42	1.3	6.6	2.1	—
Heat (MW)	—	—	—	—	—	7.41	—	0.05	0.33

certain weight content. On average, the weight fraction of the char in the oil (on oil basis) is then approx. 15 wt%. The pyrolysis gas (7.5 MJ/kg) can be used to fuel a gas engine: the electrical power output will be $0.16 MW_e$, with additional heat production of $0.21 MW_{th}$. The flue gases derived from the combustion of the char contain approximately $0.5 MW_{th}$ of sensible heat. The heat from both the flue gases and the gas engine can be used to dry the feed-stock from over 30 wt% down to the 10 wt% required for pyrolysis (air-dried wood contains approximately 25 wt% moisture).

Proprietary data indicate that for the pyrolysis process roughly 0.015 to $0.03 MW_e$ is required per $MW_{th,in}$. The exact value depends, among other factors, on whether the feedstock should be chunked, milled, and dried upon reception. About $0.02 MW_e/MW_{th,in}$ is produced on the basis of the pyrolysis gases, which is sufficient if the feedstock is delivered at certain specifications. The general mass and energy balances for the RCR are very similar, except for the recycle flow of pyrolysis gases. Only a small difference can be calcu-lated in the overall efficiency (86% for the FB versus over 88% for the RCR). The interested reader is referred to Peacocke et al. (2006) for two other (theo-retical) cases: the Wellman and the BTG fast pyrolysis process.

7.5 BIO-OIL FUEL APPLICATIONS

A key advantage of producing liquids from biomass is that its production can be decoupled in time, scale, and place from the final application. The current status of primary, secondary, and tertiary processing of pyrolysis liquids is presented further in Table 7.4. Due to its high oxygen content and the pres-ence of a significant portion of water, the heating value of bio-oil is much lower than that of fossil fuel. Nevertheless, flame combustion tests showed that fast pyrolysis oils can replace heavy and light fuel oils in industrial boiler applica-tions. In its combustion characteristics, the oil is more similar to light fuel oil, although significant differences in ignition, viscosity, energy content, stability, pH, and emission levels are observed (Shaddix and Hardesty 1999). Problems identified in flame combustion of bio-oil are related to these deviating char-acteristics, but can be overcome in practice (Gros 1996). Meanwhile, bio-oil has been used commercially to co-fire a coal utility boiler for power generation at Manitowoc Public Utilities in Wisconsin. It has also been approved as a fuel for utility boilers in Swedish district heating applications. A successful co-firing test with 15 tons of bio-oil was conducted in 2002 in a $350-MW_e$ power station in the Netherlands [some information is summarized in Wagenaar et al. (2002)]. Additional data are presented in Figure 7.18 and Table 7.5. A 4-hour co-firing session was carried at a bio-oil throughput of $1.6 m^3/h$, or an equiva-lent of $8 MW_{th}$. While co-firing bio-oil in the boiler HC61, the power output setting of the plant remained constant at about $250 MW_e$, and in the test the plant control reduced the natural gas flow to the boiler to compensate for the injection of thermal heat of the bio-oil, indeed corresponding to $8 MW_{LHV}$.

TABLE 7.4   Status of Primary, Secondary, and Tertiary Processing of Pyrolysis Products[a]

Primary Product	Secondary Processing	Secondary Product	Tertiary Processing	Final Product
Liquid	**Transport[5]**	**Fuel**	**Combustion[5]**	**Heat/steam/**
	Combustion[2]	Heat/steam	Steam turbine [5]	**electricity**
	Engine/turbine[1]	Electricity	Engine/turbine[1]	Electricity
	Stabilization[1]	Stabilized oil	Refining[2]	Electricity
	Upgrading[1]	Hydrocarbons	Refining[1,5]	Diesel/gasoline
	Extraction[1,5]	Chemicals	Refining[1,2]	Chemicals
	Conversion[3]	Chemicals	Fuel cell[1]	Chemicals
	Conversion[2]	Gas		Electricity
Gas	**Combustion[5]**	**Heat/steam**	**Steam turbine[5]**	**Electricity**
	Engine/turbine[3]	Electricity		
	Fuel cell[1]	Electricity		
Char	**Transport[5]**	**Fuel**	**Combustion[5]**	**Heat/steam/**
	Combustion[5]	Heat/power	Combustion[3]	**electricity**
	Slurrying[2]	Liquid fuel		Heat/power

Source: Bridgwater (1999a).
[a]Indices: 1, conceptual; 2, laboratory; 3, pilot; 4, demonstration; 5, commercial. The most promising options on a short time scale are indicated in bold.

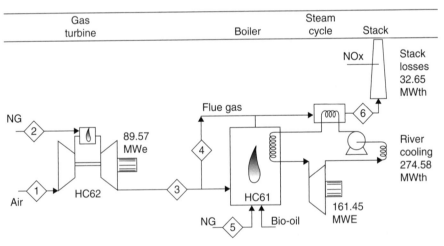

Figure 7.18   Mass and energy balances of the Harculo power station.

Oil from BTG's Malaysian plant was used routinely to replace expensive diesel for startup purposes in a fluid-bed combustor near Kuala Lumpur International Airport. No results are reported in the open literature. Since 2006, BTG has been actively involved in the combustion of bio-oil in a standard 250-kW hot-water generation unit to replace diesel and/or natural gas.

TABLE 7.5 Power Settings of Harculo Station and the M&E Balance as Indicated in Figure 7.18

	Input		Output		
	Natural Gas[a] (MW$_{th}$)	Heat (MW$_{th}$)	Power (MW$_e$)	Heat (MW$_{th}$)	Efficiency (%)
Gas turbine HC62	293.5	0	89.6	203.9 @ 520 °C	30.5
Steam turbine HC61	264.8	133.8	161.5	237.2 @ 30 °C	40.5
Total plant HC60	558.3	0	251.0	307.2 @ 30 °C	45.0

Stream no:	1	2	3	4	5	6
	Air	Natural Gas	Flue Gas	Flue Gas	Natural Gas	Flue Gas
T (°C)	16	16	520	520	16	97
P (bar)	1.00	8.45	1.06	1.02	1.2	1.00
Flow (kg/s)	358	6.67	365	123	6.02	371
LHV (MW$_{th}$)	0	293.45	0	0	264.80	0
Heat (MW$_{th}$)	0	0	203.88	70.05	0	32.65

[a]Natural gas LHV: 35.57 MJ/N·m^3; 0.808 kg/N·m^3.

For this purpose, sufficient quantities of palm-derived oil from Malaysia were transported to the Netherlands, and a dedicated oil lance was developed. Results will be reported in due course.

Generally, the production of electricity is more interesting than the production of heat because of the higher added value of electricity and its ease of distribution and marketing. Diesel engines are relatively insensitive to the contaminants present in pyrolysis oils, especially large and medium-scale engines, and bio-oil may be used. Tests have been performed by diesel (re) manufacturers such as Ormrod Diesels and Wärtsilä Diesel, in collaboration with research institutes such as Aston University, VTT, MIT, and the University of Rostock (e.g., Jay et al. 1995; Oasmaa and Sipilä 1996; Frigo et al. 1998; Shiladeh and Hochreb 2000; Baglioni et al. 2001). A complete review was prepared in 2001 by one of the present authors (Venderbosch and van Helden 2001). In general, diesel engine development and tests suffer from insufficient quantities of available bio-oil. Nevertheless, the results obtained indicate that engine deterioration can be a serious problem. However, traditional diesel engines are designed to operate on an acid-free diesel, and all engine components are manufactured in such a way and with such steel materials as to comply with these fossil fuels. Severe wear and erosion were observed in the injection needles, due to the fuel's acidity and the presence of abrasive particles. Nozzles lasted longer when filtered oil was used, but it is clear that standard nozzle materials are not adequate (see also Chiaramonti et al. 2007).

A high bio-oil viscosity and its loss of stability with rising temperatures are major problems, already referred to above. Damage to nozzles and injection systems and buildup of carbon deposits in the combustion chamber and exhaust valves are reported. Engines with larger cylinder bores (i.e., medium- and low-speed engines) are expected to be most suitable because of less stringent construction tolerances. For smaller-bore engines, reduction of the oil viscosity could be needed. Injection modification and/or a high-turbulence combustion chamber are required. Because the bio-oil has bad ignition properties (cetane index), it should be enriched by addition of cetane improvers, and application of a dual fuel system is most appropriate. Self-cleaning injectors are possibly required (Kindelan 1994). At the end of the 1990s Wärtsila stopped the development work, due primarily to the quality and quantity of pyrolysis oils at that time. Despite all these problems, it has also been reported that modifications of both the bio-oil and the engine can make pyrolysis oils quite acceptable for diesels. This would not only offer prospects for stand-alone electricity production units, but in the future potentially for the application of fast pyrolysis oils in the transportation sector (trucks, tractors, buses). A substantial RTD effort with involvement of manufacturers is required to realize this application.

7.5.1 Gas Turbines

Experience with bio-oil combustion in gas turbines is limited but promising. Known R&D projects were carried out by Orenda Division of Magellan Aerospace Corporation (Canada), ENEL Thermal Research Center (Italy), and Rostock University (Germany). Orenda is now searching actively for opportunities to run their Orenda GT2500 on pyrolysis oils. The GT2500 uses diesel oil and/or kerosene, and unlike aero-derived turbines, an external silo-type combustor is adopted. This chamber provides ready access to the main components. Several modifications are reported to be necessary (see, e.g., Chiaramonti et al. 2007):

- Complete low-pressure bio-oil supply system, including preheating and filtering of the bio-oil
- An improved nozzle design to allow larger fuel flows and dual fuel operation
- Redesign of the hot section, including section vanes and blades
- Stainless steel parts and modification of polymeric components

Despite their involvement in Dynamotive's plant in West Lorne, the nonavailability of bio-oil remains the main reason why limited test runs are carried out. A 75-kWe (nominal) gas turbine was tested in dual fuel mode by Rostock

University in 2001, showing deposits in combustion chamber and turbine blades, and higher emissions of CO and hydrocarbons.

7.5.2 Gasification

Bio-oil may have another suitable end application: its use as a fuel for gasification. It should be noted here that in refineries, gasification (next to combustion) is merely an end-of-pipe technique, using (cheap) feedstocks that cannot be used elsewhere in the process. Regarding co-gasification of biomass residues, pyrolysis could play an important role as a pretreatment technique, facilitating the cheaper transport and handling of biomass feedstocks from origin to the site of gasification over distances that biomass can never be shipped economically. Residue gasifiers can indeed be fed on bio-oil (see, e.g., Higman and van der Burgt 2003), and issues of concern are mainly the pH (feed train) and alkaline ash content. Actual data on the (small-scale) entrained flow gasification of pyrolysis oils have been reported by Venderbosch et al. (2002). Entrained flow experiments have been performed by BTG in UET's (now Choren) entrained flow gasifier in Freiberg (Germany) at about $500\,kW_{th}$ with pure oxygen, but so far no experimental results have been reported.

7.5.3 Transport Fuels

Pyrolysis oils may be used (pure or modified) as a transport fuel, and with the growing demand for bio-fuels is of strong interest worldwide. The simplest use of bio-oil may be in diesel engine, but as stated before, the oil as such is not suitable for (even) a stationary diesel engine. Upgrading of the oil to products more appropriate for further use is discussed by many organizations and institutes. In general, bio-oils are upgraded atmospherically using conventional FCC catalyst, or, at elevated pressures, by hydrotreating. FCC-like upgrading dates back to the 1990s, assuming that similar to ZSM-5 processing, oxygen may be rejected from the oil's structure as CO_2 using conventional FCC catalysts. Relevant work on this is presented by, among others Horne and Williams (1996) and Adjaye and Bakhshi (1995b). Results showed a limited yield of hydrocarbon products of about 20 wt% (or 40% energetically), due primarily to charring–coking of the feed.

Elliot (2007) recently reviewed the hydrotreating of bio-oils. The early work originates from the late 1980s, using the slow pyrolysis oils derived from carbonization or hydrothermal liquefaction processes. However, some serious (fundamental) research work is still required to understand the phenomena taking place in the treatment of pyrolysis oils. Early experiments showed that for proper dehydrogenation, temperatures on the order of 300 to 400 °C and residence times greater than 1 hour are required. The presence of water in the liquid state during the (initial) hydrotreating process seems crucial to avoid severe charring, necessitating high pressures to avoid water evaporation.

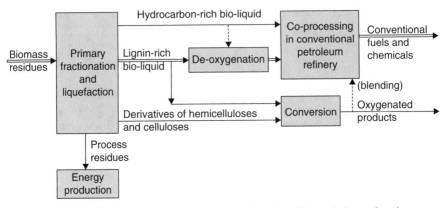

Figure 7.19   Biocoup's concept of co-refining bio-oil in existing refineries.

Until 2000, the main objectives aimed at in the literature for the upgrading of bio-oil remained a bit unclear. The overall objective was to produce transportation fuels (diesel and gasolinelike components), and the target seemed to be the reduction of the oxygen content in the oil. Since the use of methyl *test*-butly ether, butanol, and ethanol, for example, in transportation fuels, however, the common belief of petro-refineries shifted from absolutely no oxygen in the pool of transportation fuels toward the preference of adding small amounts of oxygen in the appropriate functionality (i.e., alcohol and/or ethers). Since 2000 the upgrading of bio-oil has also shifted from using it "pure" as a transportation fuel after upgrading, toward a wish to co-refine the upgraded bio-oil product with crude oil (derivatives). Samolada et al. (1998) reported that hydrotreated bio-oils could be well co-refined, with rather high efficiencies, in FCC processes. Co-refining is also the main subject in a large European project [BioCoup (www.biocoup.ev), including BTG among others; see also Figure 7.19], with the intention to produce bio-oils suitable for co-refining in standard refineries. First papers have recently been presented by Gutierrez et al. (2007) and De Miguel Mercader et al. (2008).

Other approaches to developing transport fuels include an alcohol treatment (analogous to vegetable oil esterification), reducing the oil's acidity and water content (Mahfud 2007; Mahfud et al. 2007). So far, such studies are exploratory in nature.

7.6   CHEMICALS FROM BIO-OIL

Since the earliest recorded use of the technique, bio-oil has been in use as a chemical, first in Egypt, where the product was used for sealing boats. In more recent times a number of chemicals have been derived from pyrolysis liquids (methanol, acetic acids, and liquid smoke). These liquids contain hundreds of different chemical compounds, in widely varying proportions, ranging from low-molecular-mass and volatile formaldehyde and acetic acid to complex high-molecular-mass phenols and anhydrosugars.

Approximately 300 compounds have been recognized by GC analysis as fragments of the basic compounds of biomass: that is, lignin (phenols, eugenols, and guaiacols among others) and cellulose or hemicellulose (sugars, acetaldehyde, and formic acids). Although GC analysis may not be the most appropriate analysis tool for bio-oil, large fractions of acetic acid, acetol, and hydroxyacetaldehyde are present in the oil (see also Table 7.2). Nevertheless, until now, only approximately 40 to 50% of the oil's identity (excluding the water) has been revealed. Especially the large, less severely cracked or repolymerized molecules (derived from cellulose and lignin) in the oils have not been identified. Figure 7.5 shows that all types of (oxygen) functionalities are present: acids, sugars, alcohols, ketones, aldehydes, phenols and their derivatives, furans, and other mixed oxygenates. Phenols are also present, sometimes in rather high concentrations. These phenolic fractions include phenol, eugenol, and guaiacols, and their derivatives, and the pyrolytic *lignin* (polyphenols) representing the water-insoluble components. It is questionable, however, if pyrolytic lignin contains only fragments of the original lignin or also polymerized carbohydrate (fractions).

Components in the oil interesting to consider for future chemical production are the carbohydrate fragments in the biomass. These are sugar derivatives, such as all types of anhydrosugars and oligosaccharides, formaldehyde, furfural alcohols, and hydroxyacetaldehyde. Due to the principle of GC analysis, in which only the distillable components in the oil can be identified and quantified, levoglucosan is usually referred to as an important type of sugar to be isolated. However, much more sugar (approximately 30 wt% of the oil) is present (see also Figure 7.5).

Aspects to be considered here are that the original feedstock, the process conditions, and the condensing parameters are of major importance for the types of chemicals in the oil. To complicate this further, pretreatment of wood may result in an increase of one particular component at the expense of the others. As mentioned earlier, ash (but also aging) is known to influence the reactions in the pyrolysis process and may contribute to higher yields of certain products (see, e.g., Fahmi et al. 2008).

Last but not least, analysis of bio-oil can be complicated. As an example of the variation in composition observed in wood-derived pyrolysis oil, Milne et al. (1997) remarked that not a single compound of over 100 have been identified by *all* 10 laboratories where pyrolysis oils could be analyzed. It has already been stated as well that GC analysis does not reveal the identity or quantity of components that do not evaporate in the injection system. Part of the discrepancy in analysis results from the various laboratories is caused by the continuous improvements in methodology during the last few years (increased use of GC-MS, HPLC, etc.) and the factual identification of the various components. In the following, uses for bio-oil are detailed further, beginning with applications of un-fractionated oil and with those in which fractions or isolated compounds are relevant.

7.6.1 Unfractionated Bio-oil

Resins for the Production of Particleboard or Plywood Board (MDF or OSB) Work to examine the potential use of pyrolysis oil as a raw material in wood panel manufacture is ongoing. The use of bio-oil is investigated for the replacement of formaldehyde and phenols in resins for particleboard. Due to the higher cross-linking of the lignin-derived compounds in bio-oil, a polymer with improved strength can be obtained when mixed with conventional urea–formaldehyde resins. Research in this area published at the end of 2000 concluded that bio-oils can be used in the manufacture of resins in phenol substitution rates up to 50% (Tsiantzi and Athanassiadou 2000). A review of the production of renewable phenol resins based on pyrolysis products was presented by Effendi et al. (2007) in which the authors report considerable progress but conclude that none of the phenol production and fractionation techniques yet available allow complete substitution of the resin.

Fertilizers and Soil Conditioners Reaction of bio-oil with ammonia, urea, or other amino compounds produces stable amides, amines, and so on. They are nontoxic to plants and can be used as slow-release organic fertilizers. Additional benefits are that the lignin degradation products and their reaction products are good for soil conditioning, control of soil acidity, amelioration of the effects of excess Al and Fe, increasing availability of phosphate, and crop stimulation. Furthermore, they are excellent complexing agents for nutrient metals such as Mo, Fe, B, Zn, Mn, and Cu. Other functional groups in the bio-oil-derived fertilizers are nutrients such as Ca, K, and P (Radlein and Piskorz 1998). DynaMotive has been cooperating with two major fertilizer manufacturers on the commercialization of bio-oil-derived products (Rhone 1998), but so far, no specific commercial outlets have been demonstrated.

Pure bio-oil can be mixed with lime to form BioLime, a trademark of DynaMotive corporation in Canada (Simons et al. 1996). Injection of the mixture into flue gas tunnels results in almost complete removal of sulfur oxides and a significant reduction in nitrogen oxides. After research work at the end of the twentieth century, the project seems to have been abandoned, and no references other than this have been found in the literature.

7.6.2 Fractions of Bio-oil

In wood-derived pyrolysis oil, specific oxygenated compounds are present in quite substantial amounts. The recovery of such pure compounds from the complex bio-oil may be technically feasible but are probably economically unattractive because of the high cost for recovery of the chemical and its low concentration in the oil. In the following, the relevant chemical components are presented.

Wood Flavors The only commercial application of wood-derived bio-oil known to date is that of wood flavor or liquid smoke. A number of companies produce these liquids by adding water to bio-oil. A red product is then obtained which can be sprayed over meat before further cooking. The taste, color, and smell of the meat are thus created artificially. A range of food-flavoring products, based on pyrolysis oils, have been patented and commercialized by the Red Arrow Products Company in the United States and by Chemviron in Germany. A patent is given here as a reference (Underwood and Rozum 2007).

Phenolic Compounds A part of the oil is be the *phenolic fraction*, consisting of small amounts of phenol, eugenol, cresols, and xylenols, and larger quantities of alkylated (poly-) phenols (water-insoluble pyrolytic lignin). Recoveries of phenolic compounds up to 50 wt% may have been reported, but this is from specific feedstocks only. The amount of the smaller, more expensive phenolic components in bio-oil is usually limited, probably because the original lignin in the biomass is converted only partly [Yang et al. (2007); see also Section 7.1]. Moreover, it is probably contaminated by repolymerized lignin and, possibly, sugar fragments as well.

In nature, the lignin portion acts as an adhesive to bind cellulose fibers, and it appears that the lignin-derived substance in bio-oil can be used for the development of biomass-based adhesive resins (Suzuki et al. 1997; Radlein in Bridgwater 2002). Earlier in the chapter reference was made to RTP biomass refining plants, which were producing more than 1800 tons of natural resin products annually in 2001; unfortunately, no additional information on this has been revealed subsequently. Phenolics have also been proposed for use as an alternative wood preservative to replace creosotes (Freel and Graham 2002).

Sugars As already mentioned, levoglucosan, together with levoglucosenone and hydroxyacetylaldehyde, are the few sugar derivatives present in bio-oil and detectable by GC equipment. It seems that this is the main reason that the first two components, especially, received a lot of attention. Extensive overviews on levoglucosan are given elsewhere, in particular those in separate papers of Dobele and Radlein, both published in Bridgwater (2002). Levoglucosenone is reportedly applicable in the synthesis of antibiotics and pheromones, rare sugars, butenolide, immunosuppresive agents, and whisky lactones, among others and is reportedly present in amounts up to 24 wt% (Radlein 1996). Progress in recent years to valorize bio-oil on the basis of these two interesting products is limited, though.

On the contrary, hydroxyacetaldehyde is a commercial product. It can be present in relatively large amounts in the bio-oil (17 wt%; Radlein 1996) and is used in browning food (e.g., cheese, meat, sausages, poultry, fish). A possible application is the use as a precursor for glyoxal OHC–CHO, which is an important chemical produced by oxidation of ethylene glycol (Oehr and McKinley 1994).

Calcium Carboxylates Components that can also be derived from bio-oil are carboxylic acids, from which salts such as calcium acetate and calcium formate can be produced (Oehr and Barrass 1992, 1994). In the aqueous fraction of the bio-oil, these acids are present in small amounts (up to 3 wt%). They have potential applications, such as road or runway deicing, sulfur dioxide removal during fossil-fuel combustion, or as a catalyst during coal combustion.

Furfural Derivatives Pavlath and Gregorski (1988) pyrolyzed five carbohydrate products: glucose, maltose, cellobiose, amylase, and cellulose, and showed that furfural and furfuryl alcohol up to 30 wt% and 12 to 30 wt%, respectively, were produced.

7.7 ECONOMICS

A key factor in the development to commercial implementation is the economic viability of fast pyrolysis processes. Currently, the main interest in Europe is electricity generation from biomass. CO_2 mitigation, socioeconomic benefits from re-deployment of surplus agricultural land, and energy independence are driving forces. These have led to significant fiscal incentives. Apart from such incentives, inflation, (in)direct effects of oil prices, local costs, and labor strongly affect the economics of pyrolysis plants. Therefore, it does not make sense to discuss economics in detail. General data, collected by BTG and confirmed in other studies, show that the range of capital costs for the pyrolysis plant only is between €200 and 500 per kW_{th} input biomass, depending on the technology, scale, degree of heat integration, location, and so on. The main parts of the BTG pyrolysis plant are the reactor, riser, combustor, and condenser. The costs of pretreatment, feeding, buildings, and infrastructure are not included but may add up to another 50 to 100%, depending on the initial feedstock properties (e.g., size, water content, dimensions, free-flowing behavior, bulk density). Costs related to the heat integration system (heat recovery, steam generation, drying, etc.) are usually not addressed in studies on economics.

As mentioned earlier, one of the challenges of BTG's process concept is the efficient generation and further use of the excess heat generated in the system. The Malaysian plant showed that (1) the heat required for drying of the wet feedstock is delivered by the process itself, and (2) the electricity can be generated from the excess heat available, even after use for drying. An important aspect to consider in plant economics is the observation that the cost for the actual pyrolysis reactor is just a fraction of the overall plant cost. At the same time, a proper reactor choice, in particular, offers the possibility of reducing costs upfront (e.g., in feeding and pretreatment) or in peripheral equipment. The rotating cone reactor in the Malaysian plant, for example, is about 2 to 3% of the total plant cost but reduces the overall costs significantly, as the absence of inert gases reduces the costs of secondary equipment considerably.

Studies over the years indicated that pyrolysis oils can be produced at costs in the range €4 to 14 per GJ, with feedstock costing between €0 and 100 per ton (€0 to 6 per GJ). The interested reader is referred to Peacocke et al. (2006) and Ringer et al. (2006). Such figures match quite well with the data from the Malaysian plant. But, again, it should be noted that they depend strongly on process technology, the scale of operation, feedstock, year of construction, and so on.

Generally speaking, it can be stated that the costs of pyrolysis processes should be rather low, because the operating conditions are less extreme than for combustion or gasification (lower temperatures and atmospheric pressure). However, biomass pretreatment, heat integration, and the required operational reliability can seriously increase the overall investment costs.

7.8 CONCLUDING REMARKS

Pyrolysis definitely remains an interesting pretreatment technique to permit (intercontinental) transport of large volumes of biomass. The proof of principle (reactor concept) and proof of concept (plant setup) have been demonstrated by BTG in Malaysia, DynaMotive in Canada, and Ensyn in the United States and Canada, among others. Although a number of installations have been erected, they all exhibit a lack of operational hours, and no process has really been demonstrated. The main hurdle right now is a full-proof demonstration of the concept, running multiple plants steadily more than 8000 h/y for plants with capacities above 2 tons/h. The oil should, for the time being, be used as a substitute for heat (and indirectly, power), by combustion in conventional boilers. The focus for the next few years is to produce oil, and to apply simple and cheap applications to get rid of it. Once the process (and peripherals) are proven, larger amounts of oil will become available for the development and commercial-scale demonstration of bio-oil applications, be it turbines, diesel engines, and/or further upgrading techniques.

Challenges in the coming years will focus on improving the reliability of demonstration-scale pyrolysis, improving heat transfer and heat integration and their control. Then (or in the meantime), interest should be directed toward an analysis of relevant oil properties and *improvement in the quality* (and stability) of the oil relevant for end-use application. Despite 20 years of existence of a rather uniform bio-oil, it can be concluded that only limited fundamental know-how is generated on the exact composition of the bio-oil. Much work was related to destructive GC analysis techniques, but today it is better understood that the components quantified are not necessarily present in those concentrations in the original oils. In addition, the authors believe that the compounds or fractions that are relevant in the oil, causing its specific characteristics (pH, aging, viscosity, phase separation, etc.), are not fully identified, nor are the reactions taking place understood. One particular issue to be addressed is to learn more about the exact role of the various oxygen functionalities in the oil and to establish which functionalities are (or are not) preferred, and if possible can be steered to or from either in the pyrolysis process itself or by an additional treatment (e.g., by catalysis). One important conclusion here is that it is not that the oxygen content in the oil is to be reduced but that the number of oxygen functionalities in the oil need to be limited.

For BTG's system in particular, the progress made in Malaysia from the beginning of the plant design in 2004 to date is quite convincing. From an initial set of experiments in 2003 (8 hours and maximum 100 kg/h feeding), the system has been scaled up to a factory running 24 hours/day in which a direct link has been established between the palm mill and the pyrolysis plant. In addition, the process is used for very difficult biomass feedstocks which are fluffy (not free flowing) and wet, with a high ash content (and a very low melting point). The tough problems that have been resolved dealt with boundary conditions (feeding, pretreatment, and heat recovery) rather than with the actual pyrolysis process itself.

REFERENCES

Adjaye, J. D., and N. N. Bakhshi. 1995a. Catalytic conversion of a biomass-derived oil to fuel and chemicals: I. Model compound studies and reaction pathways. *Biomass Bioenergy*, 8(3):131–149.

————. 1995b. Production of hydrocarbons by catalytic upgrading of a fast pyrolysis bio-oil: I. Conversion over various catalysts. *Fuel Process. Technol.*, 45:161–183.

————. 1995c. Production of hydrocarbons by catalytic upgrading of a fast pyrolysis bio-oil: II. Comparative catalyst performance and reaction pathways. *Fuel Process. Technol.*, 45:185–202.

Baglioni, P., D. Chiaramonti, M. Bonini, I. Soldaini, and G. Tondi. 2001. Bio-crude-oil/diesel oil emulsification: main achievements of the emulsification process and preliminary results of tests on a diesel engine. In *Progress in Thermochemical Biomass Conversion*, ed. A. V. Bridgwater, Oxford: Blackwell Science, pp. 1525–1539.

Blin, J., G. Volle, P. Girard, T. Bridgwater, and D. Meier. 2007. Biodegradebility of biomass pyrolysis oils: comparison to conventional petroleum fuels and alternative fuels in current use. *Fuels*, doi:10.1016/j.fuel.2007.03.033.

Bridgwater, A. V. 1996. Production of high grade fuels and chemicals from catalytic pyrolysis of biomass. *Catal. Today*, 29:285.

————. 1999a. *Fast Pyrolysis of Biomass: A Handbook*, Vol. 1. Berkshire, UK: CPL Press.

————. 1999b. Principles and practice of biomass fast pyrolysis processes for liquids. *J. Anal. Appl. Pyrol.*, 51:3–22.

————. 2002. *Fast Pyrolysis of Biomass: A Handbook*, Vol. 2. Berkshire, UK: CPL Press.

————. 2003. Renewable fuels and chemicals bythermal processing of biomass, *Chem. Eng. J.*, 91:87–102.

————. 2005. *Fast Pyrolysis of Biomass: A Handbook*, Vol. 3. Berkshire, UK: CPL Press.

————. 2007. *Biomass Pyrolysis*. Report T34:2007:01: IEA Bioenergy, Rotorua, New Zealand.

Chiaramonti, D., A. Oasmaa, and Y. Solantausta. 2007. Power generation using fast pyrolysis liquids from biomass. *Renew. Sustain. Energy Rev.*, 11:1056–1086.

Cuevas, A., C. Reinoso, and J. Lamas. 1995. Advances and development at the Union Fenosa pyrolysis plant. In *8th Conference on Biomass for Environment, Agriculture and Industry*, ed. Ph. Chartier, A.A.C.M. Beenackers, and G. Grassi. Tarrytown, NY: Pergamon Press.

Dahmen, N., E. Dinjus, E. Henrich, C. Kornmayer, R. Stahl, and F. Weirich. 2007. Fast pyrolysis by a twin scale mixing reactor: status of the FZK research facilities. In *Success and Vision for Bioenergy: A European Workshop on Success and Visions in Thermal Processing for Bioenergy, Biofuels and Bioproducts*, Salzburg, Austria, Mar. 22–23.

De Miguel Mercader F., A. Ardiyanti, A. Gutierrez, S. Khromova, E. Leijenhorst, S. R. M. Kersten, K. Hogendoorn, W. Prins, and M. Groeneveld . 2008. Upgrading of bio-liquids for co-processing in standard refinery units. In *16th European Biomass Conference and Exhibition*, Valencia, Spain.

Di Blasi, C. 1997. A transient, two-dimensional model of biomass pyrolysis. In *Developments in Thermochemical Biomass Conversion*, ed. A. V. Bridgwater and D. G. B. Boocock. London: Blackie Academic and Professional, p. 147.

————. 2008. Modelling chemical and physical processes of wood and biomass pyrolysis. *Prog. Energy Combust. Sci.*, 34:47–90.

Diebold, J. P. 1999. A review of the toxicity of biomass pyrolysis liquids formed at low temperatures. In *Fast Pyrolysis of Biomass: A Handbook*, Vol. 1, ed. A. V. Bridgwater. Berkshire, UK: CPL Press.

————. 2002. A review of the chemical and physical mechanisms of the storage stability of fast pyrolysis bio-oils. In *Fast Pyrolysis of Biomass: A Handbook*, Vol. 2, ed. A. V. Bridgwater. Berkshire, UK: CPL Press.

————, and A. V. Bridgwater. 1997. Overview of fast pyrolysis of biomass for the production of liquid fuels. In *Developments in Thermochemical Biomass Conversion*, ed. A. V. Bridgwater and D. G. B. Boocock. London: Blackie Academic & Professional.

DynaMotive. 2005a. DynaMotive Energy Systems Corporation: an update on the West Lorne bio-oil project. *PyNe Newsl.*, 1.

————. 2005b. An update on the West Lorne bio-oil project. *PyNe Newsl.*, 18.

Effendi, A., H. Gerhauser, and A. V. Bridgwater. 2007. Production of renewable phenolic resins by thermochemical conversion of biomass: a review. *Renew. Sustain. Energy Rev.*, doi:10.1016/j.rser.2007.04.008.

Elliot, D. C. 2007. Historical developments in hydroprocessing bio-oils. *Energy Fuels*, 21:1792–1815.

Fahmi, R., A. V. Bridgwater, I. Donnison, and N. Yates. 2008. The effect of lignin and inorganic species in biomass on pyrolysis oil yield, quality and stability. *Fuel*, 87:1230–1240.

Freel, B. 2002. Ensyn announces commissioning of new biomass facility. *PyNe Newsl.*, 14.

———, and R. G. Graham. 2002. Bio-oil preservatives. U.S. patent 6,485,841, NREL.

Freel, B. A., R. G. Graham, D. R. Huffman, and A. J. Vogiatzis. 1993. Rapid thermal processing of biomass (RTP): development, demonstration, and commercialization. *Energy Biomass Wastes*, 16:811.

Frigo, S., R. Gentilli, L. Tognotti, S. Zanforlin, and G. Benelli. 1998. *Feasibility of Using Wood Flash-Bio-Oil in Diesel Engines*. SAE Technical Paper Series 982529 Warrendale, PA: Society of Automotive Engineers.

Graham, R. G., B. A. Freel, D. R. Huffman, and M. A. Bergougnou. 1994. Commercial-scale rapid thermal processing of biomass. *Biomass Bioenergy*, 7(25):1–258.

Gros, S. 1996. Pyrolysis oil as diesel fuel. In *Power Production from Biomass II with Special Emphasis on Gasification and Pyrolysis R&DD*, VTT Symposium 164, Espoo, Finland, ed. K. Sipilä and M. Korhonen. p. 225.

Gupta, A. K., and D. G. Lilley. 2003. Thermal destruction of wastes and plastics. In *Plastics and the Environment*, ed. A. L. Andrady. Hoboken, NJ: Wiley-Interscience, pp. 629–696.

Gutierrez, A., M. E. Domine, and Y. Solantausta. 2007. Co-processing of upgraded bio-liquids in standard refinery-units: fundamentals. Presented at the 15th European Biomass Conference.

Higman, C., and M. Van der Burgt. 2003. *Gasification*. New York: Elsevier Science.

Horne, P., and P. T. Williams. 1996. Reaction of oxygenated biomass pyrolysis compounds over a ZSM-5 catalyst. *Renew. Energy*, 2:131–144.

Jay, D. C., K. H. Sipila, O. A. Rantanen, and N. O. Nylund. 1995. Wood pyrolysis oil for diesel engines. ICE Vol. 25–3. ASME Fall Technical Conference, vol. 3.

Johnson, D. A., D. Maclean, J. Feller, J. Diebold, and H. L. Chum. 1994. Developments in the scale-up of the vortex-pyrolysis system. *Biomass Bioenergy*, 7(1–6):259–266.

Kindelan, J. C. 1994. Comparative study of various physical and chemical aspects of pyrolysis bio-oils versus conventional fuels, regarding their use in engines. In *Biomass Pyrolysis Oil Properties and Combustion*, ed. T. A. Milne, Estes Park, Colorado, p. 321.

Mahfud, F. H. 2007. Exploratory studies on fast pyrolysis oil upgrading. Thesis, University of Groningen.

———, I. Melian-Cabrera, R. Manurung, and H. J. Heeres. 2007. Upgrading of flash pyrolysis oil by reactive distillation using a high boiling alcohol and acid catalysts. *Trans. IChemE B*, 85(B5):466–472.

Meier, D. 2004. New ablative pyrolyser in operation in Germany. *PyNe Newsl.*, 17.

———. 2007. Aus Holz wird Oel. *Forstmaschinen Prof.*, 15(12):26–28.

Milne, T., F. Agblevor, M. Davis, S. Deutch, and D. Johnson. 1997. A review of the chemical composition of fast pyrolysis oils from biomass. In *Developments in Thermochemical Biomass Conversion*, ed. A. V. Bridgwater and D. G. B. Boocock, London: Blackie Academic and Professional, p. 409.

Mohan, D., C. U. Pittman, and P. H. Steel. 2006. Pyrolysis of wood/biomass for bio-oil: a critical review. *Energy Fuels*, 20:848–889.

Nieminen, J. P., S. Gust, and T. Nyrönen. 2003. Forestera™ liquefied wood fuel pilot plant. *PyNe Newsl.*, 16.

Oasmaa, A. 1999. Fuel oil quality properties of wood-based pyrolysis liquids. Thesis, University of Jyvaskyla, Finland.

———, and K. Sipilä. 1996. Pyrolysis oil properties: use of pyrolysis oil as fuel in medium-speed diesel engines. In *Bio-oil Production and Utilisation: Proceedings of the 2nd EU–Canada Workshop on Thermal Biomass Processing*, ed. A. V. Bridgwater and E. N. Hogan. Newbury: UK, p. 175.

———, and E. Kuoppala. 2003. Fast pyrolysis of forestry residue. 3. Storage stability of liquid fuel. *Energy Fuel*, 17(4): 1075–1084.

Oehr, K. H., and G. Barrass. 1992. Biomass derived alkaline carboxylate road deicers. *Resources Conserv. recycl.*, 7:155.

———. 1994. Biomass derived calcium carboxylates. In *Advances in Thermochemical Biomass Conversion*, ed. A. V. Bridgwater. London: Blackie, p. 1456.

———, and J. McKinely. 1994. Glyoxal production from biomass pyrolysis derived hydroxyacetaldehyde. In *Advances in Thermochemical Biomass Conversion*, ed. A. V. Bridgwater. London: Blackie, p. 1452.

Pavlath, A. E., and K. S. Gregorski. 1988. Carbohydrate pyrolysis: II. Formation of furfural and fyrfurylalcohol during the pyrolysis of selected carbohydrates with acidic and basic catalysts. In *Research in Thermochemical Biomass Conversion*, ed. A. V. Bridgwater and J. L. Kuester. London: Elsevier Applied Science, p. 155.

Peacocke, G. V. C, A. V. Bridgwater, and J. C. Brammer. 2006. Techno-economic assessment of power production from the Wellman and BTG fast pyrolysis process. In *Science in Thermal and Chemical Biomass Conversion*, ed. A. V. Bridgwater and D. G. B. Boocock. Berkshire, UK: CPL Press.

Piskorz, J., D. Radlein, D. S. Scott, and S. Czernik. 1988. Liquid products from the fast pyrolysis of wood and cellulose. In *Research in Thermochemical Biomass Conversion*, ed. A. V. Bridgwater and J. L. Kuester. London: Elsevier Applied Science, p. 557.

Radlein, D. 1996. Fast pyrolysis for the production of chemicals. In *Bio-oil Production and Upgrading: Proceedings of the 2nd EU–Canada Workshop on Thermal Biomass Processing*, ed. A. V. Bridgwater and E. N. Hogan. Newbury: UK, p. 113.

———, and J. Piskorz. 1998. Production of chemicals from Bio-Oil. In *PyNe Final Report*, ed. A. V. Bridgwater and C. Humphreys. FAIR CT94-1857 Birmingham, UK.

Rhone, J. 1998. Dynamotive, Personal communication.

Ringer, M., V. Putsche, and J. Scahill. 2006. *Large-Scale Pyrolysis Oil Production: A Technology Assessment and Economic Analysis*. Technical Report NREL/TP-510-37779 Golden, Colorado.

Rossi, C., and R. Graham. 1997. Fast pyrolysis at ENEL. In *Biomass Gasification and Pyrolysis: State of the Art and Future Prospects*, ed. M. Kaltschmidt and A. V. Bridgwater. Newbury, UK: CPL Scientific Ltd., p. 300.

Roy, C., D. Morin, and F. Dubé. 1997. The biomass pyrocycling™ process. In *Biomass Gasification and Pyrolysis: State of the Art and Future Prospects*, ed. M. Kaltschmidt and A. V. Bridgwater. Newbury, UK: CPL Scientific Ltd., p. 307.

Samolada, M. C., W. Baldauf, and I. A. Vasalos. 1998. Production of bio-gasoline by upgrading biomass flash pyrolysis liquids via hydrogen processing and catalytic cracking. *Fuel*, 14:1667–1675.

Schöll, S., H. Klaubert, and D. Meier. 2004. Wood liquefaction by flash-pyrolysis with an innovative pyrolysis system. DGMK proceeding 2004-1 contributions to DGMK-meeting, Energetic Utilization to Biomasses, Apr. 19–21, Velen/Westf.

Shaddix, C. R., and D. R. Hardesty. 1999. Combustion Properties of Biomass Flash Pyrolysis Oils: Final Project Report, SAND99–8238, Albuquerque, New Mexico.

Shafizadeh, F. 1985. Pyrolytic reactions and products of biomass. In *Proceedings: Fundamentals of Thermochemical Biomass Conversion*, ed. R. P. Overend, T. A. Milne, and L. K. Mudge. London: Elsevier Applied Science.

———, and P. P. S. Chin. 1997. Wood technology, chemical aspects. *Am. Chem. Soc. Symp. Ser.*, 43:57.

Shiladeh, A., and S. Hochreb. 2000. Diesel engine combustion of biomass bio-oils. *Energy Fuels*, 14.

Simons, G. A., K. H. Oehr, J. Zhou, S. V. Pispati, M. A. Wojtowicz, and R. Bassilakis. 1996. Simultaneous NOx/SOx control using BioLime™ in PCC and CFBC. In *Proceedings of the 13th Coal Conference*, Pittsburgh, PA.

Suzuki, T., S. Doi, M. Yamakawa, K. Yamamoto, T. Watanabe, and M. Funaki. 1997. Recovery of wood preservatives from wood pyrolysis tar by solvent extraction. *Holzforsch. Mitt. Chem. Phys. Biol. Technol. Holzes*, 51:214.

Tsiantzi, S., and E. Athanassiadou. 2000. Wood adhesives made for pyrolysis oil. *PyNe Newsl.*, 10.

Underwood, G. L., and J. J. Rozum. 2007. Article and method for browning and flavoring foodstuffs. U.S. patent 7,282,229.

Venderbosch, R. H., and M. van Helden. 2001. *Diesel Engines on Bio-Oil: A Review.* SDE Samenwerkingsverband Duurzame Energie Enschede, The Netherlands.

Venderbosch, R. H., A. M. C. Janse, M. Radovanovic, W. Prins, and W. P. M. Van Swaaij. 1997. Pyrolysis of pine wood in a small integrated pilot plant rotating cone reactor. In *Biomass Gasification and Pyrolysis: State of the Art and Future Prospects*, ed. M. Kaltschmitt and A. V. Bridgwater. Newbury, UK: CPL Scientific Ltd.

Venderbosch, R. H., W. Prins, and B. M. Wagenaar. 1999. Flash pyrolysis of wood for energy and chemicals: 1. *NPT Procestechnol.*, 6:18–23.

———. 2000. Flash pyrolysis of wood for energy and chemicals: 2. *NPT Procestechnol.*, 1:16–20.

Venderbosch, R. H., L. van de Beld, and W. Prins. 2002. Entrained flow gasification of bio-oil for synthesis gas. Presented at the 12th European Conference and Technology Exhibition on Biomass for Energy, Industry and Climate Protection, June 17–21, Amsterdam, The Netherlands.

Wagenaar, B. 1994. The rotating cone reactor for rapid thermal solids processing. Thesis, University of Twente.

Wagenaar, B. N., W. Prins, and W. P. M. Van Swaaij. 1994. Pyrolysis of biomass in the rotating cone reactor: modeling and experimental justification. *Chem. Eng. Sci.*, 49(24B):5109–5126.

Wagenaar, B. M., R. H. Venderbosch, W. Prins, and F. W. M. Penninks. 2002. Bio-oil as a coal substitute in a 600 MWe power station. Presented at the 12th European

Conference and Technology Exhibition on Biomass for Energy, Industry and Climate Protection, Amsterdam, The Netherlands.

Wang, X. 2006. Biomass fast pyrolysis in a fluidized bed. Thesis, University of Twente.

———, S. R. A. Kersten, W. Prins, and W. P. M. van Swaaij. 2005. Biomass pyrolysis in a fluidized bed reactor: 2. Experimental validation of model results. *Ind. Eng. Chem. Res.*, 44(23):8786–8795.

Yang, H., R. Yan, H. Chen, D. H. Lee, and C. Zheng. 2007. Characteristics of hemicellulose, cellulose and lignin pyrolysis, *Fuel*, 86:1781–1788.

8

INTEGRATED CORN-BASED BIOREFINERY: A STUDY IN SUSTAINABLE PROCESS DEVELOPMENT

CARINA MARIA ALLES AND ROBIN JENKINS

DuPont Engineering and Research Technology, Wilmington, Delaware

8.1 INTRODUCTION

8.1.1 Sustainable Biofuels

As the global demand for energy continues to rise, biofuels hold the promise of providing a renewable alternative to fossil fuels. High oil prices and the threat of negative climate change impacts have sparked a surge in research and business activities. National security concerns and the desire to increase farm incomes have prompted governments around the world to enact policies in favor of biofuels. Developing countries hope to increase access to inexpensive fuel in isolated areas. Biofuels are also seen as an option in reducing air pollution in urban areas. However, the current boom has sparked controversy as well. Opponents accuse biofuels of requiring more energy inputs than their fossil counterparts and of causing more greenhouse gas emissions. Many concerns center on possible environmental degradation: erosion, deterioration of soil health and water quality, depletion of aquifers, and losses in biodiversity. Large-scale biofuel production is often regarded as a threat to food production and conservation efforts (Alles and Jenkins 2008).

Sustainable Development in the Process Industries: Cases and Impact, Edited by Jan Harmsen and Joseph B. Powell

157

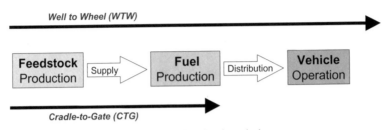

Figure 8.1   Fuel value chain.

Sustainability assessments aimed at quantifying the economic, environmental, and societal impacts can help move the often-heated debates over biofuels to a more factual level. Science-based methods such as life-cycle assessment (LCA), a holistic approach to quantifying environmental impacts throughout the value chain of a product (ISO 2006), have gained acceptance among decision makers.

To assess the sustainability of (bio)fuels, all stages of the fuel value chain have to be considered (Figure 8.1): feedstock production and supply, fuel production and distribution, and vehicle operation. An assessment of the entire value chain [i.e., well-to-wheel (WTW)] allows a fair comparison of different fuels. A cradle-to-gate (CTG) approach (here: fuel production and all associated upstream processes) is adequate to compare different technologies to make the same fuel.

8.1.2   DuPont's Commitment to Sustainability

DuPont's commitment to sustainability can be traced back to decisions made when the company was founded in 1802. The first product was gunpowder, and from the very beginning, specific safety measures were put in place to protect employees and neighbors. With each transformation since then, the company became even more focused on sustainability issues. When environmental and safety laws and regulations were introduced in the 1970s and 1980s, DuPont was dedicated to meeting those new requirements. In the late 1980s and 1990s, DuPont realized that mere compliance was not sufficient. DuPont was one of the first companies to publicly establish specific environmental goals. Today, a holistic approach to sustainability is fully integrated into all business models. The DuPont mission is *sustainable growth*: creating shareholder and societal value while reducing the company's footprint throughout the value chain. In 2006, DuPont announced two new sets of sustainability goals with a target date of 2015. The voluntary footprint reduction goals guide initiatives to decrease raw material and energy inputs into products and to reduce emissions at manufacturing sites. The market-facing goals identify opportunities to develop new products and offerings that will help meet DuPont's customers' needs and expectations for more sustainable products. Biofuels address several of DuPont's 2015 marketplace goals (DuPont 2008):

- *Environmentally smart market opportunities from R&D efforts:* "By 2015, DuPont will double our investment in R&D programs with direct, quantifiable environmental benefits for our customers and consumers along our value chains."

- *Products that reduce greenhouse gas emissions:* "By 2015, DuPont will grow our annual revenues by at least $2 billion from products that create energy efficiency and/or significant greenhouse gas emissions reductions for our customers. We estimate these products will contribute at least 40 million tonnes of additional CO_2 equivalent reductions by our customers and consumers."

- *Revenues from nondepletable resources:* "By 2015, DuPont will nearly double our revenues from non-depletable resources to at least $8 billion."

Working in alliances and partnerships with others, DuPont took up the challenge to create novel biofuels that can be produced from locally grown crops. These biofuels will provide alternatives to fossil fuels while providing economic opportunity to local farmers. DuPont promotes sustainable agriculture to ensure that the development of biofuels does not compromise critical food supply chains (DuPont 2009a).

8.2 TECHNOLOGY DEVELOPMENT FOR AN INTEGRATED CORN-BASED BIOREFINERY

8.2.1 Integrated Corn-Based Biorefinery Program

Through a $38 million partnership with the U.S. Department of Energy (DOE), DuPont initiated the integrated corn-based biorefinery (ICBR) program in 2003 to develop a cost-effective technology package for cellulosic ethanol from entire corn plants and, in the future, any biomass. This research will lead to an innovative biorefinery capable of producing ethanol fuel, performance chemicals, and materials from renewable resources.

In 2008, DuPont Danisco Cellulosic Ethanol (DDCE) was formed to accelerate the development of commercial-scale biorefineries. In October 2008, DDCE and the University of Tennessee broke ground for a pilot facility expected to produce ethanol from corn stover by the end of 2009, applying the technology developed in the ICBR program (DuPont 2009b).

Unlike traditional corn grain ethanol, the ICBR technology will use the entire corn plant (i.e., the stalks, cobs, and leaves left in the field after harvest) as opposed to only the corn kernel. DuPont and its partners are developing processes to convert the cellulose from the corncob and stalk into sugars that can be fermented into ethanol. Converting agricultural residues into fuel makes better use of limited land resources and helps to reduce the consumption of fossil fuels.

Currently, the production of ethanol in the United States is based primarily on the fermentation of sugars from corn grain. To expand ethanol production,

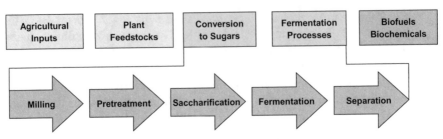

Figure 8.2 Biorefinery technology steps.

lignocellulosic feedstock alternatives, such as agricultural residues and forestry waste, have to be considered. Whereas it is comparatively easy to hydrolyze the starch in corn grain, significant research efforts are still required to develop efficient processes to extract fermentable sugars from lignocellulosic materials. Corn stover is the preferred feedstock in the ICBR program because of the current logistical advantages of harvesting, transporting, and producing ethanol in North America. Ultimately, the use of corn stover and similar agricultural residues will lead to lower production costs and expand the potential for new biorefineries.

8.2.2 ICBR Technology Concept

The ICBR concept relies on biotechnology to convert corn stover into fuel ethanol. The steps shown in Figure 8.2 form the core of the ICBR technology. Dry corn stover is milled into smaller pieces to generate a more consistent bulk feedstock. Then the stover is pretreated to separate the lignin from the plant's cellulose backbone to make the cellulose more accessible for further processing. Enzymes can now break the cellulosic materials down to fermentable sugars, in a process called *saccharification*. Novel fermentation technologies enable the conversion of both glucose and xylose from cellulose and hemicellulose, effectively converting nearly all of the useful sugars into ethanol. In a series of separation steps, ethanol is isolated from the fermentation broth and refined to a fuel-grade product.

  In the past, harsh pretreatment conditions and high temperatures were used in an attempt to break down the cellulose matrix to its individual sugar components. The ICBR technology is designed to break down cellulosic biomass into fermentable sugars through natural enzyme-based processes—replacing less efficient petrochemical processes.

8.2.3 ICBR Life-Cycle Analysis

Life-cycle assessment shows the environmental implications of different ICBR technology choices. The LCA model includes all natural resources extracted from the environment and all material releases to the environment that cross

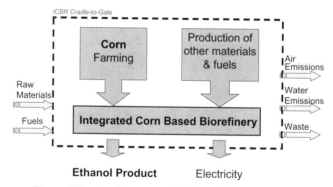

Figure 8.3 Cradle-to-gate LCA model of the ICBR.

the system boundaries, shown as the dashed line in Figure 8.3. Many of these flows are then aggregated into impact assessments, like fossil energy consumption, which includes petroleum, natural gas, coal, and lignite use, or greenhouse gas (GHG) emissions, where gases such as anthropogenic CO_2, CH_4, and N_2O are weighted by their global warming potential.

A process model of ethanol production from corn stover in an ICBR facility forms the core of the LCA model. The environmental impacts of material and energy inputs to the biorefinery are tracked back to ground using LCA databases and publicly available information to describe upstream processes. Michigan State University (MSU) provided a rigorous LCA model of corn farming, including agrochemicals manufacture and the production of fuels used in corn farming (Kim et al. 2009). Most ICBR designs assume that nonfermentable biomass provides fuel for an on-site cogeneration facility, with the option to sell excess electricity to the local grid. The LCA credit for electricity sales covers the environmental burden of electricity generation all the way back to primary energy sources (Kim and Dale 2005).

As the ICBR process development progresses, the LCA model is updated continuously. Multiple scenario and sensitivity analyses help to identify favorable design options and optimize process parameter settings.

8.2.4   Integration of LCA with Process Development

Screening of process alternatives is a critical task in the development of novel processes (see Figure 8.4). An attractive process is both economically successful and environmentally favorable. From the very beginning of the ICBR program, economic evaluation and LCA have been used side by side to guide researchers to the most sustainable ICBR process alternative. LCA is the most appropriate tool to evaluate the environmental footprint of the ICBR value chain, enabling the development team to define environmental metrics, set quantifiable environmental goals, and monitor research progress toward these competitive goals.

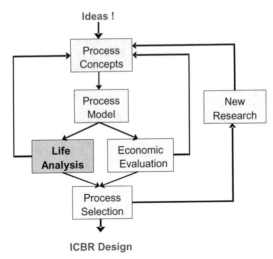

Figure 8.4   Integration of LCA into process development.

In the ICBR program, stakeholder engagement is essential to setting relevant sustainability goals. Stakeholder interests are represented by an external advisory panel of subject-matter experts from a variety of backgrounds and affiliations: for example, government agencies, academia, industry, and nongovernmental organizations. The panel members provide comments on critical issues related to the environmental sustainability of the ICBR and examine the LCA study with respect to the methods used, the data used, and the interpretations applied to the ICBR LCA results. The panel's independent, critical review of LCA methodology and results is invaluable to the ICBR program.

8.2.5   Defining Environmental Metrics

Early in the ICBR program, a broad range of possible environmental metrics was discussed with internal and external stakeholders. Resource depletion, global warming, and potential impacts on agricultural ecosystems emerged as the most relevant environmental issues. For practical purposes, metrics used to guide a technology development effort should meet the following criteria:

- The metrics should address key issues.
- The metric should be quantifiable.
- The metric should be derived from process (modeling) data.
- The metric should relate to other metrics commonly used in research and business decision-making processes.

To illustrate the integration of LCA with ICBR process development, the environmental metric cradle-to-gate fossil energy consumption is described here in more detail. Cradle-to-gate fossil energy consumption is the aggregated consumption of fossil fuels at the biorefinery itself and also in operations upstream, such as feedstock production and energy generation. Broadening the view beyond the core ICBR process facilitates an understanding of the upstream environmental impact of material and fuel inputs to the ICBR. The benefits of process efficiency are magnified in the cradle-to-gate view. Furthermore, the cradle-to-gate approach highlights the benefits of avoiding material inputs with a large environmental footprint.

Cradle-to-gate fossil energy consumption relates closely to various aspects of the environmental footprint. It is a direct measure of the depletion of fossil resources. Emissions of anthropogenic CO_2, considered a major contributor to climate change, are also linked directly to fossil energy consumption. The extraction, refining, transportation, and ultimately, combustion of fossil fuels are major causes of emissions to air, water, and land. Therefore, fossil energy consumption can be considered a leading indicator for many other environmental impacts, such as GHG emissions, water consumption, smog formation, acid rain, or heavy metals emissions.

In calculating the cradle-to-gate fossil energy consumptions of the ICBR, any fossil-fuel input along the value chain (ICBR and upstream) is tracked back to the extraction of a fossil raw material (coal, lignite, natural gas, or petroleum) from the ground. This information is collected separately for each fuel type in a life-cycle inventory (LCI). The amount of raw materials extracted as measured in mass units is converted to energy units in a life-cycle impact assessment (LCIA) using generic lower heat values. The primary energy data are then added across all fossil-fuel types to give the total cradle-to-gate fossil energy consumption.

Similarly, cradle-to-gate greenhouse gas emissions capture anthropogenic greenhouse gases (GHGs) released at the ICBR and its upstream processes. In the compilation of the aggregated GHG footprint, the various emissions are weighted with their direct global warming potentials as defined by the Intergovernmental Panel on Climate Change (IPCC 2001) before they are added together.

8.2.6 Setting External Benchmarks

The ICBR technology has to be competitive against other technologies to produce ethanol from corn. In the United States, dry mills are being built to expand fuel ethanol production from corn grain. In parallel, new technologies are being developed to produce fuel ethanol from lignocellulosic biomass such as wheat straw or corn stover. The ICBR could potentially compete with both ethanol from corn grain or ethanol from corn stover. Hence a dry mill scenario and a stover-to-ethanol scenario are both relevant benchmarks.

Publicly available benchmark data were carefully reviewed when the environmental targets for the ICBR were defined.

Over the years, most authors have come to agree that the energy balance of corn ethanol is positive: that the amount of fossil fuel required to manufacture corn ethanol does not exceed the fuel value of ethanol (Wang 2005; Farrell et al. 2006). As wet mills expanded and new dry mills were built, the production of ethanol from grain became more efficient. In the same period, farm yields continued to increase steadily. New technologies using lignocellulosic biomass to produce ethanol while generating steam and electricity have the potential to cut the use of nonrenewable energy even further.

Deviations among LCA literature data for the cradle-to-gate fossil energy consumption can largely be attributed to the following factors:

- Yield of corn farming
- Inputs to corn farming, in particular fertilizer inputs
- Ethanol yield on corn
- Energy requirements at the biorefinery, which vary with plant technology and age
- Energy credits allocated to ethanol co-products

A meaningful benchmarking process relies on consistent fundamental data and application of the same methodology across all cases studied. For the purpose of ICBR research guidance, benchmarking should focus on differences in ethanol conversion technology and eliminate differences in upstream and supporting processes. Consequently, the literature data had to be modified to bring farming and off-site energy production data to a common basis. Published information on the actual ethanol conversion was complemented with MSU data for the corn grain farming (Kim et al. 2009) and generic database modules for energy generation (Kim and Dale 2005; Ecobilan 1999).

Only a limited number of published corn ethanol studies provide enough transparency to allow the manipulations described above. When ICBR research targets were defined, Michael Graboski's report provided a rigorous, detailed analysis with current, peer-reviewed data on ethanol production in the United States (Graboski 2002; prepared for the National Corn Growers Association). Graboski's data set "2000–2004 Incremental Industry" was selected as the basis for the "Corn Grain EtOH" benchmark case. John Sheehan's study provided an excellent study on ethanol from corn stover (Sheehan et al. 2004). A process model describing the stover-to-ethanol conversion facility's performance as demonstrated at bench scale or higher provided data for the "Cellulosic EtOH Benchmark, 2002" case.

Since both corn grain– and corn stover–based ethanol are meant to displace petroleum–derived gasoline, they have to be measured against this incumbent fuel. Alexander Farrell reported well-to-wheel GHG emissions for conventional gasoline in his 2006 report on fuel ethanol (Farrell et al. 2006). His study covers the production, distribution, and combustion of gasoline in the United States.

8.3 LCA RESULTS: ICBR VERSUS BENCHMARKS

8.3.1 Fossil Energy Consumption

Biofuels are essentially a way to convert solar energy via photosynthesis into a liquid transportation fuel. One of the greatest concerns raised about them, however, is their net energy balance: whether their production requires more energy inputs from the farm to the biorefinery gate than is ultimately contained in the biofuels themselves (Worldwatch Institute 2006). To assess the energy sustainability of biofuels, their cradle-to-gate fossil energy footprint is compared to their intrinsic heating value. Figure 8.5 shows how preliminary ICBR results compare to the corn grain and corn stover ethanol benchmarks.

In all three scenarios, the cradle-to-gate fossil energy footprint to produce a gallon of bioethanol is well below the lower heat value of the fuel (i.e., the energy ultimately delivered to a vehicle). Both stover-to-ethanol cases have a smaller cradle-to-gate fossil energy footprint than the grain-to-ethanol case. Several factors contribute to this result. Compared to corn grain, corn stover comes to the biorefinery with a smaller fossil energy footprint, primarily because producing stover and grain on the same field does not require much additional effort compared to producing grain only (Kim et al. 2009). Hence, the amounts of additional agrochemicals or fuels to support farm operations associated with stover harvest alone are rather small. Nitrogen fertilizer, with

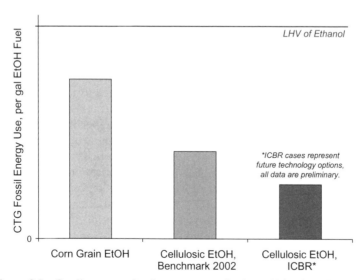

Figure 8.5 Cradle-to-gate fossil energy use of selected bioethanol options.

its large energy footprint, is of particular concern (Sheehan et al. 2004). However, only small additions of nitrogen fertilizer are required to compensate for nutrient losses associated with stover removal.

Conventional corn grain ethanol plants receive their process heat and power from fossil fuels such as natural gas and coal. Cellulosic ethanol plants are typically designed to be self-sufficient in heat and power supply, with nonfermentable residues serving as a renewable fuel for on-site cogeneration facilities. This puts cellulosic biorefineries at an advantage, even when the feed co-products from grain ethanol facilities are rewarded with energy credits for displacing other types of animal feed. Moreover, cellulosic ethanol facilities will probably produce surplus electricity. The ethanol plant would be an exporter of electricity, which potentially displaces grid electricity. Close to 80% of fossil fuel associated with producing U.S. mixed electricity can be avoided with the use of bioelectricity (Wu et al. 2006).

All these factors combined to bring the cradle-to-gate fossil energy footprint of cellulosic ethanol well below that of grain ethanol. The ICBR design capitalizes on the benefits that cellulosic feedstocks provide and takes biorefinery performance to the next level, with advanced pretreatment and fermentation technologies and optimized process integration. Mild pretreatment conditions and the targeted utilization of enzymes minimize the consumption of process heat and chemicals. High conversion rates in pretreatment, saccharification, and fermentation enable high overall stover-to-ethanol yields, which keeps the feedstock footprint at a low level. Efficient separation steps in the downstream processing of the ethanol product mean high yields and low process energy consumption. All these accomplishments are rewarded with savings in cradle-to-gate fossil energy consumption.

The rigorous application of energy efficiency and waste minimization techniques in every stage of the ICBR development process brings materials and energy consumption down to even lower levels. Savings in feedstock, fuel, or process chemical inputs to the biorefinery are magnified in the cradle-to-gate fossil energy footprint, which accounts not only for the fossil energy embedded in the biorefinery inputs themselves , but also for the fossil energy burden of the production of these inputs and associated upstream processes.

LCA sensitivity studies on selected process parameters help to identify optimal process conditions from a cradle-to-gate perspective and make it possible to set meaningful R&D targets, both for the engineers in the biorefinery process development and for biologists and biochemists in ethanologen and enzyme development. For example, the ethanol titer in the fermentation emerged as a critical success factor. An increase in ethanol titer means that less water has to be separated from the ethanol product stream. This translates directly into a reduction in the energy needed within the biorefinery and, consequently, a reduction in the cradle-to-gate fossil energy footprint.

In-depth analyses of the contributors to the cradle-to-gate fossil energy consumption also illuminate trade-offs among process alternatives. In particular, recycle loops have to be carefully evaluated in a holistic view. Internal recycling of a process chemical can significantly reduce the net consumption of this chemical and with that its cradle-to-gate fossil energy contribution. However, the implementation of recycle loops may come at the expense of additional energy and water consumption. It is common to underestimate the energy consumption of the separation steps required to return the chemical back to the process at a required purity level. The integration of LCA into the ICBR development process enables engineers to weigh carefully the benefits and penalties that come with recycle processes.

8.3.2 Greenhouse Gas Emissions

Greenhouse gas (GHG) emissions have emerged as a priority metric in policymaking (US EISA 2007; UK RTFO 2007; University of California 2007 (LCFS); EC 2008). In Figure 8.6, GHG emissions associated with the three bioethanol alternatives discussed above are compared side by side with U.S. gasoline. Since the fossil carbon contained in petroleum-derived fuels is not released until the combustion step in the vehicle engine, the analysis has to cover the entire well-to-wheels (WTW) value chain (see above), including fuel distribution and combustion.

Whenever different types of fuels are compared, differences in the energy content of the fuels have to be taken into account. Consequently, the well-to-wheel GHG results in Figure 8.6 are normalized to an equal amount of fuel energy delivered to the vehicle engine, assuming that the energy conversion efficiency in the engine remains the same for the fuel types considered. The GHG results show a similar trend to the fossil energy results discussed earlier. This is plausible since the use of fossil energy directly causes the release of

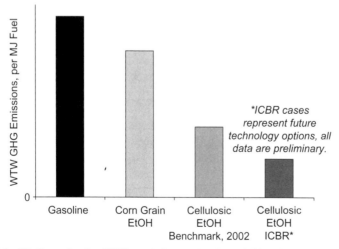

Figure 8.6 Well-to-wheels GHG emissions of selected bioethanol options versus gasoline.

anthropogenic CO_2, a key contributor to GHG emissions. Whereas in many industrial processes GHG emissions correlate in a linear fashion with fossil energy consumption, this is not the case for biomass-derived fuels, where N_2O emissions from the soil can contribute significantly to GHG emissions, as N_2O has a global warming potential of 296 CO_2 equivalents and is therefore considered a rather potent greenhouse gas (IPCC 2001).

N_2O field emissions are a key contributor to the GHG footprint of corn grain (Adler et al. 2007). By contrast, harvesting stover has the potential to reduce N_2O emissions from corn fields. Hence, corn stover comes to the biorefinery with a small GHG burden, or in favorable farming conditions even with a GHG credit, accounting for avoided N_2O emissions and possibly increased carbon sequestration in the soil. Further, corn stover's farming footprint is noticeably smaller in other environmental metrics, such as eutrophication and acidification (Kim et al. 2009). The GHG results give even stronger evidence of the importance of biomass feedstock selection in the development of sustainable biorefineries.

8.4 FINAL REFLECTIONS

Fundamental learnings from the in-depth analysis of a broad spectrum of ICBR technology options can be distilled into attributes of sustainable biorefineries in general (Alles and Jenkins 2008). The cradle-to-refinery-gate footprint of the primary biomass feedstock is a significant contributor to the overall footprint of a biofuel. Hence, choosing a feedstock with minimal environmental footprint yet a high fermentable ingredient content, is a key to success. Generally, lignocellulosic biomass has a lower environmental burden than food crops, but there are still technical and logistical challenges to overcome before lignocellulosic biomass can be converted economically into liquid transportation fuels at large scale. A breakthrough in stover-to-ethanol technology could pave the way for ethanol from other lignocellulosic feedstocks, such as perennial grasses and agricultural or forestry residues.

Using nonfermentable residues as a renewable fuel in an efficient on-site cogeneration facility is another success strategy. Measures to lower the energy consumption within biorefinery battery limits (e.g., by heat integration or equipment design) always have a positive impact on the overall biofuel net energy balance, whether they reduce the need to bring supplemental fuel to the biorefinery or enable additional energy exports. As a rule of thumb, cost-efficient measures to improve process efficiency will have a positive impact on both the economic and environmental performance of biorefineries. The common engineering goal to maximize product yield usually translates into reductions in the feedstock footprint, waste generation, and energy consumption. Increasing the effective concentration of solids, intermediates, and products in aqueous process streams not only reduces the amount of water taken from the watershed, but also reduces the burden on separation steps.

Typically, the biofuel is not the only material output of a biorefinery. If more outputs find their ways into beneficial uses, the economic and environmental burdens of the biorefinery operation can be allocated among a wider range of co-products. This could reduce both the production cost and the cradle-to-gate footprint of the biofuel. For example, lignin and other nonfermentable components of biomass feedstocks need not be disposed as wastes, but can be used as fuels to generate thermal or electrical energy on- or off-site. Other potential co-products include animal feed, fertilizer, and intermediates for specialty chemicals. The collocation of biorefineries with other facilities processing agricultural and forestry feedstocks, livestock feedlots, or power plants in industrial parks will facilitate the beneficial exchange of material and energy flows to a great extent. The possible sustainability benefits of such eco-industrial parks are largely unexplored and deserve further research.

Acknowledgments

Sustainability analysis in the ICBR program (DOE 1435-04-03-CA-70224) was a team effort, involving partners from Michigan State University, the National Renewable Energy Laboratory, Diversa Corporation, and DuPont. Interactions with researchers and leadership have been very rewarding. The program also benefited immensely from the perspectives of external stakeholders: in particular, members of the ICBR LCA advisory panel.

REFERENCES

Adler, P. R., S. J. Del Grosso, and W. J. Parton. 2007. Life cycle assessment of net greenhouse gas flux for bioenergy cropping systems. *Ecol. Appl.*, 17(3):675–691.

Alles, C. M., and R. Jenkins. 2008. Sustainable biorefineries. In *Frontiers of Engineering: Reports on Leading-Edge Engineering from the 2007 Symposium*. Washington, DC: National Academies Press, pp. 75–82.

DuPont. 2008. DuPont Sustainability. Accessed June 2008 at http://www2.dupont.com/Sustainability/en_US/.

———. 2009a. DuPont Position Statements. Accessed Jan. 2009 at http://www2.dupont.com/Media_Center/en_US/position_statements/.

———. 2009b. DuPont Danisco Cellulosic Ethanol. Accessed Jan. 2009 at http://www.ddce.com.

EC (European Commission). 2008. Proposal for a directive of the European Parliament and of the Council on the promotion of the use of energy from renewable sources, version 15.4. Jan. 23.

Ecobilan. 1999. DEAM™ LCA database.

Farrell, A. E., R. J. Plevin, B. T. Turner, A. D. Jones , M. O'Hare, and D. M. Kammen. 2006. Ethanol can contribute to energy and environmental goals. *Science*, 27(311):506–508. (Note: Contains a meta-study of recent ethanol LCAs.)

Graboski, M. S. 2002. *Fossil Energy Use in the Manufacture of Corn Ethanol*. National Corn Growers Association, Washington, DC. Accessed July 2007 at http://www.ncga.com/ethanol/pdfs/energy_balance_report_final_R1.PDF.

IPCC (Intergovernmental Panel on Climate Change). 2001. Working Group 1: The Scientific Basis. Accessed at http://www.ipcc.ch/ipccreports/tar/wg1/.

ISO (International Organization for Standardization). 2006. *Environmental Management—Life Cycle Assessment: Principles and Framework*. ISO 14040 Ed. 2. Geneva, Switzerland: ISO.

Kim, S., and B. Dale. 2005. Life cycle inventory information of the United States electricity system. *Int. J. Life Cycle Assess.*, 10:294–304.

Kim, S., B. Dale, and R. Jenkins. 2009. Life cycle assessment of corn grain and corn stover in the United States. *Int. J. Life Cycle Assess.*, Accessed at http://www.springerlink.com/content/c220515747622673/fulltext.pdf.

Sheehan, J., A. Aden, K. Paustian, K. Killian, J. Brenner, M. Walsh, and R. Nelson. 2004. The energy and environmental aspects of using corn stover for fuel ethanol. *J. Ind. Ecol.*, 7(3–4):117–146.

UK RTFO. 2007. UK Renewable Transport Fuel Obligation Order 3072, London, UK. Accessed at http://www.dft.gov.uk/rfa/aboutthertfo.cfm.

University of California. 2007. *A Low-Carbon Fuel Standard for California*. Part 1: *Technical Analysis*, May 2007. Part 2: *Policy Analysis*, Aug. 2007. Accessed at http://www.arb.ca.gov/fuels/lcfs/lcfs.htm.

US EISA. 2007. US Energy Independence and Security Act of 2007, Washington, DC. Accessed June 2008 at http://thomas.loc.gov/cgi-bin/query/C?c110:./temp/~c110q05Bgh.

Wang, M. 2005. Updated Energy and Greenhouse Gas Emissions Results of Fuel Ethanol. Accessed June 2008 at http://www.transportation.anl.gov/pdfs/TA/354.pdf.

Worldwatch Institute. 2006. Biofuels for Transportation: Global Potential and Implications for Sustainable Agriculture and Energy in the 21st Century. Accessed July 2007 at http://www.worldwatch.org/node/4078.

Wu M., M. Wang, and H. Huo. 2006 Fuel-Cycle Assessment of Selected Bioethanol Production Pathways in the United States. Accessed June 2008 at http://www.transportation.anl.gov/pdfs/TA/377.pdf.

9

CELLULOSIC BIOFUELS: A SUSTAINABLE OPTION FOR TRANSPORTATION

JEAN-PAUL LANGE, IRIS LEWANDOWSKI, AND PAUL M. AYOUB
Shell Technology Centre, Amsterdam, The Netherlands

9.1 INTRODUCTION

9.1.1 Energy Scene

Governments across the world are stimulating the utilization of renewable energies and resources, such as solar, wind, hydroelectricity, and biomass. Three major forces are driving them (Lange 2007a,b):

1. *Secured access to energy.* The world demand for energy is expected to have doubled in the middle of this century, from 400 EJ/yr today to 900 to 1100 EJ/yr in 2050. This demand cannot be satisfied by crude oil, natural gas, coal, and nuclear energy combined. Through its reliance on oil and gas, the world economy is becoming very dependent on a limited number of exporting countries.

2. *Threat of climate change.* Efforts to reduce the consumption of fossil fuel and to capture and sequester CO_2 will help reduce the CO_2 emissions in the short term. For the long term, however, CO_2-neutral energy sources are needed.

Sustainable Development in the Process Industries: Cases and Impact, Edited by Jan Harmsen and Joseph B. Powell
Copyright © 2010 John Wiley & Sons, Inc.

3. *Development and maintenance of agricultural activities.* Agricultural economies could be supported by promoting the exploitation of local (bio)resources for food, energy, and material.

Energy companies are tackling this energy challenge in two steps. On the one hand, companies and research institutes are developing renewable energies such as wind, photovoltaic, and biomass for the longer term. However, these energy sources will not deliver the volume required now and in the near future. Hence, the oil industry also needs to explore and exploit new reserves of fossil fuels to secure the near-term demand.

9.1.2 Future Fuels

The transportation sector accounts for about one-fourth of the energy demand (i.e., about 100 EJ/yr). Most of today's vehicles are driving on liquid fuels such as gasoline and diesel. A few vehicles are driving on fuels with moderate energy density such as liquefied petroleum gas (LPG) and compressed natural gas (CNG). Meanwhile, the automobile industry is developing even leaner energy carriers such as H_2 and electricity and is deploying hybrid vehicles that can switch between liquid fuels and electricity. In the long term, vehicles might be driving on renewable electricity or renewable H_2. As for the short to midterm, however, biomass is the most promising source for renewable transportation fuel, for it can provide renewable liquid fuels that are convenient in use and can benefit from the existing distribution infrastructure.

A first generation of fuels and chemicals are presently produced from sugars, starches, and vegetable oils. Although instrumental in growing the market, these biofuels are not long-term solutions, for three reasons. First, they compete with food for their feedstock and/or fertile land. They have been blamed in part for the recent price increase of foodstocks. Second, their potential availability is limited by the amount of fertile soil and by their yield per hectare. Finally, the effective savings of CO_2 emission and of fossil-fuel consumption are limited by the energy needed to grow the crop and convert it to biofuel.

Answers to these three limitations are sought in the utilization of lignocellulosic materials found as the residues of the agriculture and forestry or grown as energy crops. Lignocellulose can be grown in combination with food (e.g., as crop residue) or on nonagricultural lands. The world production of 3 to 5 gigatons/yr of these residues could provide 50 to 85 EJ/yr of energy (Klass 1998; Okkerse and van Bekkum 1999; Dale and Kim 2006; Kamm et al. 2006), which represents 10 to 20% of today's world energy demand. The net savings in energy and CO_2 emission are much larger by requiring less fertilizer (i.e., less fossil fuels to produce them), fixing CO_2 in the soil (e.g., perennial energy crops), and providing the process fuel as well. All these aspects are discussed in some length later in the chapter.

9.1.3   Lignocellulosic Conversion

Lignocellulose is much more complex to convert than are the sugars, starches, and oils. Lignocellulose is the fibrous material that forms the cell walls of a plant's "architecture." It consists of three major components (Sjöström 1993; Klass 1998; Kamm et al. 2006; Lange 2007a,b):

1. The cellulose, which consists of high-molecular-mass polymers of glucose that are held together rigidly as bundles of fibers to provide the strength of the materials. The cellulose typically accounts for some 40 wt% of the lignocellulose.
2. The hemicellulose, which consists of shorter polymers of various sugars that glue the cellulose bundles together. It usually accounts for some 25 wt% of the lignocellulose.
3. The lignin, which consists of a tridimensional polymer of propenyl-phenol that is embedded in and bound to the hemicellulose. It provides rigidity to the structure. It accounts for some 20 wt% of the lignocellulose.

Of course, the lignocellulose also contains a variety of minor components such as proteins, terpenic oils, fatty acids/esters, and inorganic materials (e.g., based primarily on N, P, and K). It should be clear by now that the structure of lignocellulose deviates severely from that of present fuels. Lignocellulose therefore needs to be depolymerized and deoxygenated as shown in Figure 9.1 (Lange 2007c). Deoxygenation via elimination of water and/or CO_2 may lead to 50 to 75 wt% loss of mass; it does not lead to important energy loss, however (Lange 2007a,b).

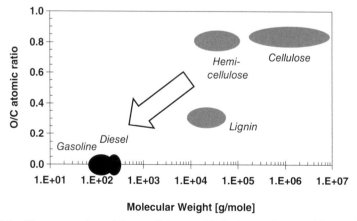

Figure 9.1   The conversion of lignocellulose to biofuels requires cracking and deoxygenation. (From Lange 2007c.)

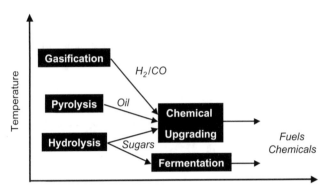

Figure 9.2   Routes for converting lignocellulose to fuels and chemicals. (Lange 2007c.)

Depolymerization and deoxygenation of lignocellulose proceeds via one of three major routes (i.e., pyrolysis, gasification, or hydrolysis), all followed by upgrading (Figure 9.2) (Lange 2007c). A first cracking step that produces a crude liquid or gaseous stream, and a subsequent deoxygenation step produces the final fuel component. The processing is not limited to these two steps, however. The intermediate cracking product stream often requires extensive cleaning to remove contaminants present in the biomass or to eliminate undesired by-products of the cracking reaction. Moreover, the solid feedstock often requires a pretreatment that may consist of sizing, drying, pre-decomposition, and so on. Finally, low-temperature processes may proceed in a liquid solvent that needs to be recycled through pumping, heating, cooling, recovery, and cleanup. All these steps will contribute to the complexity of lignocellulose conversion processes.

The simple enumeration of these various process steps suggests that lignocellulose conversion plants are complex and expensive. This perception can be sharpened further by focusing on the various fluxes of energy that are transferred during the process. Earlier analysis of fuel and chemical manufacturing processes indeed revealed that the investment cost correlates fairly well with the overall energy transfer duty of the plant (Lange and Tijm 1996; Lange 2001). The importance of energy transfer duty explains the high investment costs of process units that operate at high temperature and/or pressure, for example, with large solvent recycling (i.e., with high dilution) or that vaporize large streams. Such knowledge will be used in the present analysis to underline specific contributions to plant costs.

9.1.4   Scope of the Chapter

In this chapter we discuss two specific approaches to converting lignocellulose to biofuels: (1) production of diesel-range hydrocarbons via gasification and Fischer–Tropsch synthesis using the process developed jointly by Choren and Shell, and (2) production of the gasoline additive ethanol via hydrolysis and fermentation of the carbohydrates contained in the lignocellulose. These processes are discussed based on technical information disclosed by Choren and Iogen/NREL in the scientific literature. We then discuss the most critical issues regarding the sustainability of biomass production. The sustainabitily of the conversion processes will not be discussed further. The process data provided here can be used to assess the four key sustainability stresses proposed in the literature (Lange 2009), namely, resource utilization, waste production, hazard, and cost.

9.2 CASE STUDIES

9.2.1 Biodiesel

Chemistry   As mentioned above, biomass can be converted to synthesis gas, a valuable mixture of CO and H_2, upon heating at high temperature in the presence of inert atmosphere or steam. It is nevertheless convenient to co-feed some oxygen to burn a fraction (ca. one-fourth) of the feed [eq. (1)] to reach the required temperature (>1000 °C) and provide the heat required by the endothermic formation of synthesis gas. The gasification reaction is driven primarily by thermodynamics. Accordingly, the thermoneutral gasification of the carbohydrate and lignin fractions of biomass follows the typical stoichiometry of eqs. (1) and (2), which are characterized with >95% energy efficiency based on LHV (Lange 2007a,b):

$$C_6(H_2O)_6 + 1.5O_2 \rightarrow 6CO + 3H_2 + 3H_2O \tag{1}$$

$$C_{10}H_{13}O_3 + 2O_2 + 2H_2O \rightarrow 10CO + 8H_2 \tag{2}$$

The resulting synthesis gas can subsequently be converted to diesel-range hydrocarbons via the Fischer–Tropsch synthesis according to eq. (3), which proceeds with theoretical energy and carbon efficiencies of about 76% and 50%, respectively (Lange 2007a,b):

$$6CO + 3H_2 \rightarrow 3/n\text{-}[CH_2]_n\text{-} + 3CO_2 \tag{3}$$

It should be noted that eq. 3 applies to the ideal synthesis gas obtained from the carbohydrate fraction of the biomass. Since the lignin fraction provides a slightly higher H_2/CO ratio [eq. (2)], it should allow incorporating slightly more than 50% of the total carbon into the hydrocarbon product than suggested in eq. (3). It should indeed be realized here that lignin and carbohydrate are equally well utilized in such a process.

   In contrast to the gasification reaction, the Fischer–Tropsch synthesis proceeds at mild temperature (200 to 300 °C) in the presence of a suitable metal-base catalyst (Sie et al. 1991). Proper design of the catalyst will determine the distribution of the hydrocarbons produced. The crude Fischer–Tropsch product is not yet suitable for diesel application, as it is spread over too wide a range of chain length, from C_1 to $C_{>100}$, and consists almost exclusively of linear alkanes that tend to solidify at low temperature. The crude Fischer–Tropsch product is therefore upgraded via a mild hydrocracking step that converts the heavy fraction into a lighter diesel-range cut and slightly isomerizes the alkanes to confer on them the desired low-temperature properties (Sie et al. 1991).

Choren–Shell BtL Process   The process design, based on Choren's gasification technology (Rudloff 2007; Choren 2008; Hoffmann 2008; Kiener 2008) and Shell's Fischer–Tropsch technology (Sie et al. 1991), is presently being demonstrated in Freiberg, Germany. This β-plant is designed to convert 68 kilotons/yr of wood chips into 15 kilotons/yr of biofuel. A first commercial unit is under consideration in Schwedt, Germany. This Σ-plant would convert about 1 million tons of biomass per year into 200 kilotons/yr of biofuel, would require €800 million in capital investment, and would start up in 2012 (Rudloff 2007; Choren 2008; Hoffmann 2008; Kiener 2008). Through a detailed energy flowchart, Choren reported converting 53.3% of the energy of the feed into liquid fuels (39% to diesel and 14.3% to naphtha), 4.1% into exhaust gas (including 3.1% exhaust dryer), and 6.4% into electricity. From the energy lost, 41% is lost as cooling water and 0.7% is lost in wastewater and slag. In summary, the Choren–Shell technology is claimed to operate with mass and energy efficiencies of 22% and 53%, respectively.

Figure 9.3 is a simplified block flow diagram of the Choren–Shell biomass-to-synfuels process. More technical details on the gasification and Fischer–Tropsch technologies are provided in the literature (Sie 1991; Rudloff 2007; Choren 2008; Hoffmann 2008; Kiener 2008). It consists of the following segments:

- Feed conditioning
- Three-step gasification composed of a pyrolysis reactor followed by an O_2-blown burner to gasify the vaporized fraction of the biomass and, finally, a chemical quench that injects the char residue into the hot synthesis gas to cool it while it is being gasified
- A synthesis gas treating train that consists of a cooler, wash vessels, and a water–gas shift reactor
- A Fischer–Tropsch synthesis reactor followed by a mild hydrocracking step

Technological Challenges   Shell's Fischer–Tropsch synthesis is well described in the literature (Sie et al. 1991). Several key requirements are worthy of being mentioned here.

- It proceeds at a high rate and selectivity when the reaction heat is removed properly. Shell operates it with a fixed-bed catalyst placed in a multitubular reactor that is extensively cooled by raising steam.

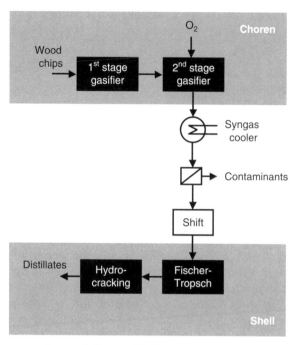

Figure 9.3 Process scheme of Choren–Shell BtL technology for producing cellulosic diesel. (Adapted from Rudloff 2007; Choren 2008; Hoffmann 2008; Kiener 2008.)

- The catalyst requires high synthesis gas pressure. It therefore operates better with gasifiers that are fired with pure O_2 than those that are fired with air and thereby provide N_2-diluted syngas.
- The catalyst is sensitive to all electronegative components, such as N, S, P, and Cl, as well as fouling components such as tar. The gasification process therefore needs to be designed such as to minimize the formation of contaminants or remove them.
- Finally, the synthesis produces hydrocarbons by converting H_2 and CO at a ratio of about 2 moles of H_2 per mole of CO. The synthesis gas composition needs to be adjusted correspondingly.

Choren's gasification process has been designed to accommodate these requirements. During gasification, the temperature pathway that a biomass particle goes through as it enters and exits the gasifier determines the chemical composition of the gas generated, including the distribution of by-product type and molecular mass. A suboptimal temperature profile typically leads to the formation of detrimental amounts of tar. The Choren–Shell process addresses these issues by using a multistep gasification process, followed by a specifically designed gas-handling train to yield a syngas product suited for further conversion into either hydrocarbons or alcohols.

TABLE 9.1 Typical Composition (vol. %) of Dry and Cleaned Synthesis Gas

	(vol%)
CO	39.8
H_2	34.1
CO_2	25.1
N_2	1.0
CH_4	0.1

Source: Data from Rudloff (2007); Choren (2008); Hoffmann (2008); Kiener (2008).

As stated above, biomass contains much oxygen and, usually, some free water, which affects the energy requirements for the conversion negatively. Thus, the physical and chemical composition of the feed to the gasifier has a large influence on heat and mass transfer, and requires close coupling among the design of the pretreatment operation, the gasification operation, and the gas-handling operation. This coupling adds to the complexity and costs of biomass gasification relative to processes based on coal and natural gas. Another important compositional aspect of biomass is its ash content, especially its alkali metals content. These form fairly low-melting ashes that require special design criteria to avoid particulate and tar conglomeration leading to plugging of the gas train. Furthermore, the higher volatility of alkali compounds presents a high risk to the catalysts of syngas conversion processes, dictating extra care in design in order to reduce the concentration of these poisons in the off-gas to very low levels. The clean synthesis gas comes out with a H_2/CO ratio of about 1 (see Table 9.1), which is finally adjusted to about 2 via a shift reactor. Thus, the resulting gas cooling and cleaning train of a gasifier is generally sensitive and expensive.

An additional factor that has a particularly negative effect on gasification routes is biomass sourcing. It is well known that gasification processes are capital intensive and therefore require very large scales, usually beyond 1 megaton/yr, to be economical. Biomass, on the other hand, is a fairly distributed commodity, requiring substantial acreage to grow. Therefore, there is a tension between the economies of scale required for a gasification process and the increase in biomass cost as the distance from its source to the manufacturing location increases. The issue is aggravated by the fact that biomass has a substantially lower energy density than that of fossil fuels: namely, about 15 vs. about 45 GJ/ton or 2 to 8 GJ/m^3 (from straw bales to straw/wood pellets) vs. about 35 GJ/m^3 for fossil fuels.

These considerations highlight several factors that make such a biomass-to-liquid (BtL) process capital intensive: namely, a large number of process steps, high-temperatures, large heat release (gasification and Fischer–Tropsch sections), and complex synthesis gas cleaning. The conclusion for gasification processes is that although energy efficiency is very important, the biggest economic challenge is in reducing capital intensity while maintaining reasonable operability.

9.2.2 Biogasoline

Chemistry Lignocellulose does not necessarily require the severe conditions applied for pyrolysis or gasification to be converted to biofuels. Polysaccharides and lignin are bounds through reactive ether links (i.e., ketal and aryl ether links that are prone to hydrolysis). Indeed, the lignin and hemicellulose readily hydrolyze at mild temperatures (<150 °C) in the presence of acids or bases (Klass 1998; Lange 2007a,b). The crystalline structure of the cellulose hinders the catalyst to access the ether links. More severe conditions are therefore required for full depolymerization. Higher temperatures result in the consecutive dehydration of the monomeric sugars into furan species such as furfural and hydroxymethyl furfural and eventually lead to the formation of levulinic and formic acids (Hayes et al. 2006; Kamm et al. 2006; Lichtenthaler 2006). All these reactions contribute to lowering the yield in sugars during hydrolysis. Moreover, if fermentation to ethanol is the ultimate goal, several degradation products, such as furfural, hydroxymethyl furfural, and lignin fragments, are inhibitors for downstream fermentation.

Alternatively to the use of acid/base-catalyzed hydrolysis, well-tuned cocktails of enzymes can hydrolyze the hemicellulose and cellulose at mild temperature and without the formation of undesirable by-products and toxins (Elander et al. 2005; Morgen 2006; Teter et al. 2006; Hayes 2008). The enzymes cannot properly access the cellulose, however. To be successful, enzymatic hydrolysis needs to be preceded by some pretreatment that predigests and tears the lignocellulose apart to render it accessible (Elander et al. 2005; Morgen 2006; Teter et al. 2006; Hayes 2008).

Once depolymerized properly, the monomeric glucose can be digested to ethanol by microorganisms such as baker's yeast. The fermentation proceeds via a complex sequence of reactions that proceed via the formation of pyruvic acid, its decarboxylation to acetaldehyde, and finally, its hydrogenation to ethanol (Figure 9.4; Klass 1998; Lange 2007a,b). The overall fermentation of glucose to ethanol is characterized by a high energy efficiency of about 97%.

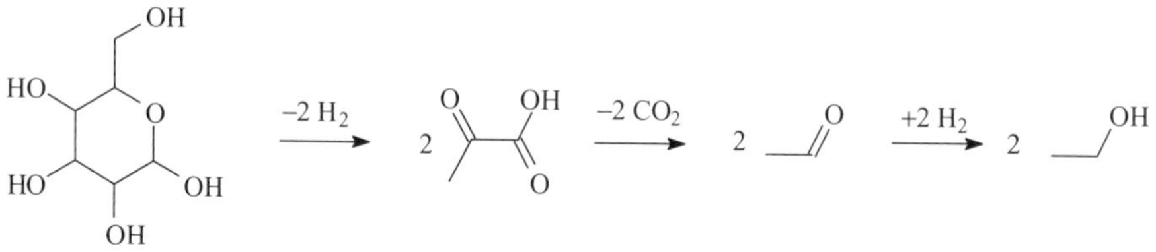

Figure 9.4 Fermentation of sugars to ethanol (H_2 is bound in the form of NADPH). (From Lange 2007a,b.)

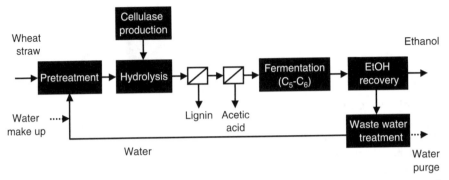

Figure 9.5 Flow scheme of Iogen's cellulosic ethanol process. (Adapted from Lawford and Rousseau 2003; Tolan 2006; Iogen 2008.)

The 3% energy lost through the process is exploited by the microorganisms to live and grow.

Recent developments of improved or novel microorganisms have extended the ethanol production to the fermentation of sugars others than glucose: namely, xylose and arabinose. These developments allow one to produce more ethanol from the biomass.

Iogen's Process The Iogen process, as described in the literature, on their web site (Iogen 2008), and modeled in the two NREL reports (Wooley et al. 1999; Aden et al. 2002), consists of the following steps (Figure 9.5):

1. A physicochemical pretreatment, based on mechanical sizing and dilute-acid steam explosion treatment at 200 to 250 °C.
2. Hydrolysis of the biomass using proprietary cellulase enzymes produced on site from the fungus *Trichoderma*. The hydrolysis is claimed to proceed to sugar with 90 to 98% yield by digesting a slurry of 5 to 15 wt% of straw for 5 to 7 days at pH 5 and 50 °C.
3. Conditioning of the hydrolysate to remove the acetic acid and lignin, which act as poison in the pentose fermentation step. The lignin is then used as process fuel.
4. Fermentation of the hydrolysate, typically 6 wt% glucose, 3 wt% xylose, and 0.3 wt% arabinose, using a proprietary bacterium of the genotype *Zymomonas mobilis* (AX101), which was developed by NREL and is claimed to convert the mixed sugars to EtOH with an efficiency of 90% of theoretical (ca. 45 wt%) and a rate of about 3.3 g/L·h, leading a brew that contains 4.2 wt% EtOH.
5. Recovery and purification of ethanol by means of distillation.

Iogen is currently operating a demonstration facility of about 13 kilotons/yr capacity (40 tons/day) in Ottawa, Canada. So far, they have accumulated about a dozen years of experience, and have produced several thousand gallons of cellulosic ethanol. The technology is claimed to produce about 0.22 ton of ethanol (75 gallons) per ton of wheat straw, which consists of about 65 wt% carbohydrates. This corresponds to mass and energy efficiencies of about 22 and 30 to 35%, respectively. In early 2007 the U.S. Department of Energy awarded $385 million of federal funding to support the commercialization of six cellulosic ethanol plants. At the time of this writing, $80 million was reserved for financing an Iogen plant of 54 kilotons/yr capacity (18 Mgal) in Shelley, Idaho.

In 2003, Iogen published improvement of its process through separated fermentation of the pentose and hexoses (Lawford and Rousseau 2003; Tolan 2006; Iogen 2008). The pentose-rich liqueur of the pretreatment is fermented using bacterium *Z. mobilis* at a rate of about 1 g/L·h to produce a brew that contains 1.5 wt% EtOH. The glucose-rich hydrolysate is fermented using a wild-type *Z. mobilis* bacterium ZM4 at a rate of 11 g/L·h to lead to 4 to 5 wt% EtOH.

Technological Challenges For biochemical processes, feed pretreatment typically involves both physical and chemical conversion operations. Sizing is always required to slurry the biomass properly and transport it through the process equipment. Furthermore, often, the total amount of water is determined by the need to turn the biomass into a pumpable slurry. Since the physical properties of the biomass have a direct effect on the rheology of the slurry, the type and degree of sizing operation must be linked to the hydraulics of the process. Note that the pumpability issue is pertinent to all aqueous-phase processes, not only those using biocatalysts.

For such processes based on biocatalysts, the amount of water required can also be strongly influenced by the tolerance of the catalyst to either reactants or products. For example, it is well known that cellulase enzymes are inhibited by glucose. Therefore, the glucose concentration in the reactor can only be allowed to reach a certain limit, thus forcing operation at lower than desired concentrations. This is aggravated by the fact that these reactors are typically of the type of a continuously stirred tank, which are known to provide poor volumetric productivities. The result is that large stirred tanks in series are required to achieve reasonable conversions and yields.

The water issue for these processes is significant from both a hydraulic loading perspective and an energy-intensity perspective. Both of these have a direct impact on the capital and operating costs of the process:

- The more water required, the higher the hydraulic load and the larger the equipment.
- Larger amounts of heating and cooling are required to handle the higher heat capacity of the streams.
- Chemicals are usually required at specified concentrations, especially acids and bases for pH control. The larger the stream, the larger the quantities of chemicals required.

- Substantially complex and expensive sets of pots and pans are required to recover and purify products and by-products, and to recycle solvents (water) and chemicals.

In fact, water is generally the most expensive ingredient in a water-based biomass conversion process having, either directly or indirectly, the biggest impact on both operating costs and capital investment. Therefore, minimizing water use is essential for the economics of these processes, and R&D efforts should be directed at reducing process water requirements to a minimum.

One way of reducing water requirements is via the cost-effective separation of the three main components of biomass into individual streams which can then be processed in the most optimal way. For example, being able to feed a cellulose-based conversion process with a stream that is very high in cellulose content rather than with the entire biomass could cut the water requirement in half, the size of the equipment in half, and result in very substantial energy savings. The key is to be able to fractionate the feed for a fraction of the costs that are saved in downstream processing. Indeed, feed fractionation is a hot topic in the biomass conversion domain (Katzen and Schell 2006). What is crucial when developing a feed fractionation process is to maintain a fit-for-purpose mentality. This means that the fractionation process should be developed keeping in mind the specific requirements of the downstream conversion process to which it will be linked. Such an approach will ensure minimum effort (cost) to provide the optimal feed for further conversion.

The cost of hydrolase enzymes has long been a major contribution to the cost of cellulosic ethanol. A collaboration between Novozyme and NREL that was funded by the U.S. Department of Energy in the early 2000 led to about a 20-fold decrease in enzyme cost (Elander et al. 2005; Morgen 2006; Teter et al. 2006; Hayes 2008). Iogen approached the problem differently by producing its hydrolase cocktails on site in a submerged liquid culture (Lawford and Rousseau 2003; Tolan 2006; Iogen 2008). The cellulase broth is filtered and sent to hydrolysis tanks without further upgrading. Such on-site production is claimed to save significant costs by avoiding purification, stabilization, and transport of the enzymes.

Another very important area of opportunity for water-based processes is the minimization of chemicals: in particular, mineral acids and bases. The recovery and recycling of these chemicals is often difficult. In most cases, people decide to recover them in the form of by-products such as fertilizers. The problem is that this complicates the overall process substantially and rarely results in the recovery of the capital investment required to build the recovery and purification sections. At best, the revenue from fertilizer sales covers the operating costs associated with use of the chemicals and the recovery and purification of the fertilizer.

More generally, although many are in favor of biorefinery concepts in which numerous products are produced and marketed, we believe that minimizing the product slate is far better, as it reduces both technology and commercial risks, particularly for a first plant of its type. For example, economics permitting, it is preferable to make one product and burn residues and side-streams for producing energy. One should not underestimate the efforts required to launch and debug new technologies. Once the main technology is validated and made robust, one can then consider selling specific by-products if the resulting incomes justify the additional costs and complexity of their recovery, purification, and marketing. Obviously, an exception should be made for (inorganic) sidestreams that cannot be burned and that need to be disposed off as waste if not sold as a by-product.

In summary, process schemes such as those proposed by Iogen are expected to be capital intensive, as they require (1) multiple process steps, some of which need to handle solids, and (2) a large amount of water, which needs to be pumped, stirred, and heated or cooled, and from which products and chemicals need to be recovered. Future improvements should come from reducing the water requirement.

9.3 SUSTAINABILITY OF BIOMASS PRODUCTION

Using renewable feedstock is no guarantee for producing transportation fuels in a sustainable manner. Sustainability has indeed many dimensions: for example, climate change, environmental, social, and economic. Different multistakeholder initiatives, such as the Roundtable for Sustainable Biofuels (RSB) or the Roundtable for Sustainable Palm Oil (RSPO), are developing criteria to ensure the sustainability of biomass production. Such criteria are also developed on a national level in various European Union (EU) member states (UK, Germany, and the Netherlands) in preparation for a legislative framework on certification of sustainable bioenergy. For example, the set of criteria on sustainable biomass production developed by the Cramer Commission in the Netherlands (Cramer et al. 2006) are reported in Table 9.2.

9.3.1 Crop Types

The performance of different biomass types against the commission's criteria depends on the type of crop that was grown to produce it. Therefore, the key characteristics of the principal crops need to be discussed. As mentioned above, the first generation of biofuels is derived from vegetable oils, sugars, or starch from crops, which were developed and are produced principally as food crops. Table 9.3 provides an overview of the most important first-generation biofuel crops.

Because of their differing ecophysiological demands (temperature, water supply, soil quality), different crops are suitable for the production of vegetable oils, sugar, or starch in different climates. Only parts of the crop (e.g., the oils in the grains) are used as feedstock. All the crops listed in Table 9.3 are food crops and are produced in systems that require input of mineral fertilizers

TABLE 9.2   Criteria on Sustainable Biomass Production Developed in the Netherlands

Climate change	Net greenhouse gas emission reduction compared with fossil reference, inclusive application, is at least 30% in 2007 and 50% by 2011.
Society	Availability of biomass for food, local energy supply, building materials, or medicines must not decrease.
	No negative effects on the social well-being of the workers and local population and no tightening of conditions, taking into account working conditions, human rights, property rights and rights of use, insight into the social circumstances of population, insight into the active contribution to improvement of social circumstances of local population, and integrity.
Environment	No deterioration of protected areas or valuable ecosystems.
	Insight into active protection of the local ecosystem.
	No negative effects on the environment in relation to waste management (no tightening), use of agrochemicals (including fertilizer), prevention of erosion and soil exhaustion, insight into the conservation of quality and quantity of surface and groundwater, and emission to air.
Economy	No negative impacts on the local and regional economy.
	Insight into the active contribution to the increase in local prosperity.

Source: Cramer (2006).

to compensate for the removal of nutrients from the soil and to maximize yields. They also require pesticides and/or herbicides to protect them from diseases and weeds. With the exception of oil palm and sugarcane, all first-generation crops are annual. This means that they are sown and harvested yearly. In contrast, sugarcane plantations can be harvested over a period of two to four years after they have been planted. Palm oil plantations can begin to be harvested three years after planting, and harvesting can continue for about 20 years before the plantation has to be replaced.

Second-generation biofuels, such as those produced by means of the Choren and Iogen technologies, are based on lignocellulosic feedstock. There are different potential sources of lignocellulose biomass: namely, agricultural residues of food crops (e.g., wheat straw, corn stover, palm kernel shells), forestry residues or other wood residues, organic wastes, and finally, lignocellulosic

TABLE 9.3 Most Important First-Generation Biofuel Feedstock Crops Globally

Feedstock	Crop	Relevant Crop Part	Growth Climate	Growth Cycle
Vegetable oil	Rapeseed, canola	40% oil in grains	Temperate	Annual
	Soybean	20% oil in beans	Subtropical	Annual
	Palm	60% oil in fruit	Tropical	Perennial (25 yr)
Sugar	Sugarcane	10–15% sugar in stem	Subtropical	Perennial (2–4 yr)
	Sugar beet	20% sugar in beet	Temperate to subtropical	Annual
Starch	Corn	60% starch in grains	Temperate to subtropical	Annual
	Wheat	60% starch in grains	Temperate	Annual
	Cassava	30% starch in tuberous root	Subtropical to tropical	Annual

energy crops based on grasses (e.g., miscanthus and switchgrass) or fast-growing trees (e.g., willow, poplar, and eucalyptus).

Compared to first-generation biofuel crops, lignocellulosic crops offer important advantages:

- The entire biomass aboveground is harvested and used for energy instead of just a part of the plant. Lignocellulosic crops thereby provide a higher yield of biomass per hectare, as discussed in more detail below.
- All lignocellulose energy crops are perennial, with plantation lifetimes of 10 to 25 years; that is, they are harvested in cycles of one to four years without being replanted since they grow again from the stocks remaining in the field after harvest. In contrast, food crops need annual tilling and planting of the soil.
- They have an internal nutrient recycling system by which they can relocate major shares of the plant nutrients from the leaves and stems into roots or rhizomes (underground shoots) in autumn, store them there over winter, and transfer them back into the newly emerging leaves of shoots in spring.
- As they have less easily digestible ingredients compared to sugar crops, for example, they are less susceptible to pest and disease attacks.

Consequently, perennial lignocellulosic energy crops provide higher biomass yield and require less labor and agrochemicals, including fertilizer and pesticides, than do annual crops. In the following sections we discuss the sustainability performance of lignocellulose feedstock in more detail.

9.3.2 Greenhouse Gas Emissions

Greenhouse gas (GHG) emissions of biofuels are calculated by summing up emissions from cultivation of the biomass, annualized emissions from carbon stock change caused by land-use change, conversion to biofuel, transport and distribution of the biomass and the resulting biofuels, fuel in use, and eventually, GHG savings achieved (e.g., from carbon capture and sequestration) (EC 2008). GHG emissions per gigajoule of biofuel are different between biofuels made from different feedstocks. Table 9.4 gives an overview of typical values for GHG emissions of different biofuels and the allocation to production, processing, and transport of these biofuels (EC 2008). The table shows significantly lower GHG emissions for the production of lignocellulosic raw materials then those for vegetable oils, sugar, and starch. Low GHG emission values for residual feedstock (e.g., straw) are due to the fact that the main part of the GHG emissions has to be allocated to the main product (e.g., wheat grains).

In contrast, the low GHG emissions of lignocellulosic energy crops (e.g., farmed wood) are due to the fact that these are perennial crops. Indeed, the emissions of GHG from soils under perennial crops are lower than under annual, intensively tilled crops, because soil tillage in perennial crops takes place only in the first year after plantations are established. This is because soil tillage allows oxygen to enter the soil, which leads to microbiological activity and the decomposition of organic matter to CO_2.

TABLE 9.4 Typical GHG Emissions of Biofuels Compared to the Fossil-Fuel Reference[a]

Biofuel	Crop	GHG Emissions ($g\,CO_{2eq}$/MJ)			
		Production of Biomass	Processing[b]	Transport and Distribution	Total
First-Generation Biofuels					
Biodiesel	Rape seed	30	15	1	47
	Palm oil	18	13 (33^c)	5	36 (56^c)
Ethanol	Sugarcane	13	1	8	21
	Sugar beet	13	27	3	43
	Corn	20	15	2	37
	Wheat	19	45	2	66
Second-Generation Biofuels					
Ethanol	Straw	3	5	2	10
Fischer–Tropsch diesel	Farmed wood	4	0	2	6

[a]Reference value for fossil fuel is 83.8 g CO_{2eq}/MJ; values from EU (EC 2008).
[b]Corrected for emission saved by exporting excess electricity from cogeneration.
[c]Including methane emissions at oil mill.

Figure 9.6 Miscanthus, a perennial biomass grass delivering lignocellulosic biomass. Photo shows the growth in one year. Taken in August in southern Germany.

Moreover, lignocellulose energy crops have a 50 to 80% lower demand for nitrogen fertilization than most annual energy crops, thanks to their internal nutrient recycling systems, discussed earlier. Nitrogen fertilizers contribute to GHG emissions through high energy consumption during their production and through N_2O emissions from soil. In general, nitrogen fertilization has a major share of CO_2 emissions in biofuel production. Nitrogen fertilization of annual crops can be responsible for $\pm 70\%$ of the CO_2 emissions in the crop production process and of more than 50% of the total biofuels production process.

Finally, energy yields per area unit are high for lignocellulose energy crops. When lignocellulosic biomass is produced, all aboveground biomass can be harvested for energetic use. When oil or starch crops are produced, only part of the crop (i.e., the grain) is harvested and only part of the grains (i.e., the oil or starch content) is used for energy. For example, only 13% of the rapeseed crop products are oil and 30% of wheat crop products are starch. Field trials show that on a good-quality site in Central Europe, about 20 tons of dry biomass can be harvested from miscanthus (Figure 9.6), compared to 4 to 9 tons of wheat grains (ca. 5 tons/ha in the EU) and 3.5 tons of rapeseed grains. On an energy basis, this results in 160 GJ/ha of BtL biofuels from miscanthus versus 42 GJ/ha biodiesel from rapeseed, with the energy losses in the conversion processes being included in the calculation.

9.3.3 The Environment

The environmental impact of biofuels can be quite complex, as it can affect the biodiversity, the water, and the soil.

Biodiversity   Soil cultivation activities in perennial cropping systems are concentrated mainly in the years of establishment, which are the first one to three
years of a plantation. Because of low soil cultivation frequency, animals living
above and below ground are less disturbed. As lignocellulosic biomass is harvested only during or after the winter, it provides animals with shelter over
winter. Since lignocellulosic crops are not attractive for pests and diseases,
they do not require pesticides and thereby enhance biodiversity by accom-
modating more insects, more birds that feed on them, and so on.

Water   Water is becoming an increasingly valuable and scarce resource
throughout the world. The impact of the biofuel economy on water consumption and contamination has therefore become an important sustainability
issue. For instance, 14% of the U.S. corn crop is irrigated and consumes some
$22,000 \, m^3/yr$ of water, which exceeds the average annual flow of the Colorado
River (Anthrop 2007). The low fertilizer demand of perennial crops reduces
the leaching of nutrients to groundwater, rivers, and lakes and thereby reduces
the degradation of water quality.

Soil   Energy crops can affect the soil, favoring its erosion and reducing its
organic carbon. Soil erosion occurs mainly after the soil has been cultivated
and is "bare," without vegetation. In perennial cropping systems this occurs
only in the first year, when the crop is planted and has yet to be established.
Since perennial crops stay in the field for 10 to 25 years without soil cultivation, their roots prevent the soil from eroding.

When left on the field, agricultural residues also help to prevent soil erosion.
They also maintain organic matter in the soil. Withdrawing all residues prevents providing enough organic matter to the soil to compensate for organic
matter losses that occur through cultivation of crops due mainly to soil cultivation. Hence, not all residues can be taken off the field. How much can be
removed depends on the type of soil, climate conditions, and eventual crop
rotation. Although it is estimated that about a third of all residues can be
removed sustainably, no rule of thumb can be given. The withdraw rate has
to be determined for the respective local conditions.

In the case of high-input farming, soil cultivation allows oxygen to come
into the soil, with the effect of destruction of valuable soil organic matter and
emission of CO_2. In perennial crops no soil cultivation is performed and
organic substance is accumulated in the form of leaves falling to the ground
or roots growing in the soil. An estimated amount of 0.6 ton of carbon per
hectare yearly is sequestered in the soil of perennial crop plantations.

Land-Use Change   Displacement effects, or *leakage*, can be defined as activ-
ity-induced changes in land use that occur outside the area in which the activity takes place (Lewandowski and Faaij 2006). The displacement by biomass
production activities will probably occur when the production of biomass
requires good-quality land that is presently used for food crop production, for

example. Change in land use can be detrimental to biodiversity and overall GHG emissions by destroying forests, grasslands, or peat lands. The release of carbon that was sequestered in and/or above ground has been shown to outweigh the potential GHG savings that could be achieved upon cultivating energy crops on the liberated land in case formerly forested or peat land is used (Smeets et al. 2006; Righelato and Spracklen 2007).

The use of residual biomass, which is a by-product of food crop production, does not lead to displacement effects because it does not require dedicated land. Perennial lignocellulosic energy crops contribute to minimizing land displacement either by using the land very efficiently (i.e., providing high yield per hectare) or by being grown on marginal or degraded lands that are unattractive or unsuitable for food production. On these lands, however, biomass yields per hectare will be lower and, consequently, production costs per ton of biomass may be higher.

9.3.4 Social Criteria

The production of biofuels could have positive social effects (e.g., the creation of jobs in rural areas) as well as negative impacts (e.g., increased scarcity of food). Also, production of biofuels should not involve child and forced labor. These aspects need to be monitored carefully.

Fuel vs. Food   The social aspect of sustainability that is being discussed most critically in the context of biofuel production is the competition between food and fuel. This competition can occur at two levels: directly by competing for the raw material (e.g., vegetable oils) and indirectly by competing for good-quality agricultural land. Increasing demand for raw material to produce bio-fuels can lead to a shortage of this raw material on the market and to an increase in their prices. The products of lignocellulosic energy crops are useful neither for food production nor as animal feed. There is, therefore, no direct competition. The production of an energy crop can, however, compete with food crop production because it needs agricultural land. Residual biomass is a by-product of food production and, therefore, does not compete with food for the raw material or the land.

There are different options to reduce the competition for good-quality agricultural land. For example, energy crops can be produced on marginal, less fertile land. Many perennial lignocellulose energy crops are suitable for biomass production on marginal lands. Switchgrass, an energy crop being developed in the United States, is an example of such a crop that is suitable for growing on marginal land. Energy crops can also be produced on land that is unsuitable for food production (e.g., because it is contaminated with heavy metal). Willows short-rotation coppice can be grown on and even contribute to the decontamination of heavy metal–contaminated land (Lewandowski et al. 2006). Multiuse crops can combine food and biomass production. Examples of such crops would be wheat varieties that combine a high yield in food grains with a high yield in straw. Presently, food crop varieties are generally bred for high grain and low straw yields. Finally, more efficient use of agricultural land by application of modern technologies, by improved crop management, and by improved varieties reduces the land needed for food crop production. This sets land free for either producing dedicated energy crop or for rotating fuel and food crops.

Job Creation   An important social aspect of biomass production and biofuel activities is the creation of jobs. In the Brazilian state of São Paulo, the production of sugarcane and ethanol is an important source of employment, both directly, as employment in sugarcane and ethanol production, and indirectly, as employment in industries that produce intermediate deliveries to the sugarcane and ethanol production sector. During the first five years of the Proalcool program, about 376,000 ha was converted to sugarcane in São Paulo, displacing crops (36%) and pastures (64%). Because sugarcane is approximately seven times more labor-intensive than pastures, this resulted in a net gain of some 25,000 worker years of employment (Smeets et al. 2006).

Job creation in sugarcane production is also exemplary for the potential trade-offs that may be encountered in balancing various social or environmental sustainability indicators. Presently, there is development toward mechanization of sugarcane harvest in Brazil. Mechanization has the advantages of reducing regional pollution (e.g., by avoiding burning of the fields), of making harvesting more efficient, and of improving the energy balance of sugarcane production. Manual harvest is difficult and unpleasant work. There are many reports on harsh working conditions and migrant labor (Smeets et al. 2006). Through mechanical harvesting these types of jobs, which are performed primarily by unskilled workers, are made redundant. The drawback, however, is a major loss of jobs in the state of São Paulo in the future.

Apart from the social criteria discussed above, a range of other social criteria needs to be considered. Table 9.5 presents a compilation of social criteria that are addressed in the drafted principles and criteria of the Roundtable for Sustainable Biofuels, Roundtable on Sustainable Palm Oil, and Roundtable on Responsible Soy. The performance of many of these social criteria is mainly region specific. A general feedstock-specific analysis would therefore be useless. The indicators that are being developed for certification systems will have to be applied to region-specific projects.

9.3.5   Economics

From an economic point of view, lignocellulosic biomass offers the advantages of larger production volumes and lower production costs than these of vegetable oil, sugar, or starch feedstock.

Abundance of Biomass   Vegetable oils, sugars, and starches are produced from crops that make specific demands on climate, water supply, and soil

TABLE 9.5 **Draft of Social Principles and Criteria of the Roundtables for Sustainable Biofuels, Sustainable Palm Oil, and Responsible Soy**

Human / labor rights	There should be responsible consideration of employees, individuals, and communities affected by biomass and biofuel activities: • Child labor should not be used. • Biofuel projects should arise through fully transparent, consultative, and participatory processes that involve all relevant stakeholders. • There should be fair payment and fair salaries for employees and contractors. • No discrimination should occur (due to gender, race, etc.). • There should be freedom of association for all employees (e.g., freedom to join associations). • Health and safety guidelines should be in the plan and implemented. • Customary rights and indigenous people's rights should be respected.
Smallholders	Smallholders should be dealt with fairly and transparently.
Community	Community relations should always be responsible.
Socioeconomic development	Activities should contribute to the social and economic development of local, rural, and indigenous people and communities.
Well-being	There should be no negative effects on the social well-being of workers and the local population.

quality. These crops are grown primarily on good-quality land. For example, oil palms grow only in tropical climates where rain forests also grow. In contrast, rape is a crop of temperate climates. The production of these crops is limited principally by the availability of suitable land for their production. In 2007 the annual global production of the three main vegetable oils used for biodiesel production was 37 megatons for palm oil, 35 megatons for soybean, and 18 megatons for rapeseed. This volume could produce 3.4 EJ of biofuels, in theory. Most of it is needed for food, however, and a smaller fraction is consumed for industrial purposes. Some increase in production could be achieved by breeding more productive oil crop varieties; breeding efforts increase yields by about 1% yearly on average. However, the potential extension of production land is limited, without converting biodiversity or carbon-rich land such as rain forest to palm or soy plantations. Several million hectares of idle land could potentially be used to grow these crops. This land is presently unused and does not belong to a high-conservation-value area.

In contrast, residual biomass is produced as a by-product of food or wood. It occurs naturally where food or wood is produced and therefore does not require additional land. Present production volumes were estimated at 50 to 85 EJ/yr a decade ago (Klass 1998; Okkerse and van Bekkum 1999; Dale and Kim 2006; Kamm et al. 2006). A more recent and thorough study (Smeets 2006) estimated that the volume of lignocellulosic residues could reach more than 75 EJ/yr globally by 2050, of which 60% are agricultural residues. However, it has to be emphasized that for technical reasons, not all residues produced can be recovered. They can be extracted from the field or forest only to an extend that allows for maintenance of soil fertility and balanced nutrients. It therefore seems more realistic to assume that less than half of this potential (i.e., <35 EJ/yr) can be used sustainably for energy.

The potential for lignocellulosic energy crops depends on the availability of agricultural land for their production and on the quality of this land. It is therefore difficult to calculate. Smeets (2006) estimated it as 215 EJ/yr by 2050, without jeopardizing food. This estimate was based on the following assumptions:

- Bioenergy crops are grown only on surplus land, which is agricultural land not needed for food and feed production.
- Modern agricultural production management systems will be in place throughout the world by 2050. Land will become available for energy crop production because of more efficient land use.
- All land available for energy crops is used to grow fast-growing trees in short-rotation coppice systems.
- Water and nutrients are not limiting.

The estimated energy potential of organic wastes is very vague. Hoogwijk (2004) estimated it to be 5 to 50 EJ of organic waste potential globally by 2050.

In summary, lignocellulosic biomass has a production potential of about 300 EJ/yr, which dwarfs that of the vegetable oils and could meet a substantial part of the global energy demand of 900 to 1100 EJ/yr expected for 2050. It should be stressed, however, that the biomass potentials mentioned here does not include conversion losses, which could amount to 45 to 65% in the production of biofuels, as illustrated by the case studies presented above. Lignocellulosic biomass might therefore provide up to 135 to 195 EJ/yr of biofuels.

Costs of Biomass Production costs for biomass include the cost of land use, crop establishment (soil preparation, planting, or seeding), agrochemicals, machinery, labor, and the fixed costs that cover maintenance of buildings, electricity, and so on. These costs obviously depend on regional cost levels as well as yields harvested. Typical production costs are reported in Table 9.6. Accordingly, the production cost of seed oils are highest (>$10/GJ), followed by beet sugar and grain starch ($6 to 7/GJ) and finally, lignocellulosic residues and crops (<$5/GJ). However, the price of biofeedstock has recently increased:

TABLE 9.6   Costs of Biomass Resources[a]

Biomass	Moisture (%)	LHV (Gj/J)	$30/bbl Oil		$60/bbl Oil	
			($/ton)	($/GJ)	($/ton)	($/GJ)
wheat grain	13	14.8	118.8	8.0	125.0	8.4
sugar beet	77	3.8	31.3	8.1	32.5	8.5
rapeseed	10	23.8	296.3	12.4	310.0	13.0
sunflower seed	10	23.8	331.3	13.9	347.5	14.6
wheat straw	16	14.4	43.8	3.0	46.3	3.1
waste wood	0	18.0	62.5	3.5	66.3	3.6
farmed wood	0	18.0	96.3	5.4	101.3	5.6

Source: Adapted from EC (2006).
[a]Assuming $1.25/euro.

about $30/GJ for vegetable oils and about $15/GJ for starches. The low cost of lignocellulosic biomass is easily understood. As for lignocellulosic residues, which are a by-product, their production cost covers mainly the recovery costs. Perennial lignocellulosic energy crops have to be established only once in a production lifetime of a plantation of about 20 years. That reduces establishment costs, which are allocated on a yearly basis. Moreover, perennial crops have a comparatively low demand for fertilizers and pesticides, which is lowered to costs for agrochemicals, for machinery, and for labor. Finally, lignocellulosic crops grow with high yields per hectare. Since sugarcane is a very productive perennial crop, it is also produced at low cost.

It has to be emphasized that a comparison of energy yields between different crops can be performed only for crops being grown under similar conditions. The productivity of oil palm, which grows in generally highly productive tropical areas, should not be compared with the yields of oil crops such as rapeseed or of lignocellulose energy crops, grown in the less productive temperate to cooler climates. The cost of biomass delivered to the plant gates also depends on the biomass density in regions, as illustrated by Figure 9.7 for agricultural residues in the Indian state of Punjab (Singh et al. 2008). These collection costs include the biomass recovery costs ($18.62/ha) and cost of transport (manual or machine transport) from the collection place to the transport unit ($6.21/ton·km). The denser the biomass production, the lower are the collection costs. Biomass density in terms of (tons/km^2) depends on the yield of the biomass per hectare and share of the area from which biomass can be harvested. With higher yields of biomass crops, not only the production costs per ton biomass, but also the supply costs are decreasing.

When comparing production costs of different biofuel feedstocks, one has to realize that cost advantages may be compensated by higher conversion costs (Lange 2007a,b). Vegetable oils have the highest production costs of all

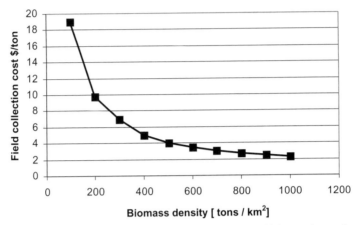

Figure 9.7 Effect of collection (= recovery and transport of biomass) cost for agricultural residues in the field versus biomass density by the example of the Indian state Punjab. (From Singh et al. 2008.)

biomass feedstocks, but have the advantage of being convertible to biodiesel easily and cheaply. In contrast, cheap lignocellulosic biomass requires comparatively costly processes for conversion into biofuels, as discussed above.

9.4 CONCLUSIONS AND RECOMMENDATIONS FOR R&D ACTIVITIES

In the present chapter we have demonstrated the role that lignocellulosic residues and perennial crops could play as sustainable feedstock for transportation fuels in the near to medium-term future. Indeed:

1. Biofuels are the only option humankind has, today and in the near future, to feed its vehicles with a fuel that is renewable, carbon-neutral, energy-dense, and affordable. Renewable H_2 and electricity are still facing major challenges in distribution and storage and are more expensive.

2. Lignocellulosic biomass has the potential to provide some 300 EJ/yr of energy or 135 to 195 EJ/yr of biofuels, which represents a sizable fraction of the global energy demand, which is expected to rise to 900 to 1100 EJ/yr by 2050.

3. Lignocellulosic residues will not compete with food for their feedstock and would not need to compete for land either. The same applies to perennial crops that are growing on land that is unsuitable for food production either because of its poor quality or because of the environmental services it provides.

4. These feedstocks have been shown to provide significant greenhouse gas savings by either being a by-product of food crops or forestry or by requiring

minimal soil cultivation and fertilization. Moreover, lignocellulosic energy crops offer additional environmental benefits: for example, in water and soil management as well as in biodiversity.

Lignocellulosic biomass is fairly cheap to produce, certainly compared to food crops. However, its conversion to liquid biofuels requires large investments. This has been illustrated with the Choren–Shell technology to produce diesel-range hydrocarbons and with the Iogen technology to produce cellulosic ethanol. These large investments result from (1) the resilience of the lignocellulose to chemical and microbial attack, (2) the need for extensive chemical transformation through cracking and deoxygenation, (3) the need for deep removal of contaminants (e.g., gasification), and/or (4) the circulation of huge amounts of water used as solvent (fermentation). Compared to first-generation biofuels, the high investment costs of lignocellulosic plants will probably offset the benefits of cheap feedstock in the initial phase, as illustrated and discussed elsewhere (Lange 2007a,b). However, as more plants are being deployed, scaled-up, and fine-tuned following the well-known experience curve, the lignocellulosic technologies will become increasingly competitive.

Cellulosic biofuels are very close to becoming reality. The biomass supply fields have been identified, logistic issues are being addressed, sustainability criteria are being developed, conversion technology is being demonstrated and governments are considering to adjusting their support to the "sustainability" performance of the biofuels. However, much still needs to be done to allow large-scale deployment at affordable cost and in a sustainable manner. Further improvements are needed throughout the entire value chain, from biomass production to fuel distribution and certification:

- Lignocellulose production
  - One needs to determine the amount of residue that can be removed from field and forest in a sustainable manner.
  - One needs to develop crops and agricultural practices that improve biomass yields and enhances its digestibility in conversion processes while reducing GHG emission and fertilizer/water utilization.
  - One needs improved machinery and practices to harvest, compact, store, and transport the biomass to the plant gates.
- Lignocellulose conversion
  - Coupling of biomass pretreatment and downstream conversion to achieve an optimally integrated overall conversion process.
  - Capital reduction for gasification is essential, as it dominates enormously the overall manufacturing profit picture for the syngas produced.
  - More "poison"-tolerant catalytic systems for all downstream conversion processes: gasification processes, milder catalytic processes and

biocatalytic processes; robust catalysts require fewer intermediate separation and purification steps and lead to cheaper processes.
  • Water reduction for water-based processes is crucial for capex reduction and energy minimization.
• Fuel distribution
  • One needs novel biofuel components that are fully compatible with present cars and fuel distribution systems.
  • One needs to revisit fuel specifications to accommodate novel, non-hydrocarbon components while guaranteeing fuel safety, emission, and compatibility.
• Sustainability
  • One needs to define agreeable and enforceable sustainability criteria and certification systems.
  • Governments need to develop systems that stimulate the most sustainable biofuels.

NOTE ADDED IN PROOF

After redaction of this chapter, Choren Industries GmbH announced that the other shareholders have acquired Shell's shareholding in the German venture. Shell remains committed to the research and development of advanced biofuels.

REFERENCES

Aden, A., M. Ruth, K. Ibsen, J. Jechura, K. Neeves, J. Sheehan, B. Wallace, L. Montague, A. Slayton, and J. Lukas. 2002. *Lignocellulosic Biomass to Ethanol Process Design and Economics Utilizing Co-current Dilute Acid Prehydrolysis and Enzymatic Hydrolysis for Corn Stover.* NREL/TP-510-32438, U.S. Department of Energy, Oak Ridge, Tennessee.

Anthrop, D. F. 2007. Analysis highlights limits on energy promise of biofuels. *Oil Gas J.*, Feb. 5, pp. 25–29.

Choren. 2008. www.choren.com.

Cramer, J., et al. 2006. Project Group Sustainable Production of Biomass: Criteria for Sustainable Biomass Production. Final Report of the Project Group: Sustainable Production of Biomass: July 14th. Accessed at http://www.globalproblems-globalsolutions-files.org/unf_website/PDF/criteria_sustainable_biomass_prod.pdf.

Dale, B. E., and S. Kim. 2006. Biomass refining global impact on the biobased economy of the 21th century. In *Biorefineries: Industrial Processes and Products*, Vol. 1, ed. B. Kamm, P. R. Gruber, and M. Kamm. Weinheim, Germany: Wiley-VCH, pp. 41–66.

EC (European Commission). 2006. *Concave, Eucar, European Commission Joint Research Centre: Well-to-Wheels Analysis of Future Automotive Fuels and Powertrains in the European Context.* Well-to-Wheels Report, Version 2b. Brussels, Belgium: EC.

————. 2008. Proposal for a Directive of the European Parliament and of the Council on the promotion of the use of energy from renewable resources. Brussels, Belgium: EC.

Elander, R. T., C. E. Wyman, B. E. Dale, M. Holtzapple, M. R. Ladish, Y. Y. Lee, and T. Eggeman. 2005. Initial comparative process economics of leading biomass pre-treatment technologies. Presented at the 15th International Symposium on Alcohol Fuels and Other Renewables, San Diego, CA, Sept. Accessed at http://www.eri.ucr.edu/ISAFXVCD/ISAFXVPP/InCPELB.pdf.

Hayes, D. J. 2008. State of Play in the Biorefining Industry. Unpublished report. Accessed at http://www.lufpig.eu/documents/StateofPlayinTheBiorefiningIndustry-DanielJohnHayes.pdf.

Hayes, D. J., S. Fitzpatrick, M. H. B. Hayes, and J. R. H. Ross. 2006. The biofine process: production of levulinic acid, furfural and formic acid from lignocellulosic feedstock. In *Biorefineries: Industrial Processes and Products*, Vol. 1, ed. B. Kamm, P. R. Gruber, M. Kamm. Weinheim, Germany: Wiley-VCH, pp. 139–164.

Hoffmann, B. 2008. *Aufbereit. Tech.*, 41:6–17.

Hoogwijk, M. 2004. On the global and regional potential of renewable energy sources. Ph.D. dissertation, Utrecht University, p. 256.

Iogen. 2008. www.iogen.com.

Kamm, B., M. Kamm, M. Schmidt, T. Hirth, and M. Schulze. 2006. Lignocellulose-based chemical products and product family trees. In *Biorefineries: Industrial Processes and Products*, Vol. 2, ed. B. Kamm, P. R. Gruber, and M. Kamm. Weinheim, Germany: Wiley-VCH.

Katzen, R., and D. J. Schell. 2006. Lignocellulosic feedstock biorefinery: history and plant development for biomass hydrolysis. In *Biorefineries: Industrial Processes and Products*, Vol. 2, ed. B. Kamm, P. R. Gruber, and M. Kamm. Weinheim, Germany: Wiley-VCH, pp. 3–59.

Kiener, C. 2008. *Erdoel Erdgas Kohle*, 124:68–71.

Klass, D. L. 1998. *Biomass for Renewable Energy, Fuels and Chemicals*. London: Academic Press.

Lange, J.-P. 2001. Fuels and chemicals manufacturing: guidelines for understanding and minimizing the production costs. *CatTech*, 5:82–95.

————. 2007a. Lignocellulose conversion: an introduction to chemistry, process and economics. *Biofuels Bioprod. Biorefin.*, 1:39–48.

————. 2007b. Lignocellulose conversion: an introduction to chemistry, process and economics. In *Catalysis for Renewables: From Feedstock to Energy Production*, ed. G. v. S. Centi and A. Rutger. New York: Wiley-VCH.

————. 2007. *Proceedings of the 12th European Biomass Conference*, Berlin, May.

————. 2009. Sustainable chemical manufacturing: a matter of resources, wastes, hazards and costs. *ChemSusChem*, 2:587–592.

Lange, J.-P., and P. J. A. Tijm. 1996. *Chem. Eng. Sci.*, 51:2379–2387.

Lawford, H. G., and J. D. Rousseau. 2003. *Appl. Biochem. Biotechnol. A*, 106(1–3): 457–470.

Lewandowski, I., and A. P. Faaij. 2006. Steps towards the development of a certification system for sustainable bio-energy trade. *Biomass Bioenergy*, 30(83):104.

Lewandowski, I., U. Schmidt, M. Londo, and A. P. C. Faaij. 2006. The economic value of the phytoremediation function. *Agric. Syst.*, 89:68–89.

Lichtenthaler, F. W. 2006. The key sugars of biomass: availability, present non-food uses and potential future development lines. In *Biorefineries: Industrial Processes and Products*, Vol. 2, ed. B. Kamm, P. R. Gruber, and M. Kamm. Weinheim, Germany: Wiley-VCH, pp. 3–59.

Morgen, C. 2006. *Integrated Biomass Utilization System*. Dong Energy Doc. 486762, Project E001123.02. Accessed at http://www.bioethanol.info/Publications/Final%20 Publishable%20Report.pdf.

Okkerse, C., and H. van Bekkum. 1999. From fossil to green. *Green Chem.* 1:107–114.

Righelato, R., and D. V. Spracklen. 2007. Carbon mitigation by biofuels or by saving and restoring forests? *Science*, 317(5840):902.

Rudloff, M. 2007. *Proceedings of the 12th European Biomass Conference*, Berlin, pp. 2250–2251.

Sie, S. T., M. M. G. Senden, and H. M. H. van Wechem. 1991. Conversion of natural gas to transportation fuels via the Shell middle distillate synthesis process (SMDS). *Catal. Today*, 8:371–394.

Singh, J., B. S. Panesar, and S. K. Sharma. 2008. Energy potential through agricultural biomass using geographical information system: a case study of Punjab. *Biomass Bioenergy*, 32(4):301.

Sjöström, E. 1993. *Wood Chemistry: fundamentals and Applications*, 2nd ed. London: Academic Press.

Smeets, E., M. Junginger, A. Faaij, A. Walter, and P. Dolzan. 2006. *Sustainability of Brazilian Bioethanol*. Report NWS-E-2006-110. Utrecht, The Netherlands: Copernicus Institute, Universiteit Utrecht.

Teter, S. A., F. Xu, G. E. Nedwin, and J. R. Cherry. 2006. In *Biorefineries: Industrial Processes and Products*, Vol. 1, ed. B. Kamm, P. R. Gruber, and M. Kamm. Weinheim, Germany: Wiley-VCH, pp. 357–383.

Tolan, J. S. 2006. Biorefineries: industrial processes and products. In *Biorefineries: Industrial Processes and Products*, Vol. 1, ed. B. Kamm, P. R. Gruber, and M. Kamm. Weinheim, Germany: Wiley-VCH, pp. 193–208.

Wooley, R., M. Ruth, J. Sheehan, K. Ibsen, H. Majdeski, and A. Galvez. 1999. *Lignocellulosic Biomass to Ethanol Process Design and Economics Utilizing Co-current Dilute Acid Prehydrolysis and Enzymatic Hydrolysis: Current and Futuristic Scenarios*. NREL/TP-580-26157, U.S. Department of Energy, Oak Ridge, Tennessee.

10

INTEGRATED UREA–MELAMINE PROCESS AT DSM: SUSTAINABLE PRODUCT DEVELOPMENT

Tjien T. Tjioe and Johan T. Tinge

DSM Research, Technology and Analysis Geleen, SRU Industrial Chemicals, Geleen, The Netherlands

10.1   SHORT SUMMARY OF MELAMINE DEVELOPMENT

Melamine is produced from urea by an endothermic reaction at a temperature of 360 to 440 °C. About 2 tons of by-product gases (i.e., ammonia, carbon dioxide) are formed per ton of melamine. In most melamine processes the hot melamine is quenched with an aqueous solution. Both the melamine and the by-product gases must be recovered from a dilute aqueous solution. Due to these features, the melamine process is capital- and energy-intensive. In the new process, liquid ammonia is used as a quenching agent. The new melamine process has lower investment and energy costs than conventional processes and produces high-quality melamine. The first commercial-scale plant, which is based on this new technology, came onstream in 2004.

Production facilities based on this new technology make a great contribution to the continuous improvement of two pillars of sustainability: eco-footprint and economics. Melamine improves the safety, durability, and quality of products such as wood-based panels, contributing to the social dimension of sustainability.

The principles used to develop the new, integrated urea–melamine process are not just limited to the development of this process but can be cited as

Sustainable Development in the Process Industries: Cases and Impact, Edited by Jan Harmsen and Joseph B. Powell

199

general approaches to sustainable development. The most important general design principles are:

- Stay away from the gas phase: gas–liquid separation is easier than gas–gas separation.
- Stay away from aqueous systems; convert directly into a solid product.
- Simplify or skip purification; optimize the synthesis section.
- Apply heat recovery.
- Apply multieffect evaporation.

10.2 CURRENT USES OF MELAMINE

DSM is the world's largest producer of melamine and is a leader in melamine technology though its catalytic gas-phase process. Melamine production technology requires sophisticated equipment and know-how, due to the demanding process conditions. The melamine industry is facing serious challenges due to the strong increase in the world's production capacity and the strong increase in energy prices. DSM has tackled this challenge by developing a new cost-competitive integrated urea–melamine process in cooperation with Melamine Chemicals Inc.

The main application for melamine is as a raw material for the production of melamine–formaldehyde resins, which are used as an adhesive of wood chips and which give laminated panels and floors their unique surface properties and attractive finishes. Based on its applications, melamine can be considered a sustainable product because it helps to conserve hardwood and natural forests by enabling the effective use of wood waste and fast-growing softwood in boards and panels.

Melamine plays a vital role in improving the quality, safety, durability, and aesthetic appearance of products such as laminated surfaces, adhesives, and resins for wood-based panels and as an ingredient in many other products. The following seven main application areas can be distinguished based on DSM (2007):

1. *Laminates.* The main application for melamine is as a raw material for melamine–formaldehyde (MF) resins, which give laminated panels and floors their unique surface properties and attractive finishes. Melamine powder is mixed with an aqueous formaldehyde solution and other substances to form a resin or adhesive. This waterproof adhesive is added to wood chips, and the resulting mixture is compressed to form chipboard. Paper printed with a wood or any other design is soaked in a similar melamine resin and pressed onto the chipboard's surface. These resins are also heat- and chemical-resistant and suitable for hygienic antibacterial surfaces. Typical applications include laminate flooring, furniture tops, kitchen and bathroom countertops, and self-assembly furniture.

2. *Wood-based panels.* Waterproof melamine adhesives are either used to glue pieces of wood together to form boards and beams, or are mixed with wood chips or sawdust and compressed to form wood-based panels. These glues are applied in the furniture, flooring, and construction industries to give laminates, plywood, MDF, OSB, or any other wood-based matrices optimal moisture resistance and integrity.

3. *Coatings.* MF resins can form efficient cross-linking systems, as they react with polyester, acrylics, and epoxies. Some benefits of these coatings are good color retention, wear resistance, scratch resistance, and glossy finish. Typical melamine-modified coatings applications include vehicle body panels, household appliances, drink cans, and coils of metal sheeting.

4. *Molding powders.* Molding powders based on melamine are produced in an entire variety of grades. In general, it is an inexpensive, hygienic, and safe material that will not break or transfer heat, and products made from it, such as tableware and picnic-ware, can be produced in a range of colors and decorative printed finishes and are dishwasher-proof. Other types of melamine molding powders do have excellent thermal and insulating properties and are used to manufacture electrical equipment.

5. *Flame retardants.* Melamine in powder form can be used to enhance the flame-retardant properties of polyurethane foam products and coatings. Melamine inhibits flame spread and reduces smoke emission. Examples of applications of foam products are soft furnishings, hospital and hotel bed mattresses, and seats in public places, and examples of flame-retardant coating include fire doors and ventilation ducts.

6. *Concrete plasticizers.* Sulfonated melamine–formaldehyde resins are used as plasticizers in concrete to improve its properties, such as stronger end product, improved flow characteristics, more workable product, reduced drying time, improved concrete quality, and faster setting. For example, the Øresund bridge that links Sweden and Denmark contains melamine-based resins as a plasticizer.

7. *Paper and textile.* MF resins provide wet-strength properties to specialty papers. Melamine-based banknotes (e.g., the euro) can be wrinkled and folded endlessly and still retain a good appearance. Other application areas are wallpaper, maps, and wrinkle-free clothing (e.g., men's trousers and travel wear).

10.3 UREA PRODUCTION

Melamine is produced in two steps. The first step, described here, is the production of urea from ammonia and carbon dioxide as raw materials. Two principal chemical equilibrium reactions take place in the formation of urea in the Stamicarbon urea stripping process:

$$2NH_3 + CO_2 \rightleftharpoons NH_2COONH_4 \qquad (1)$$

ammonia   carbon dioxide   ammonium carbamate

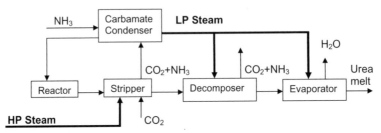

Figure 10.1 Stamicarbon urea stripping process. The heavy lines show the heat flows; the thin lines show the mass flows.

$$NH_2COONH_4 \rightleftharpoons CO(NH_2)_2 + H_2O \tag{2}$$
ammonium carbamate   urea   water

The first reaction is exothermic and the second is endothermic.

A simple block diagram of the Stamicarbon urea stripping process is shown in Figure 10.1. In the carbamate condenser, low-pressure (LP) steam is produced during the reaction of ammonia and carbon dioxide into ammonium carbamate. In the reactor the carbamate is partly converted into a urea synthesis solution according to equilibrium reaction (2).

The urea synthesis solution coming from the reactor contains a high concentration of nonconverted reactants (i.e., carbamate, ammonia, carbon dioxide), since the urea reaction is an equilibrium reaction. Most of the carbamate is decomposed and stripped off in the stripper as NH_3 and CO_2 at high temperature and pressure (140 bar, 180 °C) using CO_2 as a strip gas. Since this reaction is endothermic, high-pressure (HP) steam is required on the utility side in the stripper. The NH_3 and CO_2 gases obtained are reused in the carbamate condenser. The stripped urea synthesis solution then goes to the low-pressure decomposer, where the remaining carbamate is flashed off as NH_3 and CO_2 gases. In the evaporator, water is removed and a 99.7 wt% urea melt is produced. In the final two steps of the process, the LP steam produced in the carbamate condenser is used for the endothermic processes.

In this way, the heat supplied as HP steam in the stripper is "recovered" as LP steam in the carbamate condenser and the energy is used twice. The Stamicarbon urea stripping process requires only 50% of the steam consumption of a conventional urea process without a stripping section.

10.4 CONVENTIONAL DSM STAMICARBON GAS-PHASE MELAMINE PRODUCTION PROCESS

10.4.1 Chemistry Involved

In general, the formation of melamine from urea, via a catalytic process, is described by the following two consecutive reaction steps:

$$6 \text{ urea} \rightleftharpoons 6 \text{ isocyanic acid} + 6 \text{ ammonia} \tag{3}$$

$$6 \text{ isocyanic} \rightleftharpoons \text{melamine} + 3 \text{ carbon dioxide} \tag{4}$$

which are combined in the following overall reaction:

$$6 \text{ urea} \rightleftharpoons \text{melamine} + 6 \text{ ammonia} + 3 \text{ carbon dioxide} \tag{5}$$

The reaction temperature and pressure for the formation of melamine are approximately 400 °C and 7 to 10 bar, respectively. The reaction is catalyzed by a solid silica and alumina containing catalyst. The first step, the decomposition of urea, is a highly endothermic reaction, and the second step, the cyclization to melamine, is an exothermic reaction. The overall reaction itself is rather endothermic and requires approximately 5 GJ per metric ton of melamine produced.

Some general information on melamine is given in Table 10.1.

In addition to the desired main reaction, several side reactions occur in the reaction section during the synthesis of melamine as well as in the associated melamine recovery section. One important group of side products is made by condensation of partial deaminated melamine:

$$2 \text{ melamine} \rightleftharpoons \text{melem} + 2 \text{ ammonia} \tag{6}$$

$$2 \text{ melamine} \rightleftharpoons \text{melam} + 1 \text{ ammonia} \tag{7}$$

$$6 \text{ melamine} \rightleftharpoons \text{melone} + 8 \text{ ammonia} \tag{8}$$

In fact, these three deamination reactions are reversible, which means that the formation of these side reactions can be suppressed by applying process conditions consisting of high ammonia pressures and temperatures. The structures of the dimers melem and melam and an example of a structure of melone, which is, in fact, a mixture of several components, are shown in Figure 10.2.

TABLE 10.1 Melamine Description

CAS No.	108-78-1
Chemical name	2,4,6-triamino-1,3,5-triazine
Chemical formula	$C_3N_6H_6$
Molecular structure	
Melting point	350 °C (sublimation)

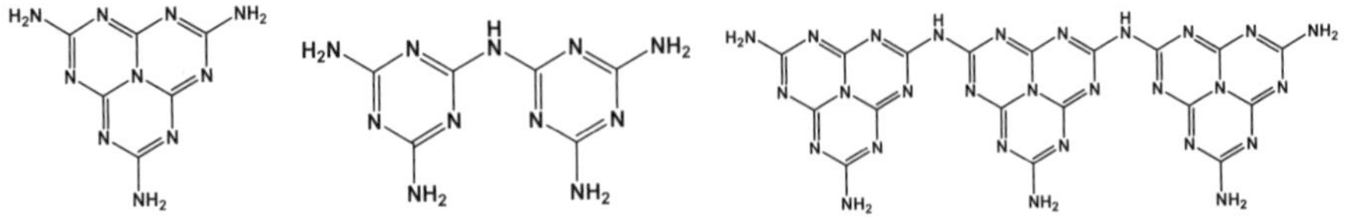

Melem ($C_6N_{10}H_6$) Melam ($C_6N_{11}H_9$) Melone ($C_{18}N_{28}H_{12}$)

Figure 10.2 Structures of the dimers melem and melam and an example of a structure of melone.

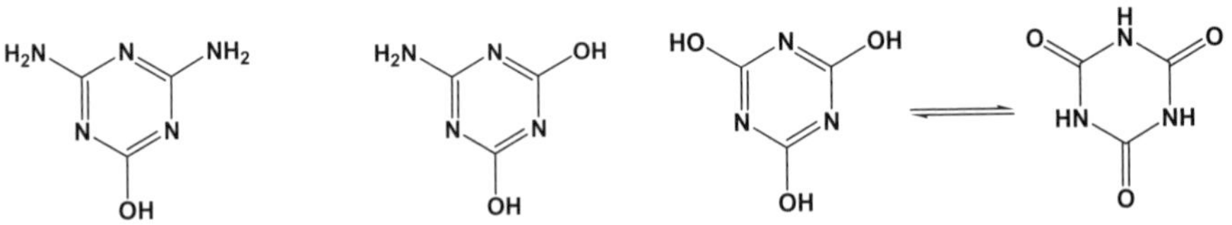

ammeline ($C_3N_5OH_5$) ammelide ($C_3N_4O_2H_4$) cyanuric acid ($C_3N_3O_3H_3$)

Figure 10.3 Structures of the side products ammeline, ammelide, and cyanuric acid.

Another important group of side products is formed by partial or complete hydrolysis of the three amino groups of melamine (Figure 10.3):

$$\text{melamine} + 1\,\text{water} \rightarrow \text{ammeline} + 1\,\text{ammonia} \tag{9}$$

$$\text{melamine} + 2\,\text{water} \rightarrow \text{ammelide} + 1\,\text{ammonia} \tag{10}$$

$$\text{melamine} + 3\,\text{water} \rightarrow \text{cyanuric acid} + 3\,\text{ammonia} \tag{11}$$

10.4.2 Conventional Process

A simple block diagram of a conventional DSM Stamicarbon gas-phase melamine process is shown in Figure 10.4. Molten urea from the urea plant is catalytically converted into melamine in the reactor at high temperature and medium pressure in the presence of additional ammonia gas. The reaction temperature and pressure are 360 to 440 °C and 7 to 10 bar, respectively. The reaction takes place in a fluidized catalytic bed reactor with only ammonia as the fluidizing gas. The heat required (the overall reaction is strongly endothermic) is supplied to the reactor by heat transfer salt (HTS). About 2 tons of by-product gases (ammonia and carbon dioxide) are formed per ton of melamine according to the overall reaction, which is described as reaction (5).

The melamine is obtained as a vapor and is cooled with an aqueous medium in the quench vessel to obtain a melamine solution or slurry and a remaining gas containing NH_3, CO_2, and H_2O. The next steps are desorption of the dissolved carbamate out of the melamine slurry/solution and the downstream processing of melamine. Downstream processing comprises dissolving

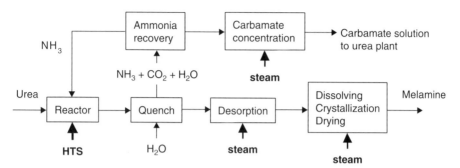

Figure 10.4 Conventional gas-phase melamine process. The heavy lines show the heat flows; the thin lines show the process flows.

of the melamine slurry, recrystallization, and finally, drying of the melamine crystals. These steps require steam as energy input. The by-product, gas out of the quench section, is partially condensed, producing a lean carbamate solution and a water-free ammonia gas (ammonia recovery section). The ammonia gas is recycled to the reactor. To be able to recycle the carbamate to the urea plant, the lean carbamate solution is concentrated, by evaporation followed by condensation, while using high-pressure steam for the evaporation. After concentration, the carbamate solution still contains 20 to 24 wt% of water.

Water has a negative impact on conversion in the urea reactor, since urea formation is an equilibrium reaction. In addition, water decreases the stripping efficiency in the urea process. Due to the presence of water in the process streams after the quench, the steam consumption required for recovery of the melamine and carbamate is high. The overall steam consumption of the melamine process ranges from 6 to 8 tons per ton of melamine. The utility consumption of a conventional gas-phase melamine process is as follows:

Natural gas	8 to 13 GJ (reactor)
Steam	6 to 8 tons
Electricity	0.4 to 0.6 MWh
Cooling water	700 tons

10.5 NEW INTEGRATED UREA–MELAMINE PROCESS

The main goal of the development of an integrated urea–melamine process is reduction of the energy and capital costs of the process. The main improvements compared with the conventional gas-phase melamine process are:

- Heat recovery from the by-products ammonia and carbon dioxide
- Export of water-free by-product gases to the urea plant without a concentration unit

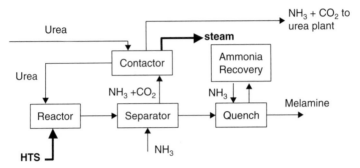

Figure 10.5 Integrated high-pressure melamine process. The heavy lines show the heat flows; the thin lines show the process flows.

- Synthesis of melamine melt instead of melamine vapor
- Integrated purification of the melamine melt without a recrystallization unit
- Water-free quench process producing dry powder directly
- Low-cost ammonia recovery, due to separation of by-product gas before the quench

A block scheme of the integrated urea–melamine process is shown in Figure 10.5. The process is operated at high pressure (150 to 250 bar) to produce melamine melt instead of melamine vapor. Urea melt coming from the urea plant is preheated in the direct contactor by the hot (360 to 440 °C) by-product gases ammonia and carbon dioxide, which were produced in the reactor. This off-gas is cooled simultaneously to temperatures below 250 °C and steam is produced in the contactor. In this way, heat from the by-product gases is recovered and can be used in the process for preheating process streams or equipment. In the reactor the preheated urea is converted into a melamine melt and ammonia and carbon dioxide gas using heat transfer salt as a heating medium. In the separator the melamine melt and the gases are separated, making it possible to recover heat from the by-product gas in the contactor. The melamine melt is purified (Wang 1999; Tjioe 2000a) in the separator by the addition of ammonia gas. The hot ammonia gas used for the purification step is also sent to the contactor for heat recovery. The purification occurs directly in the melt, and no separate recrystallization step is required. Then the melt is sprayed and quenched with evaporating liquid ammonia (Tjioe and Slangen 1998; Tjioe 2000; Best and Tjioe 1999) in the quench section. The amount of liquid ammonia is just enough to cool the melamine to the required temperature. After all ammonia is evaporated, dry melamine powder of high quality (Tjioe 1998, 1999) is obtained directly without a drying step. The evaporated ammonia from the quench is condensed in the ammonia recovery section and is reused. The ammonia recovery is much simpler than in the gas-phase process, since the by-product gas has been separated before the quench.

An extra advantage of the new melamine process is that the off-gas coming from the contactor is water-free and can be recycled directly to the urea plant without a concentration unit and without having a negative impact on the urea conversion. If the melamine process is operated at a pressure higher than the pressure of the urea plant, direct coupling (Meessen and van Wijck 1998; van Wijck 1998) with the high-pressure section in a urea plant without condensation of the gases is feasible. This results in a fully integrated urea–melamine process. The utility consumption of the new, integrated melamine process is as follows (per metric ton of melamine):

Natural gas	7 GJ (reactor)
Steam	<1 tons
Electricity	<0.4 MWh
Cooling water	<400 tons

Safety precautions are an important issue during design and operation because of the high pressure and temperature. During startup and shutdown, the process is operated at reduced pressure to minimize risks in case of a process failure. The direct coupling requires a sophisticated automatic pressure control system.

Although the high-pressure section is expensive, the total capital cost of the new process is lower than that of the conventional process. The integrated high-pressure melamine process requires only 40% of the energy consumption of a conventional gas-phase melamine process and has no negative impact on urea conversion and stripping in the urea process.

10.6 CONCLUSIONS

The main improvements of in the newly developed integrated urea–melamine process compared with the conventional gas-phase melamine process, noted in Section 10.5, have resulted in lower investment costs and a 60% reduction in energy consumption compared to conventional gas-phase melamine processes. In addition, the new melamine process produces high-quality melamine.

In this chapter we have presented an example of sustainable industrial process development. However, the principles employed to develop the new, integrated urea–melamine process are not limited to development of the process but can be utilized as general approaches to sustainable development.

REFERENCES

Best, D., and T. Tjioe. 1999. Method for preparing melamine: quenching technology: DSM. WO 99/19310.

DSM. 2007. MelaminebyDSM™: The multiplicity of melamine. http://www.dsm.com/en_US/html/dmm/applications_2.htm.

Meessen, J., and J. van Wijck. 1998. Process for preparing urea: DSM. WO 98/32731.

Tjioe, T. T. 1998. Crystalline melamine: powder technology: DSM. WO 98/55465.

———. 1999. Crystalline melamine: powder technology: DSM. WO 99/46251.

———. 2000a. Method for preparing melamine: stripping technology: DSM. WO 00/21940.

———. 2000b. Method for preparing melamine: quenching technology: DSM. WO 00/53587.

Tjioe, T. T., and H. Slangen. 1998. Method for preparing melamine: cooling technology: DSM. WO 98/54160.

van Wijck, J. 1998. Process for the preparation of urea: DSM. WO 98/08808.

Wang, Y. 1999. Method for preparing melamine: stripping: DSM. WO99/58508.

11

SUSTAINABLE INNOVATION IN THE CHEMICAL INDUSTRY AND ITS COMMERCIAL IMPACTS

JOSEPH B. POWELL

Shell Global Solutions, Houston, Texas

11.1 OVERVIEW

Through the process of "creative destruction" (Schumpeter 1975), the chemical industry constantly reinvents itself with new performance-driven products as well as lower-cost routes to existing products. Examination of U.S. Presidential Green Chemistry Challenge awards over the last decade (USEPA 2008) reveals, however, varying degrees of commercial acceptance and market penetration for recognized sustainable innovations. Sustainability is not enough, as articulated in *Economics and the Environment* (Goodstein 1999). For new technologies and products to affect society via the marketplace, consumers must be given new choices that perform as well as or better than previous alternatives, at lower net cost.[1] When these advantaged alternatives also result in a reduced environmental and societal footprint, substantial progress toward sustainability is achieved.

In keeping with the theme of case studies in sustainability, we present an overview of select developments or initiatives within the chemical industry

---

[1] A niche segment of consumers will buy at higher price and/or lower performance if sustainability is improved; however, this is often not a large enough segment to enable significant market penetration (Goodstein 1999).

Copyright © Shell Global Solutions International B.V. 2010.

Sustainable Development in the Process Industries: Cases and Impact, Edited by Jan Harmsen and Joseph B. Powell
Copyright © 2010 John Wiley & Sons, Inc.

over the period where sustainability has emerged as a concept, with emphasis on technologies exhibiting commercial success as evidenced by market penetration. We begin by taking a brief historical look at how the chemical industry has emerged over the last 300 years (encompassing the industrial revolution) relative to the concept of sustainability.

11.2 HISTORICAL PERSPECTIVE

The top 100 products (Chenier 1987) from the chemical industry are used to supply basic needs of food, housing, clothing, energy and mobility, and health. The largest volume outputs from the chemical industry have been in response to avoidance of a perpetually malnourished population, as occurred during famines of the late eighteenth century when Malthus published his treatise "An Essay on the Principle of Population" (Trewavas 2002). The work described widespread starvation resulting from "geometric" (exponential) population growth, outstripping the linear growth in capacity of the Earth to provide food. Improvements in agricultural capabilities have subsequently expanded faster than population, however, due in no small part to the Nobel prize–winning innovation of ammonia synthesis early in the twentieth century by Haber and Bosch (Aftalion 2001) for providing a human-made route to fixing atmospheric nitrogen for use by plants as fertilizer, as well as improved processes (direct contact, Frasch mining) for production of sulfuric acid, whose primary use is in the manufacture of phosphate fertilizer (Kent 1992). Thus, production of sulfuric acid, the leading chemical produced globally, can be used to gauge national economic strength (Chenier 1987). A primary role of the chemical industry has thus been to provide manufactured fertilizer so that the planet can sustain the more than sixfold expansion in population that has occurred since Malthus predicted impending disaster (Trewavas 2002), resulting instead in a 10-fold reduction in the amount of land required per capita for food production.

Shelter provides the second primal need, beyond food. The current global housing industry is supported by phenolic resins for plywood, which allows more efficient use of forest resources; insulation products derived from petrochemicals, which improve energy efficiency and reduce the CO_2 footprint; similarly derived plastics and fibers, which provide improved safety, sanitation, and hygiene while providing insulation and performance; as well as concrete and steel to provide lower-footprint, high-density housing (Kent 1992). Clothing performance and wear have been extended via innovation of manufactured fibers such as nylon, while safety and mobility have been facilitated through the production of synthetic styrene–butadiene rubber along with co-ingredients nylon or polyester used in today's tires, replacing the wooden wagon wheel. Thus, fibers and elastomers to meet societal needs for clothing and mobility comprise upward of 10% of global chemicals production (Chenier 1987).

As an example of historical chemical innovation leading to a reduction in footprint, and noting that the industrial revolution itself freed time for recreation, early billiard balls were made of fragile wood or clay, which was subsequently superseded by the more durable elephant ivory, which led to an alarming depletion of elephant populations. This issue led in 1869 to the innovation of celluloid billiard balls, the first plastic (Everton 1986; Kent 1992). Celluloid is, however, made from unstable cellulose nitrate, rumored to have resulted in explosions during play and known to cause combustion during alternative uses, such as in movie-reel film. In the march to continuous improvement in chemical products, both applications have now been replaced by safer and more stable substitutes (phenolic resins for billiards; polycarbonate compact disks or magnetic hard drives for video media), resulting in improved biodiversity via reduced stress on both elephant and human populations.

Glass itself is a chemical product developed as hunter-gatherers sought to bring light into their habitats while retaining heat. More recent chemical industry improvements include use of poly(vinyl butyrate) in safety glass (Kent 1992), or lighter and stronger glass replacements such as Lexan and polycarbonate resins for eyewear. Synthetic fibers (fiberglass) and materials have led to energy efficiency and comfort improvements in homes and automobiles, and the addition of flame retardants has improved consumer safety.

Chemical industry products have long been correlated with growth in the electronics industry, with an ongoing role in insulation materials for electronic devices and wiring. Gutta-percha, a natural latex polymer, was used to insulate the first trans-Atlantic cable (1849), and in gym shoes and golf balls, replacing expensive and short-lived leather balls stuffed with bird feathers. This polymer has now been replaced by more durable and cost-effective petrochemical-based polymer alternatives [e.g., styrene–butadiene block copolymers; poly(vinyl chloride) (PVC)] to reduce costs to consumers and provide the sustainability benefits of longer product lives. Toothbrushes are now available to the general public, following the invention of nylon to replace imported boar's hair brushes (CHS 2000b), resulting in improved general hygiene. Nylon also appears in improved foul-weather gear, in hosiery to replace fiber from silkworms, and in lower-cost and corrosion-resistant thermoplastic parts for automotive applications, among numerous applications.

The first thermoset plastic (following celluloid) was Bakelite phenolic or Novolak resin (developed by Leo Baekeland in 1907–1910), which supported the new age of electricity (radios, light bulb bases, and telephones), now partially replaced by longer-lived, less brittle performance polymers (Kent 1992; CHS 2000a). The plastics revolution has allowed safer and more sustainable indoor lighting, resulting in elimination during the late nineteenth century of whale oil as a prime fuel, thus supplanting a major global industry (whaling) generally considered unsustainable relative to biodiversity of species.

Materials contributions to the emerging age of electronics and electricity have led to reduction in the CO_2 footprint via a reduced need for physical travel as well as improved energy efficiency and enhanced consumer safety. Advances in medicine, drugs, and medical diagnostic equipment via direct or indirect underpinnings from the chemical industry have further increased life span and comfort, as evidenced by the frequent listing of the first antibiotic, penicillin, as one of the top inventions of the twentieth century.

The constant march toward improved performance products delivered at higher chemical yields with fewer by-products, coupled with lower prices to consumers and longer product life, has been a characteristic of the chemical industry. Market dynamics have driven much of the historical innovation. Stakeholder sustainability from earlier eras emphasized providing for the basic needs for food, clothing, and shelter, as well as emerging conveniences in energy, mobility, communications, and social networking.

11.3   INNOVATIONS IN THE AGE OF SUSTAINABILITY

As consumer and societal needs for the developed world matured beyond meeting basic needs of food and shelter, and given growth in the discipline of environmental science, stewardship in health, safety, and the environment has increasingly become a driver for innovation. The following presents some of the more recent trends that have occurred since the environmental movement which began in the 1960's,[2] leading to creation of the U.S. Environmental Protection Agency (EPA) in 1970, and ultimately, in the late 1980s, to the concept of sustainability. Emphasis in sustainability centered around environmental protection and resource depletion in this era, driven by improved understanding of environmental and ecosystem dynamics relative to the social and economic development emphasized by stakeholders from earlier eras.

11.3.1   Green Solvents and Coatings

A recent report (Freedonia 2004) forecasts "green" solvents, whose market penetration was expected to exceed 1 billion pounds in the United States alone in 2005, to capture up to 12% of market capacity by 2010, and comprise 20% of market value. EPA regulations driving the replacement of hydrocarbon and chlorinated solvents have spurred the growth of green solvents derived from alcohols and esters. Propylene glycol derivatives and soybean oil solvents (printing inks) represent the major component chain and fastest growth, respectively.

Similarly, substitution of waterborne polyurethanes in place of alkyd resins dispersed in volatile organic carbon (VOC) solvent is driving the growth for green coatings (87 million pounds annually in 2004, in an otherwise low-growth market) (JCT 2004). The value proposition is avoidance of issues concerning health, safety, and the environment (HSE) and the footprint associated with VOC solvents, while also achieving faster production or drying times and

[2]The beginning of the environmental movement is often attributed to Rachael Carson's *Silent Spring* (Carson 1962) leading to creation of the U.S. Environmental Protection Agency in July 1970 (http://www.epa.gov/epahome/aboutepa.htm).

improved product performance. The chemistry afforded by polyurethanes provides the performance enabler, where, in addition, substitution of aliphatic or polymeric isocyanates is being used to further "green" the value chain.

Conclusion for this case study is that the combination of improved product performance with the economic benefit of faster processing time, augmented by environmental legislation and better HSE performance, has allowed significant market penetration in an otherwise stagnant market. For this example, enhanced sustainability is imparted primarily through improved product performance rather than through a choice of petrochemical versus renewable feedstock, or through the nature of intermediates used (see below).

11.3.2 Refrigerants and Blowing Agents

Although development of commercial refrigerants has improved food storage and led to reduced footprints in food production, refrigerants themselves came under scrutiny in the 1970s for the impact on ozone depletion. Subsequently, the 1987 Montreal protocol to restrict or ban the use of ozone-depleting substances, together with the international response thereafter, has been called one of the most successful examples of international cooperation in solving a global environmental problem (USEPA 2007). The chemical industry participated in the recovery via innovation of new alternatives to the most serious of the chlorofluorocarbon and related compounds (organobromines) implicated in ozone depletion (USEPA 2007). Product substitutions have taken place in uses such as refrigerants, cleaners, propellants, and as blowing agents for production of polystyrene foams, for example. The result has been a global decrease in measured atmospheric concentrations of ozone-depletion agents, and an improvement observed in the stratospheric ozone layer, suggesting recovery by about 2075. In addition, the phase-out has led to a reduction in greenhouse gas emissions of more 8900 million metric tons of carbon equivalent per year, more than 10-fold the annual emissions from U.S. power generation.

Again, success can be attributed to the availability of acceptable replacements, which were rolled out with a consumer value proposition that included improved efficiencies and lower utility costs for air conditioners and appliances, together with legislative mandates requiring international cooperation.

11.3.3 Bioplastics and Biopolymers

Bioplastics represent biodegradable polymers and/or polymers derived from bio-based feedstocks. Use of bio-based feeds can in some cases engender reduced-toxicity intermediates for synthesis of existing polymers (Bray 2008) or be used to formulate new polymers with alternative performance properties (Mohanty et al. 2005; Wolf 2005; Wool and Sun 2005). Compostable or biodegradable polymers may be synthesized from bio-based or petrochemical feedstocks; both fall under the definition "bioplastics." World production of plastics is expected to grow from 160 million metric tons (2003) to 230 million metric tons per year by 2010 (Fuji-Keizai 2007). By contrast, the bioplastics market for Europe in 2007 was only 0.1 million metric tons relative to a total plastics market of 48 million metric tons, or approximately 0.2% of the European market, which is a prime region driving first adoption. Global production of bioplastics was 0.3 million metric tons, or about 0.1% of world plastics production (EBP 2008). In an alternative study from the European Commission (Wolf 2005), the bio-based polymer component of bioplastics in Europe was expected to grow to only 0.5 to 1.0 million metric tons by 2010 (depending on "policy and measures" incentives) out of a total market of 57 million metric tons, representing 1 to 2% of the total from a current base of about 0.1%. Some of the leading candidates comprising 100% biopolymer products include polylactic acid synthesized outside the biological plant from the corresponding bioacid, and polyhydroxyalkanoates, which can be biosynthesized directly from sugars via bacterial fermentations (Wolf 2005; Schut 2008). For other biopolymers, such as bio-derived 1,3-propanediol, comprising one of two intermediates used to produce poly(trimethylene terephthalate), the biocomponent is only a fraction (less than 40%) of the polymer, which otherwise uses petrochemical-derived intermediate terephthalic acid (Wolf 2005). Performance and structure are therefore identical to the existing polymer synthesized 100% from petrochemical intermediates, which is an advantage in market acceptance.

Overall, market penetration has been slow to date for 100% bio-derived polymers. Challenges include the difficulty in certifying and qualifying the performance of new structural polymers. Adaptation of the large, existing capitalization and infrastructure for current polymer production can also be a challenge, where modifications are often needed to produce or process a new polymer. The overall challenge is then to deliver on the fundamental customer value proposition of providing more sustainable products with equivalent or improved performance, supplied to the consumer at equivalent or lower costs (Wolf 2005; Bray 2008). Options also exist to sustain existing product lines via the manufacture of key intermediates from bio-based sources, such as ethylene and aromatics from bioethanol (Schut 2008). Such approaches sidestep the issue of qualification of performance and safety of new polymer products, and leverage the advantage of using either existing or new process routes and facilities, whether bio-based or thermocatalytic, for subsequent conversion of intermediates to desired end products.

11.3.4 Greener Production and Products

Beyond bio-based feeds, new routes and products derived from petrochemicals also provide a pathway to a reduced footprint and improved sustainability performance. Included in this category are petrochemically derived biodegradable plastics, which fall under the category "bioplastics." Process routes to mature products such as nylon are being improved to reduce the footprint.

Despite the attractive performance properties of nylon, atmospheric concentrations of nitrous oxide (N_2O), implicated in both ozone-layer depletion and global warming (Thiemens and Trogler 1991), have been linked to nylon 6,6 production, while the co-product ammonium sulfate, implicated in eutrophication, is produced in large amounts in conventional nylon 6 production. Abatement technologies to capture N_2O, and catalytic routes for production of caprolactam intermediate used for nylon 6, are seeking to reduce the footprint for next-generation manufacturing facilities (McCoy 2000; Hoelderich 2001). Recycle or "down-cycle" reuse options have also been explored, augmented by catalytic processes for depolymerization (Perkins 2007), but hindered by collection costs for reprocessing (Lave et al. 2008). Production substitutions for nylon (e.g., by poly(trimethylene terephthalate) or other polymer blends) offer the potential for footprint reduction at comparable or improved cost and performance.

The footprint required for production or manufacturing of the molecule itself may not be the best gauge of sustainability benefit. For example, the development of surfactant formulations capable of cold water detergency has reduced the demand for water heating and enabled potential CO_2 savings of 0.75% of the total U.S. footprint, or 7% to 9% of Kyoto targets (Sabaliunas et al. 2006) compared to the alternative of using bio-based oleochemicals which do not offer a performance advantage. The underlying chemistry was developed and commercialized as part of an industry partnership, using designer petrochemical-derived molecules (McCoy 2003). As this example shows, the impact of product performance on footprint reduction across the value chain can be more important than the CO_2 footprint associated with the manufacture of the performance-enhancing chemicals themselves.

Similarly, footprint reduction via elimination of phosgene ($COCl_2$) intermediate has been sought in the synthesis of polycarbonates, used in optical lenses or resins, compact disks, and performance polymers. Elimination of isocyanate intermediates for polyurethane synthesis (Szmant 1989) is also a target for green chemistry. Use of organic carbonates such as diphenyl offers the potential to eliminate phosgene in more cost-competitive process technologies for polycarbonate synthesis (Nexant 2006; Shinsuke 2007). The new process routes are capturing a majority of capacity expansion in these high-volume performance polymers. Alkyl isocyanates can also be made from dimethyl- or diphenylcarbonate, again eliminating phosgene from the process. As yet, no aromatic isocyanate is made via a nonphosgene route, although various patents exist.

11.4 SUSTAINABILITY DRIVEN BY INNOVATION AND PERFORMANCE

Although market penetration can be a challenge for new chemical products or processes, there are numerous examples which that show this form of creative destruction is indeed occurring on an ongoing basis. Compliance with environmental regulations, as well as corporate commitments toward sustainability and reduction in footprint [e.g., Responsible Care (www.responsible care.org); Reach (EC 2007)], are driving new processes using new routes and intermediates and producing high-performance products positioned to capture market share for future growth. Meanwhile, novel or improved abatement technologies improve the performance of existing plants, which is an important value proposition for existing assets. The triple-bottom-line synergy between economics, the environment, and social performance is realized via improved material and energy efficiency, as well as intermediates and feedstocks offering lower toxicity and reduced hazards. This synergy drives innovation that indeed captures market share, where sustainability needs can be met without sacrificing consumer demands for cost and performance.

Acknowledgments

Comments and a review by Garo Vaporciyan and Trevor Stephenson at Shell Chemicals are gratefully acknowledged.

REFERENCES

Aftalion, F. 2001. *A History of the International Chemistry Industry*. Philadelphia: Chemical Heritage Press.

Bray, R. L. 2008. *Bio-based Polymers*. Process Economics Program Report 265. Menlo Park, CA: SRI Consulting.

Carson, R. 1962. *Silent Spring*. Boston: Houghton-Mifflin.

Chenier, P. J. 1987. *Survey of Industrial Chemistry*. New York: Wiley.

CHS (Chemical Heritage Society). 2000a. Leo Hendrik Baekeland. Accessed Apr. 19, 2009 at http://www.chemheritage.org/classroom/chemach/plastics/baekeland.html.

———. 2000b. The Nylon Legacy: Life Before Nylon. Accessed Apr. 19, 2009 at http://www.chemheritage.org/EducationalServices/NYLON/legacy/legacy.html.

EBP (European Bioplastics). 2008. Bioplastics: Frequently Asked Questions (FAQs). Accessed at http://www.european-bioplastics.org.

EC (European Commission, Environment Directive General). 2007. Reach in Brief: Why Do We Need Reach? Accessed at http://ec.europa.eu/environment/chemicals/reach/pdf/2007_02_reach_in_brief.pdf.

Everton, C. 1986. *The History of Snooker and Billiards*. London: Partridge Press.

Freedonia. 2004. Solvents: Green & Conventional to 2007—Market Size, Market Share, Market Leaders, Demand Forecast and Sales. Study 1663: Freedonia Group (www.freedoniagroup.com). Cleveland, OH.

Fuji-Keizai. 2007. Major Trends and Issues Facing the Bioplastics Market: U.S. and E.U. Outlook. Accessed Oct. 15 at http://www.fuji-keizai.com.

Goodstein, E. S. 1999. *Economics and the Environment*. Upper Saddle River, NJ: Prentice Hall.

Hoelderich, W. F. 2001. The greening of nylon. *Chem. Innov.*, 31(2):29–40.

JCT. 2004. Polyurethane material use remains steady. *JCT Coatings Technol.*, Feb. 1.

Kent, J. A., Ed. 1992. *Riegal's Handbook of Industrial Chemistry*. New York: Van Nostrand.

Lave, L., and N. Conway-Schempf, J. Harvey, D. Hart, T. Bee, and C. MacCracken. 2008. Recycling postconsumer nylon carpet: a case study of the economics and engineering issues associated with recycling postconsumer goods. *J. Ind. Ecol.*, 2:117–126.

McCoy, M. 2000. Slowly changing how nylon is made. *Chem. Eng. News*, 78(40): 32–34.

———. 2003. Soaps and detergents: Whether for washing clothes or cleaning dishes, new products are increasingly the result of collaborative chemical development. *Chem. Eng. News*, 81(3):15–22.

Mohanty, A. K., M. Misra, and L. T. Drzal. 2005. *Natural Fibers, Biopolymers, and Biocomposites*. Boca Raton, FL: CRC Press.

Nexant. 2006. *Polycarbonate*. PERP 05/06-7. July. San Francisco, CA.

Perkins, S. 2007. Polymer breakdown: reaction offers possible way to recycle nylon. *Sci. News*, July 7.

Sabaliunas, D., C. Pittinger, C. Kessel, and P. Masscheleyn. 2006. Residential energy use and potential conservation through reduced laundering temperatures in the United States and Canada. *Integr. Environ. Assess. Manage.*, 2(2):142–153.

Schumpeter, J. 1975. *Capitalism, Socialism and Democracy*. New York: Harper & Row.

Schut, J. H. 2008. What's ahead for "green" plastics: look for more supply, more varieties, better properties. *Plast Technol.*, Feb. Accessed at http://www.PTOnline.com.

Shinsuke, F. 2007. Green and sustainable chemistry in practice: development and industrialization of a novel process for polycarbonate production from CO_2 without using phosgene. *Polym. J.*, 39(2):91–114.

Szmant, H. H. 1989. *Organic Building Blocks of the Chemical Industry*. New York: Wiley-Interscience.

Thiemens, M. H., and W. C. Trogler. 1991. Nylon production: an unknown source of atmospheric nitrous oxide. *Science*, 251:932–934.

Trewavas, A. 2002. Malthus foiled again and again. *Nature*, 418:668–670.

USEPA (U.S. Environmental Protection Agency). 2007. Achievements in Stratospheric Ozone Protection. EPA-430-R-07-001, April 26. Accessed at http://www.epa.gov/ozone/strathome.html.

———. 2008. The Presidential Green Chemistry Challenge: Award Recipients 1996–2008. 744F08008. Accessed at http://www.epa.gov/greenchemistry.

Wolf, O. E. 2005. *Techno-economic Feasibility of Largescale Production of Bio-based Polymers in Europe*. Technical Report EUR 22103 EN. Brussels, Belgium: European Commission, Joint Research Centre, Institute for Prospective Technological Studies.

Wool, R. P., and X. S. Sun. 2005. *Bio-based Polymers and Composites*. San Diego, CA: Academic Press.

12

IMPLEMENTATION OF SUSTAINABLE STRATEGIES IN SMALL AND MEDIUM-SIZED ENTERPRISES BASED ON THE CONCEPT OF CLEANER PRODUCTION

JOHANNES FRESNER AND JAN SAGE
STENUM GmbH, Graz, Austria

12.1 OVERVIEW

In this chapter we present the following aspects of sustainability as applied to small and medium-sized enterprises (SMEs):

- Appropriate strategies to motivate SMEs to develop a sustainable business approach
- An initial and sustained process of redesigning manufacturing processes with the goal of minimizing waste, emissions, and wastewater generation
- Actual improvements from the application of a sustainable strategy and involvement of key stakeholders (i.e., employees, suppliers, clients) in a SME case study on anodizing aluminum
- Strategy, methods, and learning points from the case for implementation in other companies

Sustainable Development in the Process Industries: Cases and Impact, Edited by Jan Harmsen and Joseph B. Powell
Copyright © 2010 John Wiley & Sons, Inc.

12.2 ACTIVE STRATEGIES FOR SUSTAINABLE MANAGEMENT

The management process determines a company's operations and its organization by allocating appropriate resources and combining them effectively to reach the desired results. Resources can be either human working capacity, or investments in production means, raw materials, and energy. When talking about quality management, we refer to the quality aspects of production; when talking about environmental management, we refer to management of the environmental aspects of a company. The general aim of any management system is to develop a strategy which guarantees that management determines proactively what has to be done in view of legal obligations and efficient use of resources. The next step is to ensure that this is done by applying appropriate processes, raw materials, and energy and by organizing human resources effectively.

If management systems focusing on sustainable business strategies are to be widely accepted among enterprises, they must contribute to increased profitability. This means that by the end of each business year there must be a visible positive effect on the balance sheet either through savings in raw materials and energy, through reduced costs for compliance, financing, and insurance, or through facilitation of internal procedures. In addition, productivity or sales due to a better image of the company and the products should be increased.

An effective way to start the process of including a vision of a sustainable economy in the management system of a company is implementation of the concept of *cleaner production*, which is essentially a low-level environmental management system. The cleaner production approach identifies opportunities to solve emission problems using a preventive approach (Yaacoub, 2006). The overall goal is to minimize waste and emissions and maximize product output. By analyzing the flow of materials and energy in a company, one tries to identify options to minimize waste and emissions out of industrial processes. Improvements in organization and technology help to make the best possible use of materials and energy and to avoid waste, wastewater generation, and gaseous emissions as well as waste heat and noise. Examples of cleaner production options are:

- Documentation of actual consumption
- Use of indicators and control (to identify losses from poor planning, poor education and training, mistakes)
- Substitution of raw materials and auxiliary materials (especially renewable materials and energy)
- Increase in the useful life of auxiliary materials and process liquids (by avoiding drag-in, drag-out, contamination)
- Improved control and automation
- Reuse of waste (internal or external)
- New low-waste processes and technologies

Typical elements of a cleaner production program are:

- The formation of an environmental team
- Input/output analysis providing an overview of the efficiency of the use of material and energy and a classification of waste and emissions
- Material and energy flow analyses to show the reasons for waste and emissions
- Options for improvement: by product changes, good housekeeping measures, changes in raw materials, technological changes, and internal and external recycling
- Feasibility studies to show the environmental and financial benefits of the options
- Implementation of measures and follow-up to analyze the effects of the measures

These elements help to start a process of continuous improvement by providing key tools for monitoring and control of environmental effects, quick improvement, the feeling of success, the stimulation of motivation, and creating a capacity for autonomous problem solving. This approach is then institutionalized into an environmental management system, which is at best integrated with quality management and health and safety issues. The most effective way of involving SMEs especially is apparently not on an individual one-by-one basis but by working with them in small groups, almost in a club-like atmosphere. A model case for such a club is Ecoprofit Graz.[1] A case study will illustrate the potential of this approach and the results that can be expected.

12.3   ELOXIERANSTALT A. HEUBERGER GmbH: SUSTAINABLE MANAGEMENT IN AN ANODIZING PLANT

Eloxieranstalt A. Heuberger GmbH is an anodizing company with 14 employees in Graz, Austria. The company treats the surface of a broad range of aluminum parts by electrolyte generation of a surface film of aluminum oxide. The company specializes in processing orders within a very short time. Initially, some 40,000 m² of aluminum sheet metal, profile, and small parts were treated in the plant annually. Heuberger has participated in the Ecoprofit program of the city of Graz since 1996 (Fresner 2006).

In 1997 Heuberger decided to introduce an environmental management system according to the EMAS scheme of the European Union. As a basis for introduction of the environmental management system, the work done during

[1]The Ecoprofit approach originated in the city of Graz in 1992. Today, it is employed in more than 100 cities in Austria, Germany, Italy, and Hungary as well as in India, Colombia, and Nicaragua. It is explained in more detail in the chapter appendix.

the first year in the Ecoprofit program was used. The management system today includes all aspects of business (quality, health, and safety). Anodizing is a galvanic process in which the surface of aluminum is converted to aluminum oxide, which protects the basic material against corrosion and wear. By grinding and polishing, the surface can be prepared in different decorative qualities prior to anodizing.

The project began with a review using information collected during the cleaner production project as a basis:

- Information on material and energy inputs and outputs as well as options for improvement
- Information on legal compliance
- Information on the organization of the company

From this review, a first working program was drafted, which included:

- Development of a project to guarantee compliance with current Austrian legislation
- Evaluation and written documentation of the working conditions at all workplaces to fulfill the legal requirements
- Definition of procedures for anodization, analysis of process baths, and maintenance
- Definition of responsibilities, corrective measures, and an auditing procedure
- Documentation of the management system

The analysis was carried out by the environmental team, which consists of seven members, representing all areas of the company: the manager, the production foreman, employees in charge of maintenance and packaging, and a secretary. The analysis included benchmarking with other plants and with best available technology. For this process, a consultant provided the necessary information and guidance. The findings were sometimes eye-openers to both operators and management. A variety of simple good housekeeping measures were the primary result, as was the definition of plans for a technical revamp to upgrade the plant to best available technology.

Hazardous waste was reduced to a minimum, used compressor oil being the only remaining hazardous waste. Nonhazardous waste is separated into the categories of paper, metal, plastic, organic waste, and industrial waste. Packaging materials are almost completely reused for the packaging of products. With the most important customers, returnable packaging systems were arranged. The annual quantity of industrial waste amounts to as little as 1500 kg.

Wastewater results primarily from rinsing parts after pickling and anodizing. Longer dripping times were introduced to minimize drag-outs, the amount of process solutions carried from one process bath to the next on the surface of the parts, therefore attending the requirements for rinsing. The racks were changed for the same purpose. Spray rinsing was introduced to increase the rinsing effect. The neutralization plant for treatment of the wastewater will be extended.

Electric energy is used for the anodizing process and for motors and lights. A new electronically controlled rectifier, new lights, and energy-efficient drives were installed where appropriate. Gas is used to heat process baths and during the winter to heat the workshop. Measures to reduce gas consumption included introduction of covers for the baths when they are not in use, and the reduction of heating times before production stopped at night.

The next step was introduction of the elements of the cleaner production program into the daily procedures of the company. The baths are analyzed daily to optimize the quantity of chemicals, and the quantities used are recorded and analyzed. Changes in the resulting indicators are discussed in meetings of the environmental team. The properties of the chemicals were also analyzed. A dialogue with suppliers was initiated to enhance understanding of the processes and to optimize the use of chemicals. Several dyes were changed because less hazardous alternatives were available. During the process of evaluating operators' workplaces, possibilities for accidents were analyzed and documented. Measures for prevention were defined.

The managing director paid particular attention to formulation of a convincing environmental policy. The environmental guidelines are a testimony to the commitment according to which the protection of the environment is an essential part of management, which results in objectives and procedures for everyone in the company. They were accepted very well and the employee feedback was explicitly positive after the procedures had been amended by examples showing how they would affect daily practice.

The environmental policy includes the statement: "We try to minimize the effects of our activities on the environment". This is clarified by a special paragraph to emphasize the point to employees and illustrate its meaning by addressing actual activities in the company: "We know that this is a continuous task consisting of many small steps which have to be implemented continuously. We try to do so, for example, by improving our racks to optimize utilization of the process solutions and to reduce the consumption of water and energy. We try to minimize drag-out by systematically studying dripping and improving our rinsing technology and practice."

Monthly meetings of the environmental team form the backbone of the environmental management system. In the meetings, the following topics are discussed:

- Progress of the environmental program
- Overview of new developments
- Current problems

- Compliance with existing regulations
- Training needs
- Current indicators of consumption of materials and energy
- Ideas for improvement

Documentation of the management system was kept as short as possible. The meetings are documented in minutes, and current problems and remedies are noted in special forms printed on red paper. Additionally, there is an audit form; a form for the control of consumption of water, energy, and chemicals; a form for the documentation of environmental effects; and a form for the environmental program. Checklists were developed for the key variables of the anodizing process, for adoption of orders, and for purchasing. Plans exist for training and maintenance. Each employee was trained in first aid. There is continuous training in the handling of materials and to reduce the use of chemicals.

Despite doubling its production, the company reduced actual water consumption by 50% between 1996 and 1999, a cost reduction of €20,000. Reduction in the specific (surface-related) consumption of chemicals (roughly 10%) bought a cost reduction of €2000, and the reduction of gas consumption (10%) yielded €4000 annually.

Year by year, additional measures were implemented:

- Further reduction in water consumption (closed-cycle cooling plant)
- Elimination of impurities in the dye baths (filtration plant)
- Reduction in energy consumption (reduction of peak loads, good housekeeping)
- Reduction the use of chemicals (improved production planning)

All in all, in 10 years, the following results were achieved:

- Specific water consumption was reduced by 95%.
- Specific consumption of natural gas was reduced by 60%.
- Specific consumption of chemicals was reduced by 35%.
- The error rate was reduced to less than 1%.

The following organizational changes were implemented:

- Teamwork encouraged
- Environmental team assembled (later transformed into the production improvement team)
- Team and individual bonuses granted
- Internal communication increased

- Increased service orientation established (providing product development for clients and doing consulting for clients)
- Controlling system installed (consequent data acquisition, calculation of indicators, plan vs. actual comparison)
- Green procurement strengthened (especially when selecting process chemicals)

The following technical changes were established:

- Improved rinsing by adapting the plant
- Longer dripping time to reduce drag-out of liquid on part surfaces
- Employment of an improved crane to improve dripping
- Adaptation of process schedules and heating
- Installation of a retardation plant[2]
- Installation of an ultrasonic degreasing plant for special parts

The ideas behind these measures were generated out of an intense discussion process by the environmental team members with suppliers and a consultant. Figure 12.1 shows the interrelations among problems, measures, and the

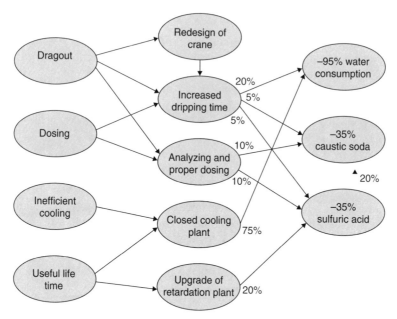

Figure 12.1   Interrelation among problems, measures, and contribution to savings.

[2]A retardation plant contains a resin that holds back metals when an acidic solution is passed through the bed. In this way the metals are extracted from the acid and the acid can be reused.

TABLE 12.1 Involvement and Benefits of Stakeholders

Stakeholder	Form of Involvement and Benefit
Regional government	Transparency, easier access to real data, cooperative problem-solving approach, development of action plans
Neighbors, general public	Transparency, open days, participation of the general manager as a speaker in public events, press articles
Employees	Transparency (indicators), increased communication, team solving approach, inclusion in decision making
Suppliers	Mutual understanding of problems, additional knowhow for supplier and company through plant tests, integration of supplier to process development
Ecoprofit Club	Group of similar-thinking people with similar problems
Clients	Information, training, dialogue regarding product design, eloxal-suitable construction, recycling of aluminum, introduction of reusable packaging

resulting savings. The involvement in the improvement process of company stakeholders is shown in Table 12.1, and input/output balances for 2001 are shown in Table 12.2.

The team formed by the employees and the director was highly motivated. This was shown by active involvement in company meetings as well as by many good and practical ideas. However, some practical problems occurred, which increased the project duration to almost two years.

- The authorities were indecisive regarding procedural questions, due to changes in legislation, so the company was very cautious regarding investments in the wastewater treatment plant.
- The work had to be done after-hours. Although this work was paid for, it reduced the employees' leisure time, a policy only partially accepted.
- Compilation of documentation on the management system should have been done by the team, but this proved to be very time-consuming. As a results, the consultant wrote most of the documentation after discussing the respective topics and procedures with the team members. Consequently, it proved difficult for the internal auditors to check the management system critically during the internal audit.

12.4 ANALYSIS OF THE RESULTS

Sustainable development has three dimensions (Figure 12.2): social, ecological, and economic. The cleaner production project focuses on primarily

TABLE 12.2 Input/Output Tables for Heuberger for 2001

	Input
Energy	
Electricity	210,000 kWh
Natural gas	50,000 m^3
Water	
Well water	17,000 m^3
City water	2500 m^3
Raw materials	
Sulfuric acid	13,000 kg
Caustic soda	12,000 kg
Pickling additive	2400 kg
Sealing additive	1500 L
Dyes	300 kg
Degreaser	300 kg
Organic acids	75 L
Auxiliary materials	
Abrasives	100 kg
Packaging materials	800 kg
Raw material	
Aluminum	65,000 m^2
	Output
Wastewater	18,000 m^3 (does not include evaporation)
Solid waste	
Industrial waste	1500 kg
Aluminum hydroxide	1400 kg
Biogenic waste	500 kg
Aluminum scrap	200 kg
Hazardous waste	
Oils	None
Emissions to air	
Evaporated water	Not recorded
Exhaust gas	500,000 m^3 (calculated)
Product	
Anodized aluminum	65,000 m^2

improvement in the economic and ecological dimensions, and helps to provide a better understanding of the dimensions of sustainable development. The management system will increasingly involve the social dimension within a company. It forms a basis for a clearer understanding of the needs of employees and defines goals by improving training and communication. Communication and problem resolving with the outside are improved by involving suppliers, authorities, neighbors, and customers step by step. The development of products and services according to sustainable criteria will follow as a bold step addressing all three dimensions.

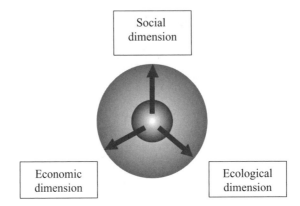

Figure 12.2   The three dimensions of a sustainable development.

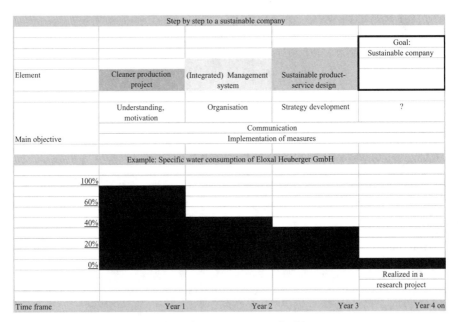

Figure 12.3   Step by step to a sustainable company.

Figure 12.3 shows the steps the company followed in its development, together with the main objectives of this phase and the time frame. Heuberger's development is illustrated using relative specific water consumption as an indicator.

Cleaner production is a strategy to reduce the environmental impact of businesses by systematic application of the principles of prevention. Cleaner production focuses on sources of waste and emissions and on changing organization, raw materials, and process technology along the product life cycle with the clear aim of reducing waste and emissions (Fresner et al. 2007b). Cleaner production projects provide a full understanding of the productive processes, a systematic analysis of waste and emissions, and include evaluation and prioritization. Management becomes more certain of where the problems are and can invest resources to resolve them effectively. Early success and financial savings provide motivation to continue. These principles can be the basis of company strategies. Active research on the roots of problems, continuous improvement, and application of best technology, where appropriate, are key principles in the success for innovative businesses.

Cleaner production tools, such as input/output, material flow, and energy flow analyses, build the basis of an information system that allows industry to determine the efficiency of material and energy flows, and to understand the properties of chemicals used and the effectiveness of measures. This makes them a valuable tool in measuring the actual improvement in environmental performance (Fresner et al. 2007a). Transparency regarding material flows gives a basis for sensitization and the creation of awareness. Training can be more effective with clear priorities and practical examples from the company itself. A cleaner production project will delineate options and measures for improvement in company performance. Such visible changes provide strong motivation to continue the process of improvement.

Within a company's own environment the principles of eco-efficiency, prevention, renewable resources, and participation are explored and solutions are developed. This process is structured and guided by consultants, so very naturally, attention is expanded to the production chain, product life cycle, and societal acceptance and integration.

A cleaner production project will add a strategy of prevention to a company's policy, which can be a powerful guideline for employees in the design of products and processes and during operations. It will provide practical experience, with problem-focused teamwork. Tools for environmental control are created and applied in practice. This guarantees a profound understanding of environmental impacts and ways of resolving them.

Essential factors for implementing an active environmental management system are:

- Commitment of management (top down)
- Committed environmental policy
- An environmental team working as a network in covering all the organization and acting as a multiplier (bottom up)
- Immediate feedback
- Increased room for action and quick change
- Documentation of relevant data
- Information for everybody involved
- Allocation of sufficient resources (especially, time)

The management system ensures consistency and continuity. For practical reasons, existing management system elements should be integrated to avoid parallel developments.

12.5   IMPLEMENTATION OF SUSTAINABLE STRATEGIES

Translating sustainable development into small steps that can be readily understood and implemented is a challenging task. The process can be handled using a stepwise strategy consisting of cleaner production, upgraded technology, integrated management, an informed supply chain, and improved product features. Thus, a learning environment is provided in which companies understand the message of sustainable development and create proprietary solutions. The eco-efficiency approach provides for easy access, as it usually pays to prevent waste and emissions. It is important to include the analysis of technical and organizational systems from the very beginning.

A cleaner production project will help to motivate management, as the results assist in reducing daily cost. It will add a strategy of prevention to a company's policy, which can be a powerful guideline for employees in the design of products and processes, and during operations. It will provide practical experience with problem-focused teamwork.

A management system focusing on teamwork and continuous improvement of quality, environmental aspects, and health and safety provides continuity. The involvement of suppliers, customers, authorities, and neighbors will, step by step, expand the scope of improvement outside the boundaries of the company. The importance of aspects of sustainable development will be recognized, new information channels identified, and information collected and interpreted. New questions will arise. In this process, creative approaches should be stimulated that expand today's system boundaries of in-company optimization. The focus should not be on incremental improvement but on redesign and rethinking of systems to supply services and benefits. Typically, potential win–win solutions for customers, companies, suppliers, neighbors, and the authorities will be demonstrated.

Questions requesting basic research (to understand how consumers perceive benefits and to design innovative sustainable services and of systems for recycling of products or product components while preserving their value) and applied research (design of efficient production systems with the aim of zero emission, zero defects, and elimination of auxiliary materials) are discussed almost naturally as a next step. However, these successful cases would not have been possible without considerable public funding. More research on the perception of benefits of sustainable strategies by consumers and enterprises regarding monetary and ethical categories seems to be necessary.

To set up a really "living" environmental management system, STENUM uses the following approach. The initial review is carried out as a cleaner production project: An environmental team is formed to do the project work within the company. Together with external consultants, the environmental effects are defined on the company level by using input/output analyses and evaluating the materials and emissions. Priority areas are defined and investigated in more detail using material and energy flow analyses. The processes are examined for possible improvement. Options are generated, recorded, and the feasibility is studied. Measures that can be realized immediately are implemented. During this phase a legal compliance audit and an organizational audit are conducted.

This review is followed by the formulation of environmental policy, which must express commitment, address the main environmental effects, and motivate and guide company employees. The policy must be communicated internally. Next, the actual management system is set up. STENUM proposes doing so by using already effective elements. These might be working instructions, process procedures, standard operating procedures, or an existing quality management system. The result should be a consistent, simple, effective system of responsibilities and procedures covering the entire organization, regarding all activities with effects on the environment.

A phase of additional training will follow, concluding with internal, then external auditing. These steps should be regarded as learning steps, in which experiences with the management system are collected and interpreted. The goal must be to make the system leaner, more effective, and more practicable. Company employees, above all the management, should be involved directly in the initial evaluation of the company. Special emphasis should be put on practical aspects of management, leading techniques and communication during training, and introduction of the management system (Fresner and Engelhardt 2001).

Through these steps, management systems with systematic continuous improvement in the use of resources following the principles of prevention will be created. Significant reductions in emissions will result, as well as reduced production costs.

APPENDIX: A SUCCESSFUL REGIONAL CLEANER PRODUCTION PROJECT

In 1991, STENUM initiated a cleaner production project for companies entitled Ecoprofit (German acronym for "ecological project for integrated environmental technology"), which was commissioned by the city of Graz (Fresner et al. 2000). It is the design of Ecoprofit Graz that made this cleaner production program a success:

- Workshops for company representatives (consisting of training units and interactive examples) on the most important environmental topics.
- Individual consulting, which ensures implementation of the cleaner production options identified.

- Continuous exchange of experience between company representatives.
- Cooperation between the Ecoprofit team (STENUM and the Department of Environmental Protection) and Ecoprofit company representatives.
- The Ecoprofit award for environmental performance, given by the city of Graz.

Fifteen years after its establishment, more than 160 companies in Graz from a variety of industrial sectors, both microenterprises with five employees and large companies from the automobile industry with more than 3000 employees, have participated in the Ecoprofit beginner's program. Furthermore, more than 60% of the enterprises have joined the Ecoprofit Club and thus remain in the program and work together for continuous improvement, not only of their environmental performance.

A12.1   Ecoprofit for Beginners

The Ecoprofit program for beginners is made up of three elements: common workshops, individual consulting, and the Ecoprofit award. The workshop program comprises 10 workshops held throughout the year on a variety of topics: the ideas behind sustainable development, input/output analysis, energy analysis, team building, policy, creativity, law and regulations, management of hazardous materials, controlling, waste management, reporting, and preparation for the award. These topics cover the basic elements of an environmental management system but also include many useful tips, such as where to save money by cutting waste, reducing water consumption, and optimizing energy consumption.

The typical structure of a workshop is the following:

- Feedback on the steps taken by company representatives since the last workshop
- Introduction to the new topic
- Interactive learning units with group work and practical examples
- Discussion of home work exercises

Ten to 15 companies generally take part in this project and utilize the opportunities for training (capacity building within companies through the participation of employees), individual consulting, good contacts with authorities, special (environmental) legal consulting through representatives of the department of environmental protection, and the possibility to communicate the company's green image by being presented the Ecoprofit award. Last but not least, they see the advantages of being an active member of the Ecoprofit Club of environmentally proactive companies.

A very good tool for the assessment of an organization's own performance is the use of indicators and comparison with other companies: in other words, *benchmarking*. Consequently, Ecoprofit Club members have decided to define and share information about certain indicators. The objective is to analyze the data relevant to these indicators (including cost data) and compare them with typical data from the relevant literature. Typical indicators that have been worked out for all companies are:

- Water consumption per employee (m^3/employee)
- Electricity consumption per employee (kWh/ employee)
- Costs per electricity consumption (€/kWh)
- Electricity costs per turnover (€/€)
- Nonhazardous waste per employee (kg/employee)
- Disposal costs for nonhazardous waste (€/kg)
- Nonhazardous waste costs per turnover (€/€)
- Heat consumption per area (kWh/m^2).

First, the indicators are an effective means of self-orientation. Companies start asking themselves questions, particularly if their data fall above or below the average. Second, they take a look at the figures of other companies. As they know the other companies to some degree, they will again begin to reflect and ask questions. If the data are not public, information exchange will be carried out face to face. The perceived relevance that comes from using known indicators is much higher in this case.

A12.2 The Ecoprofit Club

The Ecoprofit Club was developed for enterprises that want to continue working together with others on their environmental performance after having finished the beginning year. The design of the program is very similar to that for beginners; there are also workshops held throughout the year (four or five) on new topics or on topics that are treated more intensely. There are individual consulting sessions and close cooperation between the companies and the Ecoprofit team (Fresner 2000b).

In 2006, the companies that received an Ecoprofit award in Graz implemented a total of 454 measures and identified 320 improvement options for their environmental program for 2007. Improvements were made or proposed in the areas of:

- Energy use (27% of the options)
- Raw material use (15%)
- Water use (8%)
- Air pollution (3%)
- Hazardous waste (9%)

- Nonhazardous waste (15%)
- Miscellaneous other categories (23%)

As has been shown in many other cleaner production projects, it turned out that nearly 50% of the improvements were achieved due to organizational changes or better housekeeping practices; technological modification accounted for 24% of the improvements. Approximately half of the improvements had a payback period of less than two years; the payback period for another 23% of the improvements is difficult to estimate or calculate.

In addition to demonstrating impressive results, the cleaner production projects implemented by these companies reflected increased awareness and understanding of cleaner production issues. Although it is very difficult to quantify the results of the training and to establish a direct link with changes in the mindset of production staff toward cleaner production and sustainability, the degree to which the participants changed their way of discussing and thinking within the training program provided an encouraging measure of progress.

A major part of all Ecoprofit measures is implemented by the Club companies, although some of them have been awarded a tenth Ecoprofit prize by the city of Graz. For the project participants, this is clear evidence that the potential to implement cleaner production options is far from exhausted after the first project year. Thus, continuous improvement as also demanded by EMAS or ISO 14001 has become an ongoing part of their company strategies.

Examples of Club workshops during recent years are as follows:

- Energy (analysis with infrared cameras as a perfect tool for cleaner production in the energy area; insulation of buildings, funding, traffic and mobility)
- Laws and regulations (specifics and new regulations: health and safety, new water regulations, permits, IPPC, liability, waste, responsibility)
- Product design and life-cycle analysis (interactive units: evaluation of different suitcase labels; detailed evaluation of different wood chaff-cutters, including disassembling in the workshop)
- Health and safety, storage and transportation
- Motivation of employees
- Environmental management systems
- Environmental controlling
- Membrane technology (ultrafiltration, reverse osmosis, microfiltration, nanofiltration) for water recycling and treatment)
- Networking and cooperation
- Introduction to the use of new media
- Environmental costs (total cost analysis)
- Packaging (biodegradable products and packaging)

A12.3   Ecoprofit Club Networking

The success of the Club is without doubt based on the "living" network which closely connects the participating companies and project actors with each other. Additionally, this network can be seen as an important step toward sustainable development in Graz. The major characteristics of this network include:

- Regular common workshops
- Mutual company working visits
- Informal exchange of information
- Common purchasing and use
- Cooperation and common projects
- Participation in social events

Another major element of the Ecoprofit Club network is the spirit of cooperation among member companies. The company representatives know each other personally (sometimes for as long as five years), meet regularly at the workshops as well as at the social events organized within a project year (e.g., common site visits, bicycle tours, cultural activities). Thus, the Ecoprofit club has a lot of characteristics typical of a network:

- It organizes and reorganizes spontaneously.
- It is based on personal contacts.
- It is a living community based on a manifold communication among all the participants.
- Central coordination is held to a minimum.

A12.4   Ecoprofit Club Sustainability

Sustainability is built into in the Ecoprofit Club, not only because it has been ongoing since 1993 without interruption, but also because more active members are integrated into the network each year. Although the club already implements many network ideas and includes some self-organizing aspects (e.g., the working visits), it is still coordinated by the city of Graz and the STENUM consulting company, which is responsible for the workshop program, individual consulting, review, and preparation for the award. As more companies join the club each year, the financial support of the city of Graz is decreasing as the companies' portion increases (companies pay based on the number of their employees). In the long term, the fact that the club can be self-sustaining will be as unique as the institution of the club itself, and this will also be a decisive step in the direction of sustainable development. Notably, the triangle of participants will be sustained continuously, as it is exactly this form of cooperation that determines the success of the club.

Acknowledgments

The authors would like to thank the following persons: Josef Heuberger of Anodisieranstalt Heuberger GmbH, Karl Niederl of the Environmental Office of the city of Graz, Manfred Rupprecht, former environmental coordinator of the government of Styria, Wilhelm Himmel of the government of Styria, Hans Günther Schwarz and Michael Paula of the Austrian Ministry of Science and Transport, and the STENUM team.

REFERENCES

Fresner, J. 2000. Setting up effective environmental management systems based on the concept of cleaner production: cases from small and medium-sized enterprises. In *ISO 14001 Case Studies and Practical Experiences*, ed. R. Hillary. Geneva, Switzerland: ISO.

———. 2006. Galvanik ohne Abfall: ein unerreichbarer Wunschtraum? *Galvanotechnik*, July, p. 1644.

Fresner, J., and G. Engelhardt. 2001. Experiences with integrated management systems for SME's. *Proceedings of the 7th European Roundtable on Cleaner Production*, Lund, Sweden, May.

Fresner, J., P. Wolf, and M. Galli. 2000. Effective environmental management by cleaner production: experiences from Austria and Hungary. Presented at the Workshop "Efficiency Through Management of Resources: Green Productivity Programs in SMEs," at EXPO 2000, Hannover, Germany, Sept.

Fresner, J., H. Schnitzer, G. Gwehenberger, M. Planasch, C. Brunner, K. Taferner, and J. Mair. 2007a. Practical experiences with the implementation of the concept of zero emissions in the surface treatment industry in Austria. *J. Cleaner Pro.*, 15(13–14): 1228.

Fresner, J., J. Mair, H. Schnitzer, C. Brunner, G. Gwehenberger, and M. Plannasch. 2007b. Practical experiences with reducing industrial use of water and chemicals in the galvanising industry. In *Quantified Eco-Efficiency*, ed. G. Huppers and M. Ishikawa. New York: Springer.

Yaacoub, A., and J. Fresner. 2006. *Half Is Enough: An Introduction to Cleaner Production*. Beirut: Lebanese Cleaner Production Center.

13

SUSTAINABLE CONCEPTS IN METALS RECYCLING AND MINERAL PROCESSING

Nitosh Kumar Brahma

Indian Institute of Technology, Kharagpur, W. Bengal, India; IGE-Badu-Kolkata, India

13.1   OVERVIEW

Microbial engineering has recently begun to pursue the concept of sustainable design conditions in the chemical, biochemical, and bioprocess industries, especially that of hybrid and biocompatible materials development for in situ applications. The measure of sustainability has been characterized on the basis of the recycling potential of natural and hybrid materials. Bioleaching is a process in which microbes are used to separate metallic ores from a matrix of sulfide and iron complexes in an acidic (pH 1 to 2) environment in the absence of carbohydrate and in the presence of CO_2 as the sole source of carbon for the biosynthesis of protein and DNA. In this process, known as *bioenergetics*, e^- and H^+ ionic transport through the cell wall and membrane of a bacterium are used to maintain a pH 7 in the cell cytoplasm for the growth of DNA, compared to a pH of 1 to 2 in bulk solution. *Bioleaching* has recently been used intensively to recover low-grade minerals and metals from sulfide ores dumped or heaped in metal and mining industries. Such metal and mineral sulfide wastes pollute the environment by the formation of H_2SO_4, derived by the reaction of sulfide and bauxite ores. If the process of bioleaching is not used properly, pollution as well as acidity in soil and water for areas surrounding mining and metal industries will be increased. Moreover, the loss of rare elements such as copper

Sustainable Development in the Process Industries: Cases and Impact, Edited by Jan Harmsen and Joseph B. Powell

237

(Cu), gold (Au), silver (Ag), silicate (Si), and uranium (U) can be avoided via recovery of these metals by the process of bioleaching. The bacterium isolated for use in bioleaching belongs to the family Bacillaceae, and is known taxonomically as *Thiobacillus ferrooxidans*. From the nomenclature it is easily understood that the microbes (bacilli) have the potential to oxidize sulfide (S^{2-}) to sulfate $(SO_4)^{2-}$, releasing 8 e^- from the cell, to convert 8 H^+ to water (H_2O) by facilitated electron transport, such as that which occurs in cell membranes and in the bioenergetic pathway NADPH --> NADP --> ADP --> ATP to synthesize DNA and proteins, where the peptides are developed using CO_2 as the sole source of carbon.

In both microbial engineering and biochemical unit operations and their modifications, bioleaching may be used either in continuous, discontinuous, and on semibatch systems. In conventional bioleaching, copper, gold, silver, nickel, cobalt, silicate, and uranium have been extracted. The process can be modified for the synthesis of catalysts, nanoparticles, and nanobiotubes (Sunkura et al. 2003; Brahma 2005). Recently, it has been proposed that by means of bioleaching, nanoparticles of metallic ions can be produced and that bacteria can provide a more biocompatible nature for such nanoparticles and nanotube syntheses than can any other instruments used in chemical and mechanical processes (Brahma 2008). The author Nanoparticles derived in bioleaching or by microbes have given the name *biological nanotubes* or *particles* (BNTs). These nanoparticles would be more biocompatible than metallic complexes of nanocomposites or carbon nanotubes (CNTs) produced chemically. Table 13.1 presents various types of microbes that have been reproduced and characterized to date for use in bioleaching, as well as the unit operations involved, including reactors and other unit operations.

13.2 BIOLEACHING PROCESS DESIGN AND DEVELOPMENT

Mathematical modeling related to bioleaching is based principally on the growth model of *T. ferrooxidans*. The symbol μ, the specific growth rate of microbes, is used in the Monod bacterial growth model, and K_m, the Michaelis and Menten constant $[(k_{-1} + k_2)/k_1]$, is used to estimate the reaction kinetics of bioleaching toward M^+ or M^{2+} separations. Estimation of K_m in bioleaching is difficult compared to classical microbial enzyme kinetics and microbial growth because microbial growth rates in bioleaching are very slow compared to conventional microbial growth in glucose and protein substrates. In bioleaching, microbes take in general 14 days to activate the cell and for their enzyme activities to mature, depending on the size of the particles and removal of sulfide complex from metal ions. For reactor designs, the residence time τ (tau), in hours, corresponding to V_R (the volume of the reactor in liters) and the flow rate $V°$ (in L/h) have been measured, and accordingly, the growth of bacillus was determined to require 14 days. Ultraviolet-visible measurements, ranging from 260 nm for DNA, to 280 nm for protein, to

TABLE 13.1   Types of Microbes and Unit Operations Used in Bioleaching

Microbes	Unit Operational Activities in Bioleaching
1. *Thiobacillus ferrooxidans* 2. *Thiobacillus thiooxidans* 3. *Ferrobacillus ferrooxidans* 4. *Ferrobacillus thiooxidans*	Bacilli 1 to 4 used in CSTR, batch, semibatch, and continuous operations; bacilli 2 to 4 used in different experiments and basic studies of bacilli in acidophilic pheno- and genotypes
Fungal species	Used in series cascade reactors.
Algal species	Specially used in bubble column designs for agitation configurations: (a) jet air sparging; (b) air bubbling from the bottom; (c) stirring with a change of plate (propeller numbers and shape)
Genetically modified adaptive strains	Mainly used in loop BC reactors and their configuration according to the nature of leaching.
Genetically engineered strains and the difficulty in adapting their growth in bioleaching processes	Studied primarily in relation to membrane-based separation technology for concentrating metallic ions from bulk solutions as metallic sulfate ions (dissociate after leaching)
Other biomasses	Electrochemical processes

350–450 nm, were used to determine the change in concentrations of metals. All the steps noted above were applied to follow bacterial growth as a function of residence time and reactor volumes. Process design proceeded first in batch, then in semibatch, and finally, in cascade reactors, connected serially and/or in parallel, for industrial leaching of metals at ppm concentrations in bulk solutions.

Genetically engineered (GE) strains and genetically modified (GM) strains are made in two different ways. In the processing of GM strains (adaptive), genetically mutated strains are used (Mahapatra 1990; Brahma 1992; Brahma 2002; Sunkura et al. 2003; Brahma 2005). In the processing of adaptive GM strains, by increasing the concentration of metallic ions, the strains are allowed to grow the cells systematically and to use them in the process of bioleaching. In a case study (Brahma 1992; Patil 2003), the author has used concentrated copper ($CuSO_4$) solution to adapt *T. ferrooxidans* strains and to utilize them in chalcopyrite ($CuFeS_2$) bioleaching. However, in GE strains, a gene that was found to be important (i.e., rusticyanine, the iron-reducing gene of *T. ferrooxidans*), was studied. These genes exist in the form of a plasmid, which was transformed into *E. coli* K-12, the universally used auxotrophic strain. The basic problem in these systems was to adapt and maintain the growth of an *E. coli* K-12 hybrid strain at acidic pH (1 to 2), leaching various metallic ions.

Therefore, mutants of *T. ferrooxidans* were searched, isolated directly from concentrated copper or other metallic ion–leached solution as activated seeds, and were then used in the process of leaching.

However, for conventional genetically engineered strains, we have used *E. coli* K-12 as an experimental model. The hybrid strains of *E. coli* K-12 were then systematically trained to grow in copper or any highly concentrated metal solution. In searching for plasmids with specific genes of *T. ferrooxidans*, wild-type mutants and antibiotic markers were also searched (Silverman and Lundgren 1959; Brahma 1992, 2001, 2002; Tsuchiya 1978; Sunkura et al. 2003). The difficulties that are commonly observed are associated with the cell-wall functions of *T. ferrooxidans* at acidic pH. The reason is that the cell-wall and membrane properties of the microbes found responsible for bioleaching were involved primarily in electron transport mechanisms in the form of oxidoreductase–cytochrome, similar to mechanisms of sulfide and iron conversions in the form of $S^{2-} + 8e^- \rightarrow SO_4^{2-}$, whereas

$$Fe^{2+} \rightarrow Fe^{3+} + e^-$$

and

$$2H^+ + 2e^- + \frac{1}{2}O_2 \rightarrow H_2O$$

are used for water formation. These transfers of slip genes are not properly modified in acidic environments with hybrid *E. coli* K-12, and not with bacilli, so further attempts has been made to isolate GE bacilli and fungi or algae.

E. coli K-12 is involved basically in conversions, transformations, and growth in organic substrates and not in the inorganic transformations of toxic metal ions or substrates which are involved in bioleaching. Figure 13.1 represents the schematic pathways of membrane electron transport in the form of facilitated transport. The mechanisms of oxidation and reduction of Fe^{2+} and Fe^{3+} in the presence of cytochrome and oxidoreductase enzymes as developed on the surface of the membrane, especially in the case of *Thiobacillus*, were found to be involved in electron transport. They are characterized by the schematic pathways shown in Figure 13.1, which also shows the relations of Fe^{2+} and Fe^{3+} in the process of electron transport through a membrane. The steps that may be required for oxidation and reduction of Fe^{2+} and Fe^{3+} ions include (Iyanagi and Mason 1973; Hutchins et al. 1988; Appia-Ayme et al. 1999; Patil 2003):

1. Support for the bioenergetics of *Thiobacillus*, namely formation of the sequence ATP --> ADP --> and NADPH --> liberation of H^+ in the form of $NADP^- + H^+$
2. Conversion of S^{2-} to SO_4^{2-} and formation of $Fe(OH)_3 \cdot H_2SO_4$
3. Formation of water and oxygen inside the cell and the metabolic activities of the cell at pH 1 to 2, to reduce the pressures of the electron motive

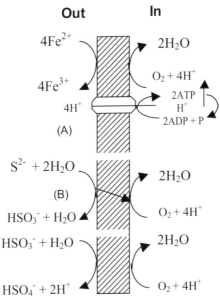

Figure 13.1 Outer membrane of *Thiobacillus ferrooxidans*, showing clearly the neutralization process, the maintenance of pH 7 in the cytoplasm of *T. ferrooxidans*, pumping proton H^+ transport from the cell through the membrane, and reactions with electrons (e^-) that result in formation of sulfate from sulfide during bioleaching and by formation of H_2O in the sequence DNA --> RNA --> protein of *T. ferrooxidans*.

force (e^-) on the H^+ ions that are generated during the process of leaching in the presence of CO_2, the latter serving as the sole carbon source in a chemolithotrophic, obligatory environment

13.3   BIOLEACHING REACTOR DESIGN: APPLICABILITY OF THE CORE PARTICLE MODEL

Design of a bioleaching reactor using the core particle model requires (Pogliani et al. 1990; Niemelä et al. 1994; Porro et al. 1997; Rawlings 1997; Cancho et al. 2007) knowledge of the exact parameter of cell growths. The model has been used for the estimation of chalcopyrite ($CuFeS_2$). Figure 13.2 shows a typical reactor model with sparging capacity. The reactor design requires the measurement of average particle sizes, which change during bioleaching, to estimate the required mathematical relations. Growth rate is described by

$$\mu = \mu_{max}\frac{C_s}{K_s + C_s} \tag{1}$$

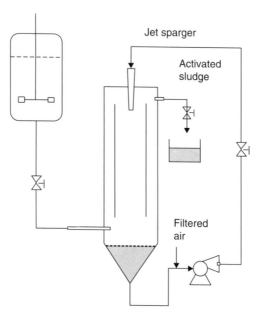

Figure 13.2 Semibatch air-jet (sparge) reactor in bioleaching of chalcopyrite. Oxidoreductase chemolithotrophic activities of *T. ferrooxidans*, considered to be enhanced due to an increase in the residence time by reverse fluidization, and sufficient mixing. The method will also provide a reduction in the number of reactors, which need to be optimized by particle size and types of metals, minerals and microbes (bacterial, fungi, or algae) involved in the process. (From Brahma 2002, 2005.)

where μ is the specific growth rate, μ_{max} the maximum growth rate at infinite supply of nutrient, C_s the concentration of limiting nutrient, and K_s is a constant (van't Reit and Tramper 1991).

Instead of using multiple stages of stirred reactors, a jet-sparged column reactor (Figure 13.2) would be useful for generating activated microbes in bulk solutions, leached at pH 1 to 2. The process parameter in this case can be manipulated, using CO_2 and O_2 mixtures, sparged to the bulk leaching solution from the top (Figure 13.2). In this method, the lag-phase growth of *T. ferrooxidans* could be manipulated and could be reduced, activating the growing bacterial seed in a semibatch continuous-CO_2-sparged loop bioreactor. Due to increasing turbulence in the case of sparging from the top of the loop reactor, the dissolution of particles of chalcopyrite is also enhanced. For experimental design at pH 1 to 2, artificial 9K Lundgren media (Silverman 1959) were used to dissolve chalcopyrites. For extraction or separation of diluted copper solution at ppm levels in the leached bulk solution, Fe metal chips, membrane-based separation technology and liquid surfactant membranes (LSMs) can also be used. LSMs could be deployed in a bubble column to bind metallic M^{2+} ions on the hydrophilic-tail side surface, with immobilization of entire cells via an organic solvent for the head part of the

TABLE 13.2   Postulated Input and Output Data for Bioleaching with 100 Tons/Day of Feed Containing Chalcopyrite Ore

Feed Materials Present	In Reaction Froth Flotation	Final Pulp Density[a]	Stoichiometric Calculation of Air, CO_2, and Fe Reacted[b]
Cu: 1000.00 kg Fe: 571.43 kg S: 875.14 kg Gangue material (silicate calcinate + aluminum): 428.57 kg Total: 2857.15 kg Material in feed = 11,430 kg/day	Cu, 35%; Fe, 20%; S, 30%; gangue material, 15% Material underflow = 792.85 kg/ day × 100/95 = 834.58 kg/ day Material overflow = 11,430 − 834.58 = 10,595.4 kg/day	Water to be added = 2857.15 × 80/20 = 11,428.60 kg/day	Copper production = 63.546/159.5) × 2112.78 = 841.74 kg/day

[a]Feed is considered 20%.
[b]Total solid materials in outlet = 792.85 kg/day.

TABLE 13.3   Postulated Tank Volume and Height, Cell Growth, and Energy Requirements for One Reactor

Energy Requirement for Ingot Making	Cell Growth in the Presence of Iron	Power Requirement	Volume and Height of Each Tank
$mC_p\Delta T$ + latent heat of fusion: 134.8 kcal/day	$\mu = \mu_{max} \cdot [Fe^{2+}]/ (K_{Fe^{2+}} + [Fe_{2+}])$ $= 1.1 \times 10^{-3}$ g/cm^3	61.75 kW	41 m^3 and 4.0 m; connected serially

LSM. All the unit operations and processes noted above are discussed elsewhere. Using this approach, design of a 100-metric ton/day bioleaching process for feed containing chacopyrite ore is postulated in Table 13.2. Tank volume and height, cell growth, and energy requirements are specified in Table 13.3.

13.4   INDUSTRIAL APPLICATIONS

The Regional Research Laboratory (RRL), Bhubaneswar, Orissa, India, is intensively involved in designing a variety of pilot plants for bioleaching

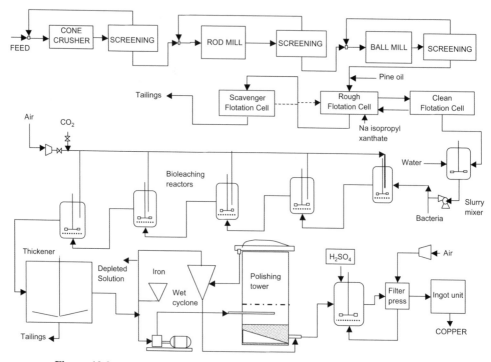

Figure 13.3 Process design of bioleaching of nickel and copper sulfide ores.

(Ritcey and Ashbrook 1984; Pogliani et al. 1990; Aldrich and van Deventer 1993; Porro et al. 1997; Rawlings 1997; Schnell 1997; Rawlings et al. 1999; Rossi 1999; Biswal 2003; Brahma 2009; Katr et al. 2003; Mohanty et al. 2003; Narayana et al. 2003). The research group of Misra, Sukla, and Mohanty is attempting to design and develop methods for isolating silicate and nickel from sulfide iron ores. They are using different sources of iron-based ores to separate Ni, since Fe^{3+} and Fe^{2+} are used by the microbes to activate a carbon source from CO_2 for metabolic and growth activities (Hutchins et al. 1988; Pogliani et al. 1990; Niemelä et al. 1994; Brahma 2002; Patil 2003; Cancho et al. 2007). Serial cascade and parallel reactors (Figure 13.3) are used for industrial applications. The main objective is to develop and sustain the growth of *A. ferrooxidans* microbes (14-day growth). The main objective of the pilot process is for use in a continuous mode to establish the durability of using activated cells in bioleaching, and finally, to displace the Fe^{3+} hydroxide clay used in civil or commercial applications. The temperature effects of bioleaching are also important when large-scale production in situ is considered (Pogliani et al. 1990). However, microbial leaching is basically dependent on GM and GE microbes adapted for mineral metal leaching in acidic environments (Ritcey and Ashbrook 1984; Bastin and Dochain 1990; Venkatachalam 2003). Continuous reactors (Mahapatra 1990; Niemelä et al. 1994; Cancho et al. 2007), shown in Figure 13.3, represent one potentially effective design to validate industrial leaching potential. The author developed the concept during 1990 at the Indian Institute of Technology, Kharagpur, India (Mahapatra 1990; Brahma 1992; Patil 2003). Cascade serial reactors will support the fundamental adaptive control of leachable strains belonging to an acidophilus genus in the family Bacillaceae. The system will ensure applications of bioleaching for adaptive control of fungi and other microorganisms, adapted by means of GM, at high concentrations of iron, copper, and other mineral ores (Bastin 1990). Electrochemical precipitations, flotation, and ultrasonication may also be deployed to break the core shell of sulfide dissociate particles and to extract leachable metals such as Cu^{2+}, Au^+, Ag^+, and Ni^+ (Ritcey and Ashbrook 1984; Bastin and Dochain 1990; Rawlings et al. 1999; Rossi 1999; Venkatachalam 2003).

13.5   CONCLUSIONS

The contamination of soil due to environmental pollution will perhaps be the biggest challenge for industrial sustainability and ecological balance in this millennium. Chalcopyrite recovery with the proposed bioleaching process shown in Figure 13.1 includes cascade bioreactors such as CSTRs or bubble columns (Silverman and Lundgren 1959; Tsuchiya 1978; Mahapatra 1990; Brahma 1992, 2001, 2002; Sunkura et al. 2003). The process concept may be useful for large-scale industrial leaching. The cell-wall labile protein (a rusticyanine or cytochrome similar surface) grows mainly in the absence of carbohydrate in CO_2-saturated broth, to provide a solution for leaching of $FeSO_4$ and $CuSO_4$, and represents a new type of biochemical reaction through which the real solution and recovery of minerals occurs by means of bioleaching or as bioremediation (Iyanagi and Mason 1973; Appia-Ayme et al. 1999). The understanding of bioenergetics in the absence of carbohydrates but in the presence of CO_2 at an acidic pH 1 to 2 requires multiple studies with various metal leaching approaches and the use of microbes with eukaryotic and prokaryotic origins. A proper understanding of molecular biology applicable in both the genetic engineering of microbes and in reactor design would be essential, including thorough work on the molecular biology of *T. ferrooxidans*, fungi, and algae groups. For sustainable design in the field of metal and mineral handling, bioleaching and bioremediation would be essential first steps, followed by enrichment or enhancement of reactor designs for recovering industrial metals and minerals from low-grade pollutants or wastes. The method would be recognized as a measure of pollution control (Sunkura et al. 2003). Problems of biochemical reactions with *T. ferrooxidans* are to be incorporated into the bioenergetics of *Thiobacillus* at pH 1 to 2. Moreover, bioleaching may also provide a compatible environment for the generation of nanowires and nanoparticles (Sunkura et al. 2003; Brahma 2005).

REFERENCES

Aldrich, C., and J. S. J. van Deventer. 1993. The use of neural nets to detect systematic errors in process systems. *Int. J. Miner. Process.* 39(3–4):173.

Appia-Ayme, C., N. Guiliani, J. Ratouchniak, and V. Bonnefoy. 1999. Rusticyanine, a high molecular weight cytochrome *c*, the cytochrome *c4* (c552) and a cytochrome *c* oxidase genes are organized in a polycistronic unit. *Appl. Environ. Microbiol.* 65:4781–4787.

Bastin, G., and D. Dochain, 1990. *On-line Estimation and Adaptive Control of Bioreactors.* Amsterdam: Elsevier.

Biswal, S. K. 2003. Flotation column: a novel technique in mineral processing. In *Minerals Processing and Engineering*, ed. V. N. Mishra, G. S. Yadav, and K. S. Rao. Kolkata, India: Indian Institute of Chemical Engineers.

Brahma, N. K. 1992. The utilization of low concentration of urea in bioleaching of chalcopyrites. *J. Ind. Chem. Eng.* 32(3):22–29.

————. 2001. Microbial control of environmental pollution. In *Environmental Pollution and Management of Wastewater by Microbial Techniques*, ed. G. R. Pathade and P. K. Goel. Jaipur, India: ABD Publishers.

————. 2002. The importance of bioleaching in mineral processing, specially copper (Cu), gold (Au), uranium (U) and other chalcopyrite similar ores. In *Mineral Biotechnology*, ed. L. B. Sukla and V. N. Misra. New Delhi, India: Allied Publishers.

————. 2005. Large scale production of bionanotube organometallic composite thin film. In *Chemcon 2005*, New Delhi, India.

————. 2008. Bioleaching and nano-particle: a breakthrough concept to develop nano-clay and recovering biocompatible (ferro)-nano elements. *Chemcon 2008*.

————. 2009. *Design and Use of Microbial Technology.* New Delhi, India: Lakkshmi.

Cancho, L., M. L. Blázquez, A. Ballester, F. González, and J. A. Muñoz. 2007. Bioleaching of a chalcopyrite concentrate with moderate thermophilic microorganisms in a continuous reactor system. *Hydrometallurgy*, 87(3–4):100.

Hutchins, S. R., J. A. Bierley, and C. L. Bierley. 1988. Microbial pretreatment of refractory sulfide and carbonaceous ores improves the economics of gold recovery. *Mining Eng.*, 40:249–254.

Iyanagi, T., and H. S. Mason. 1973. Some properties of hepatic reduced nicotinamide adenine dinucleotide phosphate–cytochrome *c* reductase. *Biochemistry*, 12(12): 2297–2308.

Katr, R. N., L. B. Sukla, and V. N. Misra. 2003. Perspectives of mineral biotechnology. In *Minerals Processing and Engineering*, ed. V. N. Mishra, G. S. Yadav, and K. S. Rao. Kolkata, India: Indian Institute of Chemical Engineers.

Mahapatra, S. C. 1990. The production of copper from low grade sulphide-ores by bacterial leaching. B.Tech. thesis, IIT, Kharagpur, India.

Mohanty, G. N., S. K. Biswal, S. R. Reddy, P. Vibhuti, and N. Misra, Eds. 2003. *Role of Chemical Engineering in Processing of Minerals and Materials.* New Delhi, India: Allied Publishers.

Narayana, K. L., K. M. Swamy, and V. N. Misra. 2003. In *Minerals Processing and Engineering*, ed. V. N. Mishra, G. S. Yadav, and K. S. Rao. Kolkata, India: Indian Institute of Chemical Engineers.

Niemelä, S., C. Sivelä, T. Luoma, and O. H. Tuovinen. 1994. Maximum temperature limits for acidophilic, mesophilic bacteria in biological leaching systems. *Appl. Environ. Microbiol.*, 60:3444–3446.

Patil, S. K. 2003. Reactor design and process evaluation of bioleaching of chalcopyrite waste water treatments. B. Tech. project, Pune Vishkarma Institute of Technology.

Pogliani, C., G. Curutchet, E. Donati, and P. H. Tedesco. 1990. A need for direct contact with particle surfaces in the bacterial oxidation of covellite in the absence of a chemical lixiviant. *Biotechnol. Lett.*, 12:515–518.

Porro, S., S. Ramírez, C. Reche, G. Curutchet, S. Alonso-Romanowski, and E. Donati. 1997. Bacterial attachment: its role in bioleaching processes. *Process Biochem.*, 32(7):573.

Rawlings, D. E, Ed. 1997. *Biomining: Theory, Microbes and Industrial Processes.* Berlin: Springer-Verlag.

Rawlings, D. E., N. J. Coram, M. N. Gardner, and S. M. Deane. 1999. *Thiobacillus caldus* and *Leptospirillum ferrooxidans* are widely distributed in continuous flow biooxidation tanks used to treat a variety of metal containing ores and concentrates. In *Biohydrometallurgy and the Environment Toward the Mining of the 21st Century*, ed. R. Amils and A. Ballester. Amsterdam: Elsevier.

Ritcey, G. M., and A. W. Ashbrook. 1984. *Solvent Extraction: Principles and Applications to Process Metallurgy*, Part I. Amsterdam: Elsevier.

Rossi, G. 1999. The design of bioreactors. In *Biohydrometallurgy and the Environment Toward the Mining of the 21st Century*, ed. R. Amils and A. Ballester. Amsterdam: Elsevier.

Schnell, H. A. 1997. Bioleaching of copper. In *Biomining: Theory, Microbes and Industrial Processes*, ed. D. E. Rawlings. Berlin: Springer-Verlag.

Silverman, M. P., and D. G. Lundgren. 1959. Studies on the chemoautotrophic iron bacterium *Ferrobacillus ferrooxidans. J. Bacterio.*, 77:642–647.

Sunkura, M. K., S. Vddiraju, and G. Bhima Sasetti. 2003. Bulk synthesis strategies for inorganic nanowires and nanotubes. In *Role of Chemical Engineering in Processing of Minerals and Materials, Chemcon 2003*, ed. G. N. Mohanty, S. K. Biswal, S. R. Reddy, P. Vibhuti, and N. Misra, New Delhi, India: Allied Publishers.

Tsuchiya, H. M. 1978. Microbial leaching of Cu–Ni sulfide concentrate. In *Metallurgical Applications of Bacterial Leaching and Related Microbiological Phenomena*, ed. L. E. Murr, A. E. Torma, and J. A. Brierley. New York: Academic Press.

van't Reit, K., and J. Tramper. 1991. *Basic Bioreactor Design.* Boca Raton, FL: CRC Press.

Venkatachalam, S. 2003. Electro flotation and its applications. In *Minerals Processing and Engineering*, ed. V. N. Mishra, G. S. Yadav, and K. S. Rao. Kolkata, India: Indian Institute of Chemical Engineers.

14

INDUSTRIAL ECOSYSTEM PRINCIPLES IN INDUSTRIAL SYMBIOSIS: BY-PRODUCT SYNERGY

QINGZHONG WU

Environmental Technology Center, The Dow Chemical Company, Plaquemine, Louisiana

14.1 INTRODUCTION

14.1.1 Industrial Ecology

To quote from a recent Gordon Research Conference dedicated to this theme, "the multidisciplinary field of Industrial Ecology" has "its roots in the idea that biological systems can provide models for the design and functioning of industrial systems by using the wastes from one process as useful inputs to another." Evolution of the discipline requires "a deepened understanding of environmental challenges and how they can be addressed" (Duchin and Lifset 2008). In another view, industrial ecology asks us to "understand how the industrial system works, how it is regulated, and its interaction with the biosphere; then, on the basis of what we know about ecosystems, to determine how it could be restructured to make it compatible with the way natural ecosystems function."

Industrial ecology "provides a powerful prism through which to examine the impact of industry and technology and associated changes in society and the economy on the biophysical environment. It examines local, regional and global uses and flows of materials and energy in products, processes, industrial sectors and economies and focuses on the potential role of industry in reducing environmental burdens throughout the product life cycle" (ISIE 2008).

14.1.2 Definition and Principles of an Industrial Ecosystem

The discipline *industrial ecology* uses a systematic and holistic approach to scrutinize and examine both industries and the ecosystems on which they rely for resource extraction and emission depository. The industrial ecosystem can thus be defined as *local/regional systems under industrial ecology study where multiple industrial entities are actively involved* (derived from Korhonen and Snäkin 2005). For an industrial ecosystem to be sustainable, there are several principles that must be followed to govern, regulate, and guide various industrial activities: roundput, diversity, locality, gradual change, and cooperation. As explained by Korhonen (2007), *roundput* refers to recycling of materials, cascading of energy, and sustainable use of renewables; *diversity* denotes involvement of many different systems components and actors; *locality* is a spatial scale of the system, meaning local product cycles, and actors taking part are local; and *cooperation* means a symbiotic and cooperative relationship between the actors or system components. The principle of *gradual change* can be understood as "gradual development of the system diversity" (Korhonen 2001).

14.2 RELATIONSHIP BETWEEN INDUSTRIAL SYMBIOSIS AND SUSTAINABLE DEVELOPMENT

Industrial symbiosis, or *by-product synergy* (BPS) as it is called by some researchers and practitioners, is a cooperative systematic approach to achieving synergy among diversified industries to match generators of secondary materials (co-product, by-product, and even "waste") with potential users. The ultimate results are mutual economic benefits and reduction of the total environmental footprints, including but not limited to energy savings, global warming potential reduction, and natural resources conservation.

If we put industrial symbiosis or by-product synergy in the larger context of sustainable development for the entire planet, we can realize that it contributes to sustainable development through dematerialization and substitution to meet two of the four conditions that enable the status of sustainability: (1) Nature is not subject to systematic increase in concentrations of substances extracted from the Earth's crust, and (2) nature is not subject to systematic increase of concentrations of substances produced by society. A strategic sustainable development model, four conditions to meet the status of sustainability (Robèrt et al. 2002), and how industrial symbiosis helps sustainable development are all illustrated in Figure 14.1.

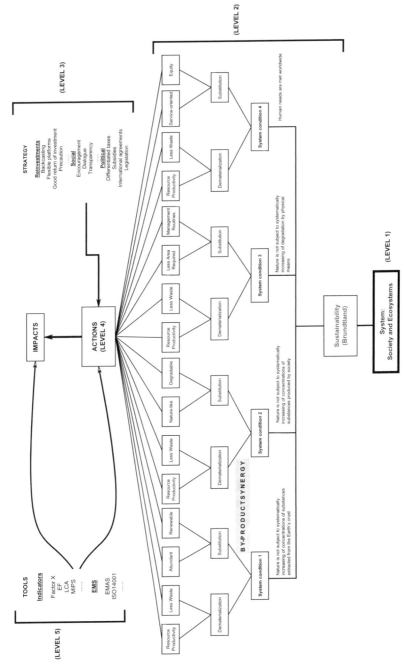

Figure 14.1 Strategic sustainable development model. (Adapted from Robèrt et al. 2002, with permission.)

14.3 CHALLENGES, BARRIERS, AND COUNTERMEASURES IN EXPLORATION, EVALUATION, AND IMPLEMENTATION OF INDUSTRIAL SYMBIOSIS

Dow Chemical is at the forefront of by-product synergy (BPS) research and practice, which is a growing success within the company. Based on Dow's experience and learning, for by-product synergy to succeed, it is suggested that efforts should focus on (1) following the principles of locality, diversity, and gradual change, (2) trying to cultivate a cultural change, and (3) realizing the challenges and barriers constantly and conscientiously and working out countermeasures to address the challenges and remove the barriers (Wu 2008).

By-product synergy does not come automatically. For successful identification and implementation of industrial symbiosis, two factors are indispensable: the system factor and the people factor. The *system factor* calls for the social environment, economic situation, and physical layout of the industries involved; the *people factor* entails education, experience, expertise, value system, and mindset. For the people factor, the researcher or practitioner of industrial symbiosis, as well as the players involved, need to realize the challenges and barriers and work out countermeasures to address or remove the barriers. Only through this effort can an opportunity be turned into reality. Generally speaking, the system factor determines whether a potential for by-product synergy exists; the people factors turn the potential into reality. The challenges and barriers in industrial symbiosis can be categorized as follows (Wu et al. 2005; Wu 2008):

- Cultural
  - Greedy (over product) and throwaway (after product use) consumption culture
  - "Out of sight, out of mind" culture or mindset toward environmental problems
  - Secondary materials not regarded as potential alternatives to raw materials but considered as wastes that do not deserve our efforts—just dispose of them!
- Economic
  - Unfair economic structure across different geographic locations and among different industrial segments
  - Unfair cost structure on waste management
- Legal and regulatory
  - Legal barriers between companies, preventing effective and efficient information exchange
  - Legal barriers imposed by government that deter waste reuse, recycle, and recovery
  - Regulations that do not meet the needs of resource conservation and environmental protection

- Technical
  - Current product manufacturing technologies that generate "wastes" not amenable for by-product synergy
  - Insufficient technology capability on the user side to employ secondary material beneficially

Realizing the challenges and barriers is very instrumental in working out corresponding countermeasures to address the challenges and/or remove the barriers. This requires examination of both the system and people factors. Generally speaking, if the challenges and barriers for a particular synergy are systematic, there is a need to take an evolutionary rather than a revolutionary approach to changing the current system or planning a new system; if the challenges and barriers are due to people factors, it is easier to address than the system factor.

14.4 WHAT BY-PRODUCT SYNERGY IS AND IS NOT

By-product synergy is about:

- Exploration of alternative raw materials or products from secondary materials (in contrast to the traditional virgin raw materials or products)
- Cooperation between secondary materials generators and potential users
- Research to solve technological, environmental, and commercial issues that prevent BPS from happening
- Finding new ways of dematerialization and substitution to achieve sustainable development

By-product synergy is not:

- A sales activity to get rid of waste
- A one-way street from secondary material generator to end user
- Something that the entire society is going to adopt over night, but gradually will adopt
- A cure-all to solve the environmental problems that we human beings are facing today—which requires other approaches, such as technology innovation, fair and just political and economic policy frame, rational (more sustainable) consumption modes, and social mindset change

It must be pointed out that industrial symbiosis is also about business—all parties involved need to benefit economically. The economic viability for each party in the by-product synergy project needs to be evaluated under both the current economic situation and conditions in the future, when economics may not favor some of the players in the by-product synergy project. One approach to consider in evaluating the long-term feasibility of by-product synergy is to decouple economics from the environmental footprint and conduct environmental life-cycle assessment (LCA). If the LCA results indicate a net reduction in the environmental footprint, and if the economic evaluation favors every party, this synergy is probably going to sustain a long-term benefit (until the next generation of technology emerges that changes some of the data used for LCA, in which case the previous LCA needs to be reexamined and updated). Even if the current economic evaluation does not favor all parties, while LCA indicates a net reduction in the environmental footprint, the synergy is still feasible and may become reality in the future.

14.5   WORK PROCESS AND SUCCESSFUL CASES OF INDUSTRIAL SYMBIOSIS

The Dow Chemical Company is actively engaged in by-product synergy and has begun to see the benefits: with accomplishments, experiences, lessons, and a clear path forward. Some of the principles derived from industrial ecology have been followed in its practice of by-product synergy: locality, diversity, and gradual change. Because of the company's long-term sustained efforts in pollution prevention, waste minimization, and site integration (both within one site and across sites), most of our current successful BPS projects are between Dow and outside collaborating companies or agencies.

Dow's vision for BPS is to be a strong enabler to achieve Dow's 2015 environmental health and safety sustainable development goals and even beyond. Dow's BPS mission is to help evolve a complete culture change across the company on waste management practices by constantly challenging the practice status quo:

- What if BPS is perceived as business opportunities rather than just cost reduction?
- What if we began to speak in terms of 100% product instead of zero waste?
- What if every gram of raw material became product?
- What if our so-called "wastes" weren't wastes at all but raw materials for other industries?

Through Dow's continuous efforts in studying and practicing by-product synergy, a work process has been designed that has proved to be instrumental in guiding BPS activities. A simplified version of the work process is shown in Figure 14.2. As stated in Section 14.4, industrial symbiosis is good not only for the environment but also for business and should greatly drive business value. As an example, Figure 14.3 indicates the value delivery of by-product synergy

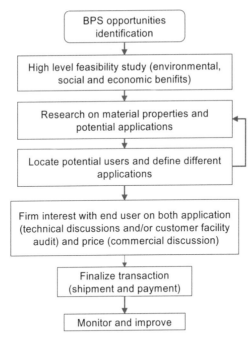

Figure 14.2 Simplified version of the by-product synergy work process of the Dow Chemical Company.

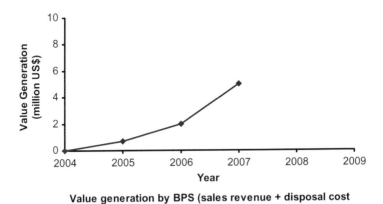

Figure 14.3 Demonstrated results through BPS activities (indicative of the results led by the Dow Environmental Technology Center, in the United States alone).

(indicative of the results lead by Dow Environmental Technology Center in the United States alone).

14.5.1 Synergy Between the Chemical and Water Industries and the Local Community

A case study of by-product synergy among the triad of chemical industry, water industry, and the local community, is described as follows:

- *Secondary material name:* municipal wastewater
- *Secondary material generator:* community (with a population of around 55,000) in Terneuzen, the Netherlands
- *Secondary material quantity:* around 3,000,000 m³/yr
- *Secondary material end user:* Dow's integrated R&D and production site at Terneuzen
- *Results of by-product synergy*
  - From 2007 onward, the municipal wastewater treatment plant effluent that was previously discharged into the sea (Western Scheldt) is now reclaimed and reused by a chemical plant.
  - Dow's integrated R&D and production site at Terneuzen won the European Responsible Care Award in 2007 for innovative industrial reuse of municipal wastewater.

This is an example of how a by-product synergy that is driven by system factors gradually evolves and is ultimately turned into reality by innovative strategic planning, investigation, research, and a public–private partnership. Figure 14.4 illustrates the key players involved and their respective roles in this industrial symbiosis. The characteristics of the symbiosis are detailed below.

Evolution   In the mid-1990s, Dow Benelux enlarged its production capacity at the Terneuzen site significantly. This production expansion required corresponding expansion of the site's water facilities. Given the fact that the region of Zeeuws-Vlaanderen in the Netherlands, where the Dow Terneuzen site is located, is structurally short of fresh water, Dow's higher water demand made it necessary to review the water supply in the entire region. Therefore, Dow and Evides, Terneuzen's local water purifier, joined their efforts to sustainably control the regional water balance. Improving water efficiency by reducing reliance on the increasingly scarce fresh water has been a long-standing priority for the Dow site. Working closely with Dow, Evides Industriewater conducted several studies to evaluate various water sources besides water conservation (water reuse and recycling) practices at the site. In 2000, these studies resulted in the construction of water treatment facilities producing various types of water from six different water sources. The

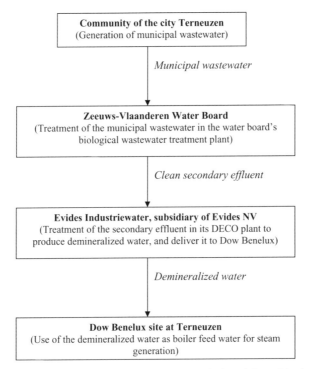

Figure 14.4 Key players and their respective roles in industrial symbiosis of municipal wastewater reuse by the chemical industry.

water sources for the production of demineralized water included seawater, effluent from the municipal wastewater treatment plant, river water from the river Maas (Biesbosch water), and sweet surface water from Belgium. From 2007 onward the seawater source was abandoned and the Evides' Integrated Membrane System plant was refurbished to support the treatment of a new source, which is the effluent from the municipal wastewater treatment plant.

Collaboration Among Multiple Organizations   The current successful symbiosis status could not be achieved without close cooperation among Dow Benelux, Evides Industriewater, the Zeeuws-Vlaanderen water board, the community of the city of Terneuzen, and the research organizations that conducted the various water treatment studies. The sustained success still calls for close cooperation among all parties involved.

Innovation   The current status of the successful reuse of municipal wastewater for high-value industrial applications on such a large scale required innovative thinking and strategic planning. These innovations demonstrate how to change or improve the following system factors in order for the symbiosis to occur:

- The regional infrastructure had to be adapted, requiring investment for channel crossing and 6 km of pipeline from the municipal wastewater treatment plant to the Evides pumping station.
- The diurnal fluctuation of the flow, which is typical of municipal wastewater, had to be dampened (equalized).
- The existing reverse osmosis (RO) and pretreatment facility needed to be modified to accommodate the source water change from seawater to biologically treated municipal wastewater.

Thanks to the powerful people factor in this project, all the system constraints were overcome. Scientific research verified the technical and economical feasibility of the municipal wastewater source to the RO process. The existing usable infrastructure is now used for water conveyance from the municipal wastewater treatment plant to Evides' DECO plant (about 6 km). The diurnal fluctuation of the water flow has been overcome by installing an equalization tank. The result is a win–win–win symbiosis.

- Reuse of around 2.5 million m^3/yr of treated municipal wastewater from the city of Terneuzen (therefore, a corresponding 2.5-million m^3/yr reduction in the freshwater intake from the region when the seawater-to-RO process was abandoned)
- Energy saving at the DECO water demineralization facility; 65% reduction in energy use compared to the previous operation, when seawater was used to feed the RO desalination system
- Reduction in the consumption of chemicals (and corresponding environmental burdens associated with making these chemicals from a life-cycle perspective) used for membrane fouling control
- Reduction of municipal wastewater discharge and associated environmental emissions to the receiving water body
- Support for the continued growth and development of both the Dow Benelux Terneuzen site and the Terneuzen community

Following is an excerpt from the CEFIC news release on the European Responsible Care Award for this project (CEFIC 2007):

"This innovative water project demonstrated a commitment to the local community and to the environment and showed the industry going above and beyond what is required," the judges commented. They also noted that it overcomes the huge prejudice of reusing treated sewage water. Overall, the project is innovative because this is the first time that municipal wastewater is being reused on such a large scale in the industry. And what's more, both the concept and the technology have the potential to be applied by other companies to similar situations at other locations. Dow Benelux is strongly committed to solving problems around scarcity of fresh water. The focus is on the availability of fresh drinking water for people in urban areas. In the near future more people will live in cities than in rural areas. This requires effective management of water supplies and water chains for which the award-winning concept can be a solution.

14.5.2   Synergy Within the Chemical Industry

By-product synergy for an off-spec formaldehyde product case study is described as follows:

- *Secondary material name:* off-spec formaldehyde
- *Reason for being off-spec:* high water content, high paraformaldehyde content
- *Secondary material quantity:* 330,000 lb (150 metric tons), one time
- *Secondary material generator:* Dow Chemical
- *Secondary material end user:* proprietary
- *Application of the secondary material:* raw material in the end user's chemical manufacturing process

The uniqueness of this synergy included: (1) a very short distance between the Dow site and the end user (system factor), (2) economics that are avorable for both parties (system factor), and (3) the fact that people working on this secondary material from both companies have a very strong background in environmental engineering and science, strong commitment to resource conservation and environmental protection, and very good persuasive communication skills to bring key stakeholders in their respective companies to the same level of passion and commitment (the people factor).

14.5.3   Synergy Between the Chemical Industry and Its Upstream or Downstream Industries

The case study for crude cellulose ether polymer (Methocel, a Dow trademark) is summarized as follows:

- *Secondary material name:* crude cellulose ether polymer (Methocel)
- *Reason for generating this crude cellulose ether:* deviation in particle size, etc.
- *Secondary material quantity:* in excess of 500,000 lb (227 metric tons) per year
- *Secondary material generator:* Dow Chemical
- *Secondary material end user:* proprietary

- *Application of the secondary material:* unique applications for moisture retention and substance binding outside the chemical industry

It took nearly four years from the beginning of evaluation on all potential applications of this secondary material until real synergies occurred. In this case, both the system and people factors played important roles. In terms of the system factor, there are no nearby end users because of the local climate and industry setup in the vicinity of the generator. The synergy is achieved between the generator and the current consumers, who are located far away. However, both the economic value and environmental benefits justify the synergy. In terms of the people factor, this synergy cannot be achieved without teamwork supported by various functions within Dow Chemical who enjoy working together not only for the results but also for the journey itself; the customers stood firmly and work very closely with Dow in the course of evaluation and never give up during trials both in the lab and on the field scale.

Methocel (www.dow.com) has very diversified properties and functions, and this has opened the door for many potential applications. The key is to find which application by which end user can generate the most value to both the generator and the end user, both economically and environmentally.

Methocel is a cellulose derivative (Figure 14.5) with a high molecular mass that bears both hydrophilic and hydrophobic functional groups. Methocel cel-

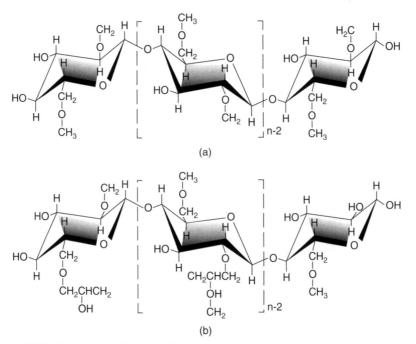

Figure 14.5 Structures of Methocel polymers: (a) methylcellulose (Methocel A products); (b) hypromellose (Methocel E, F, J, K, and 4-Series products).

lulose ether products are available in two basic types: methylcellulose and hypromellose, both of which have the polymeric backbone of cellulose, a natural carbohydrate that contains a basic repeating structure of anhydroglucose units. Methocel belongs to the general group called water-soluble polymers, which are used primarily to disperse, suspend (thicken and gel), or stabilize particulate matter.

Methocel has the following general properties and functions (not inclusive):

- No ionic charge
- Water retention
- Thermal gelation
- Enzyme resistance
- pH stability
- Binding
- Dispersing, suspending, stabilizing capability
- Film formation
- Lubrication and friction reduction
- Rheology modification and control

14.5.4 Synergy Among Various Geographic Regions (Across Country Borders)

Under certain circumstances, synergy can be achieved between two remotely located partners in two different countries if:

- There are no competent partners close by.
- The material is of high commercial value and/or manufacture of the materials requires a large environmental footprint (considering non-renewable resources from and environmental emissions to the Earth).
- LCA evaluations justify long-distance transportation, so that environmental benefits associated with prime product and raw material substitution far exceed the environmental burdens associated with material transportation.
- All relevant regulations are in full compliance.

14.6 CONCLUSIONS AND RECOMMENDATIONS

From industrial symbiosis (by-product synergy) idea generation to its successful implementation, the following are important enablers in turning the symbiosis or synergy from theory to reality.

- *Motivation:* motivation of all parties involved to the same level of passion for and commitment to sustainability
- *Validation:* validation of ideas or beliefs through down-to-earth investigation and research, including investigation of synergy feasibility considering all the system factors required, and validation of environmental benefit claims
- *Collaboration:* collaboration among generators, end users, and all other parties involved who will benefit from the synergy
- *Innovation:* innovation for breakthroughs, including novel applications of the material, new processing technology to enable the material's applications in the current market, or a combination of new processing technology and novel applications
- *Communication:* timely, transparent, and effective communication of all information that is required for the success of the symbiosis or synergy
- *Professionalism:* a win–win attitude and professionalism during collaboration

The challenge facing the industrial symbiosis practice in general is lack of diversity in the secondary material reuse–recycle–recovery industry network at the local scale (such as in North America). However, the biggest challenge is the current cultural environment and its associated price structure, developed around the production and consumption of products. Other barriers preventing successful by-product synergy identification and implementation include level of education, experience and expertise of industrial symbiosis practitioners, and the legal system and regulations.

Industrial symbiosis researchers and practitioners need to realize that there are two indispensable factors governing successful symbiosis or synergy: the system factor, which determines the synergy feasibility, and the people factor, which transforms the synergy from potential to reality. The ultimate industrial ecosystem may take a long time to evolve, but it is and should be our humanity's journey toward sustainable development.

Acknowledgments

This contribution would not have been possible without the strong commitment to sustainable development by The Dow Chemical Company. The author acknowledges the support of the company, particularly of Dow's Environmental Technology Center, in writing and sharing our experiences and conclusions regarding the widespread practice of industrial symbiosis. Appreciation is due to all the reviewers, both those from Dow and external reviewers, for comments and suggestions for improvement of this chapter. It is to be noted that the views and opinions expressed herein do not necessarily endorse, state, or reflect those of The Dow Chemical Company.

REFERENCES

CEFIC (European Chemical Industry Council). 2007. European Responsible Care Award, Budapest, Hungary, Oct. 6, 2007. Accessed at http://www.cefic.org/Files/NewsReleases/071002-C%20Award%20Press%20Release.pdf.

Duchin, F., and R. Lifset. 2008. Industrial ecology: transforming the use of energy, materials, water and wastes. *6th Gordon Conference in Industrial Ecology*, Colby–Sawyer College, New London, NH, Aug. 17–22. Accessed Nov. 1, 2008 at http://www.grc.org/programs.aspx?year=2008&program=industeco.

ISIE (International Society for Industrial Ecology). 2008. A History of Industrial Ecology. Accessed Nov. 1, 2008 at http://www.is4ie.org/history.html.

Korhonen, J. 2001. Four ecosystem principles for an industrial ecosystem. *J. Cleaner Prod.*, 9:253–259.

Korhonen, J. 2007. Environmental planning vs. systems analysis: four prescriptive principles vs. four descriptive indicators. *J. Environ. Manag.*, 82:51–59.

Korhonen, J., and J.-P. Snäkin. 2005. Analysing the evolution of industrial ecosystems: concepts and application. *Ecol. Econ.*, 52:169–186.

Robèrt, K. H., B. Schmidt-Bleek, J. Aloisi de Larderel, G. Basile, J. L. Jansen, R. Kuehr, P. Price Thomas, M. Suzuki, P. Hawken, and M. Wackernagel. 2002. Strategic sustainable development: selection, design and synergies of applied tools. *J. Cleaner Prod.*, 10(3):197.

Wu, Q. 2008. By-product synergy: Dow Chemical's successful experience. Presented at the *American Chemical Society 235th National Meeting*, New Orleans, LA, Apr.

Wu, Q., K. C. Lee, Z. Bell, and A. Mangan. 2005. "Sustainable development through by-product synergy. *Proceedings of the 2005 ACEEE Summer Study on Energy Efficiency in Industry*, pp. 4–170.

INDEX

Adhesive, 200
Adipic acid, 27
Agriculture, 45, 47, 109, 122, 160, 172, 192
AIChE, 1, 6, 9, 10
Algae, 75, 240, 245
Aluminium, 221
American Institute of Chemical Engineers,
    see AIChE
Ammonia, 26, 146, 199, 201
  synthesis, 210
Animal feed, 169
Anodizing, 222
Antibiotics, 147
Aquaculture, 45
Arabinose, 180
ATP, 240
Auto shredder residue, 86

Bacterium, 181
  genetic engineering, 239
Baekeland, Leo, 211
Bakelite, 211
Benchmarking, 17, 164, 222, 233
Biodiesel, 49, 109, 194
Biodiversity, 188, 211
Biofuel, 49, 54, 109, 157, 159, 171–198
  cellulosic, 171, 195
  feasibility, 194
  greenhouse gas emissions, 186
  lignocellulosic, 192
  second generation, 110

Biogas, 47
Biogenic resource, 40
Bioleaching, 237–246
  reactor, 241
Biolime, 146
Biological nanotubes, 238
Biomass, 41, 74, 84, 109, 123, 149, 171, 174,
    178, 182
  lignocellulosic, 163, 164, 187
  production costs, 192
  thermal decomposition, 111
Biomass Technology Group, see BTG
Bio-oil, 139, 142
  chemicals, 144
  gasification, 143
  health and safety, 120
  hydrotreating, 143
Bioplastics, 213
Biopolymer, 214
Biorefinery, 48, 110, 157, 159, 168, 182
Bio-remediation, 245
Biosludge, 64
Boustead model, 14
BPS, 94, 99, 103, 104, 106, 250. See also
    By-product synergy
  barriers, 94
  economic challenges, 96
  network, 91, 97
BTG, 109, 122, 129, 131, 132, 140, 150
Business Council for Sustainable
    Development for the Gulf of Mexico, 85